INTERNATIONAL RULE OF LAW AND PROFESSIONAL ETHICS

This book makes a strong case for the recognition of the importance of rule of law both in domestic law and courts, as well as the conception of international rule of law, where the international tribunals have been critically examined. This original volume recognizes the linkages between domestic and international rule of law and connects them with ethics and governance. The substantial contribution goes beyond the analysis of statutory law and develops a strong jurisprudential foundation for protecting the rule of law. It is written by scholars with outstanding records of publications, who significantly contributed to the advancement of knowledge in a number of related fields. This explains the authoritative nature and the intellectual rigour, the strong thematic framework and policy focus all throughout, which does not lose sight of the scholarly arguments that are essential in a book of this nature.

C. Raj Kumar, O.P. Jindal Global University, India

The United Nations is the symbol of humanity's aspirations for a rules-based international order, whether this be in security, human rights or environmental governance. Just as the organization provides a platform where the weak and the powerful can interact on formally equal terms, so law mediates relations between unequals by acting as a constraint on capricious behaviour and setting limits on the arbitrary exercise of power. This admirable book traces the progressive internationalization of the rule of law, offering along the way intriguing insights into how various professions have helped to develop and implement international ethical standards.

Ramesh Thakur, Australian National University, Australia

T0348032

Law, Ethics and Governance Series

Series Editor: Charles Sampford, Director, Key Centre for Ethics, Law, Justice and Governance, Griffith University, Australia

Recent history has emphasised the potentially devastating effects of governance failures in governments, government agencies, corporations and the institutions of civil society. 'Good governance' is seen as necessary, if not crucial, for economic success and human development. Although the disciplines of law, ethics, politics, economics and management theory can provide insights into the governance of organisations, governance issues can only be dealt with by interdisciplinary studies, combining several (and sometimes all) of those disciplines. This series aims to provide such interdisciplinary studies for students, researchers and relevant practitioners.

Recent titles in this series

International Rule of Law and Professional Ethics

Edited by
VESSELIN POPOVSKI
United Nations University Institute for
Sustainability and Peace (UNU-ISP), Japan

Routledge
Taylor & Francis Group

LONDON AND NEW YORK

First published 2014 by Ashgate Publishing

Published 2016 by Routledge
2 Park Square, Milton Park, Abingdon, Oxfordshire OX14 4RN
711 Third Avenue, New York, NY 10017, USA

First issued in paperback 2016

Routledge is an imprint of the Taylor & Francis Group, an informa business

Copyright © Vesselin Popovski and the contributors 2014

All rights reserved. No part of this book may be reprinted or reproduced
or utilised in any form or by any electronic, mechanical, or other means,
now known or hereafter invented, including photocopying and
recording, or in any information storage or retrieval system, without
permission in writing from the publishers.

Notice:
Product or corporate names may be trademarks or registered trademarks,
and are used only for identification and explanation without intent to
infringe.

Vesselin Popovski has asserted his right under the Copyright, Designs and Patents Act,
1988, to be identified as the editor of this work.

British Library Cataloguing in Publication Data
A catalogue record for this book is available from the British Library

The Library of Congress has cataloged the printed edition as follows:
International rule of law and professional ethics / by Vesselin Popovski.
   pages cm
   Includes bibliographical references and index.
   ISBN 978–1–4724–2803–5 (hardback : alk. paper)
   1. Professional ethics. 2. Professions – Law and legislation. 3. Rule of law.
   4. Law and globalization. 5. International and municipal law.
   I. Popovski, Vesselin, editor of compilation.
   K4360.I58 2014
   174'.3–dc23   2013033241

ISBN 13: 978-1-138-26993-4 (pbk)
ISBN 13: 978-1-4724-2803-5 (hbk)

Contents

Notes on Contributors

John Barker is Fellow of the Lauterpacht Centre for International Law, University of Cambridge, and Chairman of the UK Foreign Compensation Commission, London. With professional experience in Southern and West Africa spanning 28 years, he advises governments, international development agencies and non-governmental organizations on administrative justice, human rights and justice sector reform.

Simon Chesterman is Dean and Professor of the National University of Singapore Faculty of Law. He is also Editor of the *Asian Journal of International Law* and Secretary-General of the Asian Society of International Law.

Frédéric Mégret is Associate Professor of Law and Associate Dean of Research at the University of McGill, Canada, and the Canada Research Chair on the Law of Human Rights and Legal Pluralism.

Vesselin Popovski is Senior Academic Programme Officer, Head of Peace and Security Studies, at the United Nations University Institute for Sustainability and Peace (UNU-ISP), Tokyo.

Charles Sampford is Foundation Dean and Professor of Law and Research Professor in Ethics, Griffith University, Brisbane, Australia, and Director of the Institute of Ethics, Governance and Law.

William A. Schabas is Professor of International Law at Middlesex University (London) and Professor of International Criminal Law and Human Rights at Leiden University. He is also Honorary Chairman of the Irish Centre for Human Rights and Professor Emeritus at the National University of Ireland, Galway.

Vasuda Sinha is a litigation associate with Norton Rose Fulbright Canada LLP, where she focuses on complex commercial disputes. She has held the Fox Scholarship to train as a barrister at the Middle Temple in London, England. She also has experience in administrative, regulatory and international trade and investment law and maintains a strong interest in public policy and public interest matters.

Lorne Sossin is Dean and Professor at Osgoode Hall Law School, York University. His teaching interests span administrative and constitutional law, the regulation of professions, civil litigation, public policy and the judicial process.

Chandra Lekha Sriram is Professor in Law at the University of London, School of Oriental and African Studies. Her areas of teaching expertise include war and human rights, public international law, international criminal law, human rights, and conflict prevention and post-conflict peace-building.

Introduction

The rule of law is a long-standing ideal developed over millennia which demands that all people – rich or poor, powerful or weak – should respect the law and be equal before the law. The ideal is expressed in different ways as a concept, value, ideal, principle with a range of cultures going back at least as far as the riverine civilization of Babylon. It has been developed to become a central ideal in systems of protection against tyrannical power. The law is respected by all and applies equally to all and entails that the highest officers of the state will be investigated and prosecuted in the same courts of law, within the same jurisdiction, penal code and procedure, and by the same judges, as anyone else. The rule of law is not only a high ideal, but also a method of daily governance; it regulates the separation and independence of the legislative, executive and judicial branches of power, and as such it is a solid guardian against potential arbitrariness of rulers, against temptation to abuse power and violate citizens' rights. The 'rule of law, not of men' elevates the law above the rulers, requires that every official obeys the rules, and this supremacy of the law above the powerful and the rich of the day is crucial in the fight against tyranny, corruption, criminality and is an indispensable part of good governance. The rule of law demands that the laws are clear, consistent, stable, accepted and known by all; that the institutions are transparent, accountable, efficient and legitimate; that the tribunals are independent, impartial, unbiased, and issues fair judgments.

However, if the rule of law ideal is generally understood and in many cases established at the national level, at the international level the concept is still in its infancy. However, there are many who want it to grow, mature and strengthen. They have been boosted by the 2005 declaration of the United Nations General Assembly supporting not only the rule of law in domestic affairs but the rule of law in international affairs. The United Nations and its University have been particularly active in pursuing this agenda. In 2006, Nicolas Michel, then United Nations General Counsel and Under Secretary-General for Legal Affairs approached Ramesh Thakur, then Senior Vice Rector of the United Nations University (UNU), about the best ways to promote the international rule of law. Ramesh and I contacted Charles Sampford, a distinguished international lawyer and Director of the Institute for Ethics, Governance and Law (IEGL) established as a joint initiative of the UNU and Griffith University at his instigation in 2004. Sampford prepared a range of proposals and we determined the scope and methodology of how to pursue this project.

Another prominent UN figure to press for the international rule of law was Hans Corell, with whom I worked on the Princeton project on universal jurisdiction, producing 'The Princeton Principles on Universal Jurisdiction' (2001). As Assistant Secretary-General for Legal Affairs in the UN, he strongly encouraged us to undertake a study on the still under-developed concept of international rule of law, and how it can evolve and be supported. Then Dame Rosalyn Higgins, at that time President of the International Court of Justice, came to UNU to give a lecture entitled 'International Rule of Law' in April 2007. She pointed out that the international rule of law is still not developed and even not properly defined yet as a term in international law, and she invited us to undertake more research and publications on this theme. 'If the rule of law does not mean much for an international lawyer', Higgins said, 'we can look at what the term means to a domestic lawyer, and start from there'. She reminded us also that in the 1950s there was an 'international rule of law movement', which saw the United Nations system, a very young organization at the time, as a precursor to international rule of law and even to a world government.

Inspired by such legal colossuses, we redoubled our determination to pursue the project. Ramesh moved to the Center for International Governance Innovation (CIGI) in Waterloo, Canada, and soon after CIGI also joined as institutional partner, contributing a total of $150,000 in cash and $285,000 in kind, to the generous $300,000 linkage grant from the Australian Research Council (ARC). The project convened three workshops, resulting in three edited collections. The first workshop was held at CIGI in October 2009 and examined the ethical supports for the rule of law in the professional and institutional ethics of key players. The second workshop, held at Old Government House in the Queensland University of Technology in November 2011, looked at the institutional supports for the international rule of law. The third workshop, held at Bond University in October 2012, looked at the issue of access to international justice. In addition, two conferences were held on Rethinking International Justice in 2012 – one in Istanbul and one in Sydney. In each workshop the participants shared their draft papers, discussed them in depth at the workshop and then developed them to produce an integrated volume. This book is the result of the first workshop and exchange of papers.

This book's main argument is that the rule of law, developed originally and entirely within the jurisdiction of sovereign states, can be understood and applied at the international level; however, such border-crossing is not automatic – the international rule of law needs to be designed, crafted and continuously supported, both ethically and institutionally. The process of internationalization of the rule of law relies on the ethics of the 'professions beyond borders' – international civil servants, members of international commissions, diplomats, officials of international organizations, judges in international tribunals, as the chapters of the book demonstrate. During the research and writing of this book we found that more issues emerged and these issues need further research, for example that the international rule of law develops not only as a set of principles to subject the power to the law and to resolve disputes through legal process, but also as a set of institutions that support and apply the rule of law and give citizens access to justice.

The development of the international rule of law and international access to justice and the building of support for these processes can be examined from a macro perspective – the practice of international organizations, such as the United Nations and international tribunals – and can also be examined from a micro perspective – defined as the ethical behaviour of individuals working in international institutions, or in different related professions, applying ethical codes of conduct, impartiality and supporting the development of the international rule of law.

The gradual acceptance of the rule of law as a governing principle by more countries around the world leads to its internationalization, we argue, and this can be illustrated with the adoption of processes and practices that apply the law – independently, equally, without bias – in the rulings of domestic and international tribunals. In this context the link between the rule of law and ethics becomes crucial – what makes the law legitimate is a consideration beyond the law itself; it is contextual and brings with it a set of ethical considerations, human perceptions. This 'humanization' of the law with the ethical behaviour of international professionals, makes it not only legitimate and acceptable, but also practical and applicable. The ethical commandments exist beyond the law, but they form the contextual background for the laws to develop. The law can rule above the kings and the presidents because all people share common ethics, norms and rules that evolve and materialize in written laws, which all respect. One of the central arguments of this book is that the international rule of law has been, and can be further, substantively supported with ethical and institutional developments. The international rule of law is a gradual ascendance of law above power internationally and this can be illustrated by gradual global acceptance of the principles of rule of law and by repeated rulings of international tribunals, re-affirming that the supremacy of law places it above political, economic or other considerations.

The chapters of this book, summarized in the conclusion, are united in problematizing the international rule of law, finding insufficiencies – conceptual and practical – in the progress of the internationalization of the rule of law, but also in searching for potential supports for the international rule of law, coming from ethical codes of various international professions and professionals engaged in international organizations. The book demonstrates that ethics, rules, codes and their implementation – either integral or imposed – can offer those supports and strengthen the international rule of law. The impartiality and independence of employees in international organizations and tribunals represent one such solid platform for international rule of law to flourish. And on the opposite, corruption, lack of transparency, bias, lack of accountability, etc., would jeopardize the advancement of the international rule of law. As presented in the book, the rule of law has evolved over centuries at the national level, but only in recent years has it become a principle, internationally accepted and adhered to. What, however, is central is that even when applied at different levels – national, regional or international – the main purposes of the rule of law remain the same: to ensure that all actors obey the law equally and consistently, to restrict temptation towards dictatorial power, to serve as a tool safeguarding against the perils of unjustness and arbitrariness.

This micro approach is indeed novel and offers opportunity for discussions on how professional ethics has developed, how codes of conduct have been adopted, how citizens have been empowered, how particular individuals maintain impartiality, integrity, professionalism and competence when serving in international organizations, tribunals, peace missions, international panels and commissions. The ethics of the professionals in international organizations and tribunals in terms of its contributions to the international rule of law has not been addressed sufficiently both in the academic literature and in the UN documents and statements. We argue in this book that the ethics of professionals, and in particular those in 'professions without borders', has served as a driving force for the development of international rule of law from the micro perspective. In fact the process of internationalizing of some of these professions – diplomats into international civil servants; soldiers into UN peacekeepers; investigators, prosecutors, judges, defence lawyers from domestic courts moving to work in international tribunals – has been in itself a building element of international rule of law.

Colleagues and interns at UNU helped me for the successful completion of this book – Johanna Stratton, Peter Nadin, Kae Sugawara, Marleen Maat and Katalin Kekesi deserve my deep gratitude in preparing the manuscript. The workshop at CIGI was kindly helped by Anne-Marie Sanchez and Briton Dowhaniuk, and also by Valentin Hadjiev, Rachael Williams, Carmel Connors and Melea Lewis from the Griffith University in Australia. Charles Sampford helped immensely not only with the initial planning and driving the project through all hesitancies towards its successful end, including writing two of the chapters for the book and inspiring others, but also with approaching the publisher – Ashgate – where Alison Kirk and Sarah Horsley were extremely professional and efficient in accepting the manuscript and providing the necessary guidance throughout the production process. I would like to formally acknowledge that the research was supported under ARC Grant (LP09900) 'Building the Rule of Law in International Affairs', as well as by UNU and CIGI. The views expressed are entirely those of the authors and not of the ARC, UNU or CIGI.

Chapter 1

From Domestic to International Rule of Law: A Long and Unfinished Journey

Vesselin Popovski

The rule of law is a notion with a long historical genealogy.[1] It suggests that the law should rule, not the royals. *Lex Regia*. Law is supreme, elevated above the power, above the arbitrary will of kings and princes, above the momentous emotions of people. The rule of law 'means that citizens and those who govern them should obey the law'.[2] As such, it defends against tyranny and makes the government accountable, regularized, fair and stable. An antonym of the rule of law would be the 'rule of the jungle' where the powerful would impose a dictate without limits and control. The law, standing above the rulers, guarantees order and justice and protects human rights against violations. The rule of law subjects the exercise of power to legal rules, tested, adopted and respected as such.

The notion of the rule of law dates from ancient times. In a famous dialogue between the Persian King Xerxes and the Spartan King Demaratus, the latter explained why the Spartans were stronger soldiers: '… though they are free men, they are not entirely free. They accept Law as their master, and they respect this master more than your subjects respect you'.[3] In 350 BC the Greek philosopher Aristotle advocated that there should be government of law, not of men: 'It is more proper that law should govern than any one of the citizens: upon the same principle, if it is advantageous to place the supreme power in some particular persons, they should be appointed to be only guardians, and the servants of the laws.'[4]

The idea of the rule of law developed as a characteristic feature of the Roman civilization, ideologically divisive, but useful for the Empire to contrast itself with what they called 'barbarians', living beyond its borders. The Romans prided themselves on being governed by the law, not by the monarch. The Roman philosopher and statesman Cicero (106–43 BC) developed the concept, similarly to Aristotle expressing the idea, that it is the law that rules, not the man, who happens to be judge – 'a magistrate is a speaking law and law is silent magistrate'.[5] Cicero also writes '*Omnes legum servi sumus ut liberi esse possumus*' (We serve the law to be free) – people are genuinely free only when the law rules, when the guardians of the law also obey the laws. A similar link between law and liberty later is made by John Locke in his famous expression: 'When the law ends, tyranny begins'[6] and also in the writings of the French liberal philosopher Montesquieu.[7]

In 1215 King John of England, defeated by the French army and fearing civil war, agreed with a document known as *Magna Carta* (Great Charter of the

Liberties of England) that sought to rebalance the power between him and his subjects. For the first time in British history, the king made the concession of being under, not above, the law. The *Magna Carta* became the symbol of the rule of law in England – it not only resolved the political crisis by limiting the power of the king, but became the foundation stone of essential and interrelated public goods, such as liberty, equality, order and justice. It also set the principle of protecting the rights of the individual, by pronouncing that no man – regardless of birth, social rank or power status – should be denied the right to justice.[8]

Rule of Law in Domestic Constitutions

The rule of law evolved during the Renaissance (1400s–1700s) and the Enlightenment (1700s–1800s), firming a set of principles, ensuring supremacy of law above the will of the monarchs, the stability and justness of governance, and the resolution of disputes through due process. The Scottish theologian Samuel Rutherford inverted the old expression *Rex Lex* (king is the law) to its opposite – *Lex Rex* (law is the king).[9] Thomas Paine also referred to *Lex Rex* in his famous pamphlet 'Common Sense'[10] congratulating the establishment of the United States of America as a model for elevating the law above the king. One of the seven founding fathers of the USA, John Adams, enshrined the rule of law in the Constitution of the State of Massachusetts, invoking Aristotle's formula of 'government of laws, not of men.'[11] When entering into office every new President of the USA takes an oath: 'I do solemnly swear that I will faithfully execute the office of President of the United States, and will to the best of my ability, preserve, protect and defend the Constitution of the United States'[12] (the oath imposes presidential duty to protect and defend only the Constitution, not the people, of the United States). The rule of law, as a foundational stone of the American Constitution, would later be rooted also in the Polish, French and other European constitutions.

Throughout the Enlightenment, the idea of the rule of law developed not only as a set of principles to subject the power to the law, and to resolve disputes through legal process, but also as a set of institutions. The emphasis on the latter was the establishment of a governance framework by which liberty, equity, order and justice – these essential societal goods – could be ensured. Simply declaring that everyone is equal before the law and that no one can be punished outside the law – as the ancient philosophers did – would do little without building institutions to uphold the rule of law. The task therefore was to define not only what the rule of law is, but also how the rule of law can be maintained, how judicial decisions can be enforced against those who defy the laws.

The Oxford Vinerian Professor Albert Venn Dicey is considered the one who coined the modern definition of rule of law.[13] He suggested three meanings, the first and second of which are more of crystallizations of the historically evolved notions listed above: no man is punishable except for a distinct breach of law, established in court of law; and every man – no matter how high in rank – is subject to the same law and amenable to the same tribunals. The third meaning is Dicey's truly great contribution – the general principles of the Constitution, he wrote, 'are with us as a result of judicial decisions, determining the rights of private persons in particular cases brought before the Courts'[14] – the rule of law, developed historically as a set of principles, should be applied as such by institutions, courts and judges in their daily practice. In other words, the rule of law remains a high constitutional ideal, but Dicey emphasized that what matters more is how the rule of law is applied day by day, case by case, judge by judge. Without such daily implementation of the rule of law by institutions and courts, the concept will remain an abstract, nebulous, theoretical, even meaningless notion,[15] abused by politicians to win elections and to parade as good citizens.[16]

The concept of the rule of law enshrined in domestic constitutional regimes has historically corresponded with other related notions, such as separation of powers (checks-and-balances), independence of judges, democracy, justice and fairness, respect for human dignity and human rights. The concept has accordingly developed in both interdependent dimensions as a limit on absolute power and also as the best ruling method that should govern the state. The rule of law in French (*état de droit*) and German (*Rechtstaat*) would be translated in English exactly as 'law-governed state'. The law, placed above the power and controlling the rulers, creates a consistent and just framework to resolve disputes, a tool for good governance, thus detaches the government – and governance more generally – from the perils of arbitrariness, irrationality and extreme emotions. The rule of law is an instruction for governments not to abuse power and treat all citizens equally with respect to human dignity; and also an instruction for judges in the courts to act impartially, to remain independent ('blind') from political influence, prejudices, and even from human emotions.[17] In the famous biblical story, Pilate asked the assembled crowd whether to execute or forgive Jesus, and he followed the whims of the people, brainwashed by the priests and elders, shouting 'Let Him be Crucified!'[18] This is not what one would expect from governors and judges applying the rule of law. The rule of law must be elevated not only above the will of the powerful, but also above the will of the people – which could be emotional, brainwashed, manipulated.

Testing the Rule of Law

The rule of law requires uniformity, stability, consistency, equality and non-prejudicial applicability.[19] The law, as supreme authority, has to be impartial, independent from momentous sentiments. Judges should follow the law without bias, without influence from the politics or the economics of the day, from media or public campaigns. This is a major test for the rule of law, first because the political environment and the economic circumstances are powerful factors that may affect the judges' own societal positions, and second because the media perception on a particular issue can bring additional pressures on magistrates and juries. Courageous independent judicial rulings would be distanced from the will of the powerful and the interests of the rich. Magistrates should make independent and fair judgments, based only on the laws and the factual evidence, presented in the courtroom. This is a challenge, particularly when judges might be put in a situation to decide on essential, even crucial, political issues. One such situation occurred in December 2000 when the judges, not the voters, decided effectively who would be the next President of the United States. The Florida Supreme Court ordered a manual recount of the votes in Florida, but a 5–4 Supreme Court decision in *Bush v. Gore* overruled that the Florida recount was unconstitutional and *in extremis* gave Bush the presidency. The vote of one judge in an extremely short period of time decided who would be the President of the most powerful country in the world for the next eight years. After her retirement Justice Sandra Day O'Connor regretted taking the *Bush v. Gore* case. In an interview for *Chicago Tribune*, she said:

> we took the case and decided it at a time when it was still a big election issue. Maybe the court should have said: 'We're not going to take it, goodbye …' Obviously the court did reach a decision and thought it had to reach a decision … It turned out the election authorities in Florida hadn't done a real good job there … And probably the Supreme Court added to the problem at the end of the day.[20]

This is an acknowledgement, also shared by the top British judge Lord Bingham,[21] that the rule of law does not suggest that lawyers should be top decision-makers.

Another test for the rule of law is whether there can be limits in the application of the rule of law. The Roman Emperor Ferdinand I (1503–1564) was reported as saying: '*Fiat justitia et pereat mundus*' (Let's do justice, even if the world perishes) – an extreme and unyielding approach to the rule of law. Shall one apply the law if the skies are falling? And can there be emergency circumstances, when the rule of law might be relaxed? I would answer both with 'Yes' and 'No'. One might defend Ferdinand I's position, that under no circumstances should the rule of law be suspended because this will open the door for abuses. The formula 'if the skies are falling' is an ambiguous standard, a dangerous invocation of emergency powers that might be used randomly by governments to undermine the rule of law and impose restrictive authoritarian policies. The imposition of emergency laws, particularly when endlessly extended over a long period of time,[22] is an example of possible manipulations, rendering emergency exceptions into rule.

However, one might also argue that the law does not exist in a vacuum; it has to be placed in a contextual framework. There are other principles, apart from the rule of law, that govern human societies and actions. We would always stop our cars at red traffic lights, but if a tsunami is mounting behind our back and could kill us, we may not respect the red lights.[23] It could be argued that the rule of law can be relaxed in some extreme emergencies but, if so, the threshold for relaxation would need to be extremely high. Societies should continue to apply the law unless there is clear evidence suggesting that people would suffer immensely as a consequence of the application of the law. An example of an extreme test of the rule of law is presented in Shakespeare's play *The Merchant of Venice*.[24] The merchant Shylock wants to cut a pound of flesh from Antonio because of an unpaid debt, as stipulated in the legal contract between them. All Venetians are terrified with such an outcome, until a solution is found by judge Portia, who interestingly neither denies the legal contract, nor pronounces it anti-human, but rather interprets it in a way that makes it impossible to implement. Portia rules that the contract indeed allows Shylock to remove one pound of solid flesh, but it does not allow to remove a single drop of liquid blood with it; and also Shylock is entitled to remove exactly one pound of flesh – no gram more or no gram less. Shylock, facing an impossible task, concedes and Antonio survives.

The rule of law has developed over centuries not only as a legal principle, but also as a governance principle, exercising control over government and safeguarding governance against tyrannical inclinations. The rule of law invokes strict legality, but it has also developed in parallel with other concepts, such as the separation of powers, democracy, justice, human rights, accountability and legitimacy. These concepts have commonality in their genesis and are directly relevant to good governance. I discussed disconnections between legality and legitimacy in a recent book[25] and argued that legitimacy would most often support legality, but it can also challenge legality, when the laws are regarded as abusive and discriminatory, and accordingly are gradually contested and suspended. Hitler and Stalin also invoked the law – the Nazi law and the Soviet law – to justify their dictatorships. Legality and legitimacy are not identical. Oppressive regimes can adopt oppressive laws – the practices of racism and apartheid in South Africa were written in laws; however, being seen as discriminatory and illegitimate, these were challenged and abolished in 1992 under domestic and international pressure.[26] The rule of law has survived, whereas the laws of dictators and oppressive systems have gradually collapsed.

The test of otherwise undisputed rule of law therefore arises from the legality-legitimacy challenge: can law be a subject of a higher standard, which provides its legitimacy? If so, what should this higher standard be, and how can it be assessed? These questions present us with a challenge how to evaluate different laws, particularly examining the long journey from domestic to international rule of law. One way to address this challenge is by utilizing the two main conceptions of the rule of law: the formalist conception (a 'thin' definition) and a substantive conception (a 'thick' definition).[27] The 'thin' theory of the rule of law does not make a judgment about the fairness of the law itself; rather, it defines specific procedural attributes and legal frameworks necessary to be in compliance with the rule of law. The 'thick' theory of the rule of law goes beyond that and includes substantive rights based on, or derived from, the rule of law. In this context the link between the rule of law and ethics becomes crucial. What makes the law illegitimate is a consideration beyond the law itself; it is contextual and brings with it a set of ethical considerations, human perceptions. The Ten Commandments of the Bible are ethical demands with enormous power, stronger than the legal canons. They exist beyond the law, but they also can form the contextual background for the laws to develop. The law can rule, but so can the ethics. One of the central arguments of this book is that the international rule of law has been substantively supported with ethical and institutional developments.

International Rule of Law

The rule of law has followed a long evolutionary tract from being a normative idea in ancient times to its codification in modern liberal constitutions. Throughout this historical voyage the crystallization of the rule of law at the domestic level has evolved significantly, whereas at the international level it is still in its infancy.[28] As Sampford suggests the concept of the rule of law is well-developed at the national level; however, when applied to an international setting, it is conceptually nebulous – both as status, and as application.[29] There are no adequate methods by which international legal systems can be evaluated, and no standardized parameters to assess and synthesize 'rules of law' in different cultural or social contexts. In actual fact, the term 'international rule of law' seems to be in itself problematic, taking into consideration the lack of wider application of concepts such as 'international democracy', 'international welfare', or 'international freedom of speech'. Does 'international rule of law' mean 'rule of international law above domestic law'? Or does it mean 'domestic rule of law, accepted and spread internationally'? It seems that in addition to definitional questions, simultaneously functional context appears to be significant. Is the international system able to effectively restrict sovereign powers and impose the rule of law on states, including the most powerful ones? What can serve as a benchmark or standard of the role and function of international rule of law? Which institutions can support the internationalization of the rule of law? Taking into account that the proper answers for those questions still need to be formulated, it seems that the current status of the international rule of law is still immature, far from determined and even less unified. The journey from domestic to international rule of law has been a long and arduous one, but there is no finishing line visible ahead. What one can confidently say is that the central premises of the rule of law should not be different at national and international levels. At both levels – domestic or international – the law should be supreme, above the powerful, and respected by all. However, at the national level the rule of law applies primarily in a vertical relationship between citizens and governments, whereas at the international level, where actors are mostly states and international organizations, they act horizontally, even anarchically. For the international rule of law the most serious challenge is how states, including the most powerful states, as main actors at the international level can be subjected to obeying the law.

A further complexity arises from the uncertain status of international law itself, as compared to domestic law. In a famous expression, the international law is at the vanishing point of law,[30] and accordingly focus and priority is given to the process and the reality in international affairs, rather than to purist legal principles and interpretations. As we discussed above, the rule of law may mean different things for different people, but even more this would apply to international rule of law, which is even less crystalized and can be interpreted differently in different countries and cultures. The international rule of law could be equated, or confused – for example with the concept of the supremacy of the international law above the national law. Many modern constitutions would prescribe that obligations arising from international treaties and conventions prevail over domestic legal obligations; a concept, defined as monism, or 'supremacy of international law',[31] but this is a different – though related – concept to what we defined as international rule of law. The supremacy of international law over domestic law has endured a long evolution with both procedural and substantive developments. The procedural requirements emphasize rules for creation, application and enforcement of the law, adjudication of the rights and duties created by the law.[32] The substantive developments involve concepts of justice, equality, respect for human rights and human dignity. It is ironic that some who neglect international law would have been safer if they had accepted and complied with its precepts. One example was in October 2011 when the Libyan rebels discovered where Muammar Gaddafi was hiding, and, enraged by his long and brutal rule, tortured and murdered him. Instead of hiding in Libya, Gaddafi could have gone to a very safe place – The Hague – and handed himself over to the International Criminal Court (ICC). And even if the ICC had refused to accept Gaddafi, the Netherlands may have found it difficult to repatriate Gaddafi back to Libya, due to its adherence to the European Convention of Human Rights, prohibiting extradition to a criminal jurisdiction applying the death penalty. The international law, which Gaddafi despised and ignored, could have saved his life.

Like the domestic rule of law, the international rule of law can be defined in a variety of ways, incorporating elements of both process and substance. Simon Chesterman offers three interpretations of the international rule of law: (1) functionalist understanding of how and why the rule of law is used; (2) formal understanding of what the rule of law means; (3) the manner in which the rule of law is articulated at the international level; and concludes that the international rule of law serves rather as a political ideal, not as a normative reality. Because it is the political power and not the law that governs international relations, the international rule of law is about means rather than ends.[33] To follow from Sampford's and Chesterman's writings, I would argue that the international rule of law can be defined only to a certain extent as a status and procedural understanding, and its strong practical orientation and value should also be perceived as an important dimension. The international rule of law is in development, in movement, in gradual recognition of the principle that law must be supreme and that all persons should be equally accountable before the law. Furthermore, international rule of law needs to be institutionalized to be able to serve as a global governance tool, and ensure equity, justice, stability, consistency, independence and impartiality in the international arena. There has been a large international recognition – in rhetoric more than in implementation – of the principle that the law must rule above political, economic and other considerations. There have been also efforts to promote the rule of law internationally,[34] but still there is a long way ahead to support this principle, both from a macro perspective – developments in international institutions and tribunals – and from a micro perspective – ethical behaviour and impartiality of professionals, working in these international institutions and tribunals.

In summary, the rule of law as a matter of core principles is, or should be, the same at the domestic and at the international level; however, as a matter of practical implementation, it faces challenges at the international level because of the anarchical nature of the international society, where states may agree to respect the rule of law most of the time, but sometimes may also disagree to do so. The '*Rule of Law: A Guide for Politicians*' prescribed that 'The rule of law in the international society requires that laws are made public, accessible, clear and prospective and that the law-making process is guided by clear rules. There is no difference in this respect between the rule of law at the national level and the international level'.[35] Well written for sure; however, looking at the international law-making and the practice of the international organizations, one would certainly see differences and challenges in meeting the demands for clarity, publicity and accessibility of the laws, not to mention compliance and enforcement.

Development of the International Rule of Law from a Macro Perspective: United Nations

The rule of law is not explicitly spelled out in the UN Charter and the closest reference is the text in the Preamble, stating the UN determination to establish conditions under which justice and respect for the obligations arising from treaties can be maintained – a similar respect is also expressed with regard to peace, human rights and other values. The centrality of the rule of law, however, can be found in the Preamble of the Universal Declaration of Human Rights (1948), which states that 'human rights should be protected by the rule of law'.[36] The 1970 UN Declaration on Friendly Relations also makes reference to the concept.[37] On 20 December 1993, following the World Conference on Human Rights, the UN General Assembly adopted a resolution titled *Strengthening the Rule of Law* recognizing that the rule of law is essential to the protection of human rights and expressing its intention to assist institution-building necessary for the maintenance of the rule of law. In many UN documents, the rule of law is regarded as fundamental to achieving global other and the other related purposes – peace and security, respect and promotion of human rights, sustainable economic progress and development.

In 2004 the UN Secretary-General issued a report *Rule of Law and Transitional Justice in Conflict and Post-Conflict Societies* proposing the following definition of rule of law:

the rule of law refers to a principle of governance in which all persons, institutions and entities, public and private, including the State itself, are accountable to laws that are publicly promulgated, equally enforced and independently adjudicated, and which are consistent with international human rights norms and standards. It requires, as well, measures to ensure adherence to the principles of supremacy of law, equality before the law, accountability to the law, fairness in the application of the law, separation of powers, participation in decision-making, legal certainty, avoidance of arbitrariness and procedural and legal transparency.[38]

This definition is globally accepted and often expressly emphasized by states in their statements to the UN General Assembly and referred to by various UN organs and agencies. The principle that all entities – states, individuals and corporations – should be held accountable to publicly promulgated and equally and independently adjudicated laws is a solid underlying foundation that can inform and guide the work of the UN. The understanding of the rule of law as accountability of all – states and international bodies – creates a solid constitutional link between UN organs – the General Assembly, the Security Council, the Secretariat, the International Court of Justice – they all have essential roles, derived from the provisions of the UN Charter. As the UN applies rule of law both statutorily and functionally, it can be in itself seen as a macro example of both defining and practising the rule of law internationally, but also empowering states to develop their own domestic rule of law institutions.

The UN General Assembly placed the rule of law on its agenda for the first time in 1992, and the adoption of regular resolutions on the matter began from 2006 (A/RES/61/39, A/RES/62/70, A/RES/63/128, etc.). The Security Council in the last decade has often engaged in thematic debates and adopted statements on generic topics, addressing rule of law in many presidential statements (S/PRST/2003/15, S/PRST/2004/2, S/PRST/2004/32, S/PRST/2005/30, S/PRST/2006/28, S/PRST/2012/1). Many thematic Security Council resolutions also emphasize the importance of rule of law in different contexts – women, peace and security (SC Res 1325, SC Res. 1820), children in armed conflict (SC Res 1621), protection of civilians in armed conflict (SC Res 1265, 1296, 1674). The Peacebuilding Commission has also regularly addressed rule of law issues that are integral to the peace-building activities in the countries on its agenda – Sierra Leone, Burundi, Guinea-Bissau and others. The UN judicial mechanisms, including the International Court of Justice (ICJ), ad hoc criminal tribunals (ICTY and the ICTR) and hybrid tribunals (Special Court for Sierra Leone, Extraordinary Chambers in the Courts of Cambodia, and the Special Tribunal for Lebanon) are also regarded as fundamental building blocks of the international rule of law.

On 28 October 2011 an independent, non-profit organization 'Security Council Report' issued a cross-cutting report on the rule of law, examining more generally the relationship between international law and the Security Council and its treatment of the rule of law.[39] It analysed two main aspects of this relationship – the degree to which rule of law has been incorporated in the Council's work in conflict and post-conflict situations (such as DRC and Liberia) and the degree to which the Council has been guided by the rule of law while imposing sanctions, also taking into account the rights of those affected by the Council's decisions. More recently, the Security Council has requested the Secretary-General to provide a report on the UN system's support for the promotion of the rule of law in conflict and post-conflict situations[40] and at the time of writing the Secretary-General report is expected to offer a focus on measuring the effectiveness of UN support for the rule of law. In a preliminary oral briefing to the Security Council on the subject, the Deputy Secretary-General, Ian Eliasson, argued that:

> evaluating the impact of our work is not easy ... Rule of law work also demands a holistic approach that links justice, security and development, and that aims to reach vulnerable groups in society. While there has been a significant progress in measuring impact in many sectors of development, the rule of law continues to lack the benefit of systematically collected and analysed information with which to measure the impact of interventions.[41]

It is encouraging to see how the UN Secretariat and other UN organs are making efforts in contributing more to the promotion of the rule of law all over the world with a particular emphasis on peace-keeping operations and other peace and security activities, including actions, authorized and mandated by the Security Council. The promotion of the rule of law at macro level entails also a greater support for promotion of human rights, accountability mechanisms, reinforcement of norms of justice, strengthening security institutions, placing greater emphasis on gender equality and other UN agendas. It is desirable for the UN to identify and promote its best practices in strengthening the rule of law at the international level and also its best practices in respect and protection of human rights, transitional justice and domestic accountability, and to evaluate the impact of the rule of law activities to these practices, so as to ensure that the strengths and weaknesses of its current rule of law policies and strategies are effective.

In January 2013 the 'Security Council Report' issued a second cross-cutting report entitled, *The Rule of Law: The Security Council and Accountability*[42] which focused on the Council's practice with regard to individual accountability for international crimes and human rights violations, using eight case studies to examine the way in which the Council dealt with accountability for such crimes. One of the key findings of the report is that despite rhetorical commitment to accountability as a principle, and the understanding that accountability is a powerful practical tool to promote peace and security, the Council has been inconsistent in its approach to this issue. The report shares a disappointment that the Council does not show readiness to discuss how to ensure more effective implementation of its decisions on individual accountability for international crimes. One recommendation, highlighted in the report, suggests that the Council during its briefings and consultations should keep track more consistently and systematically of specific developments on accountability, as well as attempt to use more often the *Arria formula*[43] meetings.

These institutional developments signal that more rule of law activities have been embraced by more UN entities with the aim to develop, promote and implement international norms and standards in most fields, and to support a general framework of international rule of law. As of 2013, over 40 UN entities are engaged in rule of law issues in more than 110 countries, the majority of which are conflict and post-conflict situations, in all regions of the globe, with the largest presence in Africa. The purpose is to reach a clear and consistent international legal framework; strong institutions of justice, governance, security and human rights that are well structured, financed, trained and equipped. Responsibility for the overall coordination of the UN work rests with the Rule of Law Coordination and Resource Group,[44] chaired by the UN Deputy Secretary-General. The Group developed some broad policy guidance documents: *UN Approach to Rule of Law Assistance*; *UN Approach to Justice for Children*; *The UN and Constitution-making*. These documents place an emphasis on the notion that a strict adherence to the rule of law is crucial for building the legitimacy and trust in governments, in particular in post-conflict zones. Strict adherence extends to all elements of the rule of law – including the supremacy of law, equality before the law, legal certainty, fairness in application of the law, avoidance of arbitrariness, procedural and legal transparency, protecting the rights of victims and providing them with access to justice, and the provision of legal assistance.

Development of International Rule of Law from Micro Perspective: Professional Ethics

As presented above, the rule of law has evolved over centuries at the national level, but only in the last 60 years has it crossed the boundaries of states to become a principle, internationally accepted and adhered to. Applied on different levels – national, regional or international – the main purposes of the rule of law remain similar – to demand that all actors obey the law equally and consistently, to restrict temptation towards dictatorial power and serve as a tool to safeguard against the perils of arbitrariness. The development of the international rule of law and the building of support for this process can be examined from a macro perspective – the practice of international organizations, such as United Nations; and it can also be examined from a micro perspective – defined as the ethical behaviour of individuals working in international institutions, or in different related professions – e.g., lawyers, diplomats, international civil servants, prosecutors and judges in international tribunals – applying codes of conduct, impartiality, unbiased behaviour, etc., supporting the development of the international rule of law. This micro approach is indeed novel and offers opportunity for discussions on how professional ethics has developed, how codes of conduct have been adopted, how citizens have been empowered, how particular individuals maintain impartiality, integrity, professionalism and competence when serving in international organizations and tribunals or other international bodies. The ethics of the professionals in international organizations and tribunals in terms of its contributions to the international rule of law has not been addressed sufficiently both in the academic literature and in the UN documents and statements. The ethics of professionals, and in particular those in 'professions without borders', has served as a driving force for the development of the international rule of law from a micro perspective. In fact the process of internationalizing some of these professions – diplomats into international civil servants, soldiers into UN peace-keepers, judges moving from domestic courts to work in ICJ or ICC, etc., has been in itself a building element of the international rule of law.

Yet not everything is optimistic; there is a tension, or rather duality, between promoting the rule of law internationally – based on the 'thin' formalistic concept of the rule of law, detached from ethical considerations – and establishing the international rule of law as a 'thick', substantive concept, attached to ethics, human rights and good governance. Many professionals in international settings have supported the establishment and development of the international rule of law by being truly independent international citizens, by applying high ethical codes and standards, impartiality and competence, and all these offer support and strength to the international rule of law. From a micro perspective and in contrast with the domestic rule of law, I would argue that the international rule of law is never just 'thin', procedural and value-free. The work for international organizations carries with it ethics, values, impartiality, human rights and gender awareness and cultural sensitiveness. Ultimately, a balance must be struck between the domestic and the international settings, and between the macro and the micro perspectives – institutions and individuals.

To conclude, the development of the rule of law at the national level has been long, at times difficult, but gradually accepted and enshrined in constitutions. At the international level the rule of law is still maturing slowly, controversially and it does not yet represent an established governance method in the international arena. Although international rule of law is not yet a 'state of affairs', it has some attractiveness and remains a useful tool, a language, a means within the international context. It serves a function, shows ascendancy and acceptance of the principle internationally, but is still far from defining a global constitutionalism, a global governing framework. What at this stage can be done is to help the maturity process, to demonstrate the progress towards internationalization and institutional developments from a macro perspective and to emphasize the role of the ethical behaviour of various professions in the internationalization of the rule of law.

References

1   See Brian Tamanaha, *On the Rule of Law: History, Politics, Theory* (Cambridge University Press, 2004).

2   *Rule of Law: A Guide for Politicians* (Raoul Wallenburg Institute, 2012), p. 10.

3   From http://history-world.org/Greek%20Sparta.htm (last accessed June 2013).

4   Aristotle, *The Politics* (350 BC) 3.16.

5   Cicero, *The Laws,* Book III, 2–3, p. 151.

6   John Locke, *Second Treatise of Government* (1690).

7   Montesquieu, *The Spirit of the Laws* (1748).

8   From http://www.salisburycathedral.org.uk/history.magnacarta.php (last accessed June 2013).

9   Samuel Rutherford, *Lex, Rex* (1644).

10 Thomas Paine, *Common Sense: Addressed to the Inhabitants of America, on the Following Interesting Subjects (1776).*

11 Massachusetts Constitution, Part First, Art. XXX (1780).

12 USA Constitution, Article Two, Section One, Clause Eight.

13 See Tom Bingham, *The Rule of Law* (Penguin, 2011).

14 Albert Venn Dicey, *An Introduction to the Study of the Law of the Constitution* (Macmillan, 1885), p. 172.

15 Such criticism has been offered by several scholars. See Joseph Raz, 'The Rule of Law and its Virtue', in Raz (ed.), *The Authority of Law: Essays on Law and Morality* (Oxford University Press, 1979); Judith Sinclair, 'Political Theory and the Rule of Law', in A. Hutchinson and P. Monahan (eds), *The Rule of Law: Ideal or Ideology* (Carswell, Toronto, 1987).

16 Brian Tahamana (2004) gives several quotes from statements of respect for the rule of law, including by current dictators –Tamanaha, *On the Rule of Law*, pp. 2–3.

17 The relationship between laws and mores (opinions, habits, emotions) might be closer – the law can be seen as a kind of universalized opinion – the preferences of the majority, applied to everyone.

18 From the New Testament (Matthew 27:11–26).

19 Bingham, *The Rule of Law*.

20 *Chicago Tribune*, 27 April 2013, Interview, 'O'Connor questions court's decision to take Bush v. Gore'.

21 Bingham, *The Rule of Law*, p. 7.

22 Egypt was governed under Emergency Law (Law No. 162 of 1958) almost continuously since 1967.

23 Some observers noted that Japanese – extremely law-abiding people – driving away from the murderous Tsunami on 11 March 2011 in Tohoku stopped at red traffic lights.

24 Written from 1596 till 1598.

25 Richard Falk, Mark Juergensmeyer and Vesselin Popovski (eds), *Legality and Legitimacy in Global Affairs* (Oxford University Press, 2012).

26 Ibid., p. 389.

27 Paul Craig, 'Formal and substantive conceptions of the rule of law: An analytical framework', *Public Law* (1997), 467.

28 Visible also from very limited space on the international rule of law in otherwise fundamental books on rule of law – see Tamanaha, *On the Rule of Law*, and Bingham, *The Rule of Law*.

29 Charles Sampford, chapter 1, 'Re-Conceiving the Rule of Law for a Globalizing World', in S. Zifcak (ed.), *Globalisation and the Rule of Law* (Routledge, 2005), pp. 9–31.

30 Attributed to Professor Hersh Lauterpacht's lectures at Cambridge University in the 1930s.

31 For such interpretation, see Mattias Kumm, 'International law before national courts: The international rule of law and the limits of the internationalist model', *Virginia Journal of International Law* 44 (2003), 19.

32 H.L.A. Hart, *The Concept of Law* (Oxford: Clarendon, 1961).

33 Simon Chesterman, 'An international rule of law?', *The American Journal of Comparative Law* 56 (2008), 331–61.

34 Thomas Carothers (ed.), *Promoting Rule of Law Abroad* (Carnegie, 2006).

35 *Rule of Law: A Guide for Politicians*, p. 32.

36 Universal Declaration of Human Rights (1948).

37 A/RES/2627(XXV).

38 S/2004/616.

39 http://www.securitycouncilreport.org/cross-cutting-report/lookup-c-glKWLeMTIsG-b-7829857.php.

40 S/PRST/2012/1.

41 DSG/SM/SC 10905 (30 January 2013), available www.un.org/News/Press/docs/2013/dsgsm653.doc.htm.

42 http://www.securitycouncilreport.org/atf/cf/%7B65BFCF9B-6D27–4E9C-8CD3-CF6E4FF96FF9%7D/cross_cutting_report_1_rule_of_law_2013.pdf.

43 Arria Formula enables one member of the Council to invite other members to an informal meeting, held outside the Council chambers and chaired by the inviting member. The meeting is called for the purpose of briefings by experts in a matter of concern to the Council. The Arria Formula meetings are informal and allow for more interaction between the Council members, civil society, UN agencies, and others on international peace and security issues.

44 The members of the Group are Department of Political Affairs, the Department of Peacekeeping Operations, Office of the High Commissioner for Human Rights, the Office of Legal Affairs, United Nations Development Programme, The United Nations Children's Fund, The Office of the United Nations High Commissioner for Refugees, the United Nations Development Fund for Women and the United Nations Office on Drugs and Crime.

Chapter 2

"Unqualified Human Good" or a Bit of "Ruling-Class Chatter"? The Rule of Law at the National and International Level

Simon Chesterman

The rule of law is almost universally supported at the national and international level. The extraordinary support for the rule of law in theory, however, is possible only because of widely divergent views of what it means in practice. This chapter surveys the evolution of the term in discrete cultural traditions before exploring its formal, substantive, and functional conceptions. It then turns to how the rule of law at the national level has been implemented through international organizations, and the extent to which those international organizations have internalized the rule of law in their own procedures. Finally, it examines what, if anything, may be signified by terms such as "the international rule of law" or "the rule of international law".

Introduction

> We ought to expose the shams and inequities which may be concealed beneath the law. But the rule of law itself, the imposing of effective inhibitions upon power and the defense of the citizen from power's all-intrusive claims, seems to me to be an unqualified human good.
>
> (Thompson 1977, p. 266)

> It would not be very difficult to show that the phrase "the Rule of Law" has become meaningless thanks to ideological abuse and general over-use. It may well have become just another one of those self-congratulatory rhetorical devices that grace the utterances of Anglo-American politicians. No intellectual effort need therefore be wasted on this bit of ruling-class chatter.
>
> (Shklar 1987, p. 1)

What, if anything, is meant by terms such as "the international rule of law"? At the United Nations World Summit in 2005, Member States unanimously recognized the need for "universal adherence to and implementation of the rule of law at both the national and international levels" and reaffirmed their commitment to "an international order based on the rule of law and international law" (2005 World

Summit Outcome Document 2005, para. 134). The rule of law has been embraced across the political spectrum: on the right, Friedrich Hayek placed it at the heart of development policy (Hayek 1960, pp. 220–33); on the left, the Marxist historian E.P. Thompson called it an "unqualified human good" (Thompson 1977, p. 266). It is a term endorsed by both the World Social Forum and the World Bank.

Such a high degree of consensus on the virtues of the rule of law is possible only because of dissensus as to its meaning. At times the term is used as if synonymous with "law" or legality; on other occasions it appears to import broader notions of justice. In still other contexts it refers neither to rules nor to their implementation but to a kind of political ideal for a society as a whole. This chapter will briefly survey its evolution in discrete cultural traditions before exploring these formal, substantive, and functional conceptions of the rule of law (Stephenson 2001). It will then turn to how the rule of law at the national level has been implemented through international organizations, and the extent to which those international organizations have internalized the rule of law in their own procedures. It will conclude with an examination of what may be signified by terms such as "the international rule of law" or "the rule of international law."

To conceive of the rule of law in a manner coherent across the many contexts in which it is invoked requires a formal, minimalist understanding that does not seek to include substantive political outcomes—democracy, promoting certain human rights, redistributive justice or laissez-faire capitalism, and so on—in its definition. These outcomes are more properly sought in the political realm (Raz 1990). Nevertheless, examination of the functional manner in which the rule of law is deployed in international forums suggests important qualifications on how the rule of law may be adapted as a meaningful concept at the international level. In other words, agreement on the *meaning* of rule of law requires a formal conception of its content, but how that content is applied to international law—where the primary challenge is not the vertical relationship of subjects to a sovereign, but the horizontal relationship of subjects to other subjects—requires a functionalist understanding of its *use*.

Evolution of the Rule of Law at the National Level

The early history of the rule of law is frequently conflated with the history of law itself. The Code of Hammurabi, promulgated by the king of Babylon around 1760 BC, was one of the first sets of written laws; the fact that it was inscribed in stone and made publicly available was a significant advance toward a legal system (Viel 2005). Yet few would argue that Babylon was governed according to the rule of law in any modern sense. That modern conception may be understood at its most basic by a distinction from the "rule of man," implying power exercised at the whim of an absolute ruler, and from "rule *by* law," whereby a ruler consents to exercise power in a non-arbitrary fashion. In neither case is the ruler him- or herself bound by law in any meaningful sense.

Plato held in the *Republic* that the best form of government was rule by a philosopher king, but allowed that rule by law was a second option warranted by the practical difficulties of locating an individual with the appropriate qualities to reign (Plato 1892).[1] Aristotle surveyed various Greek constitutions before concluding in *The Politics* that "the rule of law" was preferable to that of any individual (Aristotle 350 BC, p. III.16), a position later quoted by John Adams on the eve of the American Revolution as the definition of a republic: that it is "a government of laws, and not of men" (Adams 1775).

Throughout this early period, however, law continued to be seen largely as a means by which to rule rather than a constraint on the ruler as such. Despite occasional doctrinal assertions to the contrary, the development of norms and institutions that might actually bind the sovereign took some centuries.

The Anglo-American Tradition

The rule of law took root in England in theory before it did in practice. Though the 1215 Magna Carta established some limits on the exercise of power by the king with respect to the liberties of freemen,[2] it was not until the seventeenth century that the notion of the king himself being subject to law began to be taken seriously. In an extraordinary exchange with James I in 1607, Sir Edward Coke, Lord Chief Justice of the Common Pleas, rebuffed the king's argument that he could withdraw cases from the judiciary and decide them himself: the king ought not to be subject to man, Coke argued, quoting Bracton, but subject to God and the law (Bracton 1968). Due in large part to such impertinence Coke was later dismissed from the bench, but returned to the legislature where he played a role in drafting the 1628 Petition of Right, also seeking to limit the prerogatives of the Crown (Boyer 2004; Reid 2004).

In the 1644 publication *Lex, Rex*, Scottish theologian Samuel Rutherford outlined a more general theory of limited government, including concepts such as the separation of powers—his book was burned and he was cited for treason, dying before he could be tried (Rutherford 1644). A more acceptable position

---

1   By *The Laws*, Plato endorsed a stronger position: "Where the law is subject to some other authority and has none of its own, the collapse of the state, in my view, is not far off; but if law is the master of the government and the government is its slave, then the situation is full of promise and men enjoy all the blessings that the gods shower on a state." Plato, *The Laws* 715d (Trevor J. Saunders trans., Penguin, 1970) (360 BC).

2   Article 29 of the Magna Carta (1215) provided that "No Freeman shall be taken, or imprisoned, or be disseised of his Freehold, or Liberties, or free Customs, or be outlawed, or exiled or any otherwise destroyed; nor will we pass upon him, nor condemn him, but by lawful Judgment of his Peers, or by the Law of the Land. We will sell to no man, we will not deny or defer to any man either Justice or Right." Available at http://www.yale.edu/lawweb/avalon/medieval/magframe.htm.

was that of Thomas Hobbes' *Leviathan* (1651), who argued that the rule of law, even in the limited sense of government being founded on a rule or set of precepts, was logically impossible. To be subject to the law, Hobbes argued, a sovereign must subject himself to a greater power. This implies some other sovereign who is free of the law unless subject to another sovereign and so on (Dyzenhaus 2001; Hobbes 1914, ch. 29).

It took a civil war, the beheading of one monarch, and the overthrow and exile of a second before the Bill of Rights Act was adopted in 1689.[3] This provided, among other things, that it was "illegal" for the sovereign to suspend or dispense with laws, to establish his own courts, or to impose taxes without parliamentary approval. It also provided that election of Members of Parliament should be free, and that parliamentary proceedings should be subject only to parliamentary scrutiny. The monarchy remained powerful and institutions supporting the rule of law weak, however—judges were given security of tenure only in 1701;[4] deprivation of trial by jury was one of the abuses cited in the American Declaration of Independence in 1776;[5] Bills of Attainder were abolished only in 1870.[6] Political participation in Britain remained deeply flawed through the nineteenth century: the Reform Act of 1832 abolished infamous rotten boroughs such as Old Sarum, which elected two members to the House of Commons despite having only 11 voters (none of whom was a resident), but the franchise became universal only in 1928.[7]

In the face of this inconstant practice, the modern conception of the rule of law in the Anglo-American tradition is frequently tied to the British constitutional scholar A.V. Dicey, writing in 1885, who referred to it also as the "supremacy of law"(Dicey 1885, p. 171). His three-point definition is frequently quoted:

---

3   An Act Declaring the Rights and Liberties of the Subject and Settling the Succession of the Crown 1689 (Engl.) ("Bill of Rights 1689"). Charles I was executed in 1649 during the English Civil War (1642–51). Charles II eventually regained the throne and died in 1685. James II succeeded him but was driven into exile during the Glorious Revolution of 1688. Before William and Mary were affirmed as rulers in 1689, they affirmed a Declaration of Right that was subsequently embodied in the Bill of Rights Act.

4   The 1701 Act of Settlement provided, among other things, that judges enjoyed tenure during good behavior rather than at the pleasure of the Crown. For a modern discussion, see Cheryl Saunders and Katherine Le Roy, eds, *The Rule of Law* (Sydney: Federation Press, 2003) (discussing responses to a 1992 decision by the Victorian Parliament in Australia to abolish the Accident Compensation Tribunal and revoke the appointments and commissions of its members).

5   Declaration of Independence 1776.

6   Forfeiture Act of 1870 (U.K.). The procedure does not appear to have been used in the nineteenth century, however, with the last such bill passed in 1798 against the Irish rebel Lord Fitzgerald. Cf. U.S. Const. art. I, § 9, cl. 3; U.S. Const. art. I, § 10, cl. 1.

7   Equal Franchise Act 1928.

We mean, in the first place, that no man is punishable or can be lawfully made to suffer in body or goods except for a distinct breach of law established in the ordinary legal manner before the ordinary Courts of the land ...

We mean in the second place ... not only that with us no man is above the law, but (what is a different thing) that here every man, whatever be his rank or condition, is subject to the ordinary law of the realm and amenable to the jurisdiction of the ordinary tribunals ...

[Thirdly,] the constitution is pervaded by the rule of law on the ground that the general principles of the constitution (as for example the right to personal liberty, or the right of public meeting) are with us the result of judicial decisions determining the rights of private persons in particular cases brought before the Courts. (Dicey 1885, pp. 172, 77–78, 208)

Dicey's three aspects of the rule of law—regulating government power, implying equality before the law, and privileging judicial process—are commonly regarded as basic requirements of a formal understanding of the rule of law.

Continental Europe

Continental European jurists developed a slightly different understanding of the role law plays in ordering society, placing less emphasis on judicial process than on the nature of the State.[8] This is reflected in the terms commonly used for "rule of law"—*Rechtsstaat, État de droit, stato di diritto, estado de derecho*, and so on.[9] An important substantive distinction was the role of constitutionalism: whereas Britain never developed a written constitution, in Europe the establishment of a basic law that constrained government came to be seen as axiomatic.[10] This distinction lives on in the different approaches to legal interpretation epitomized by common law precedent-based argument, and civil law doctrinal analysis. It also survives in the

---

8   Dicey himself noted that his third aspect of the rule of law was somewhat specific to England.

9   There are occasional exceptions to such translations. See, e.g., the translation of "rule of law" as *"le rétablissement de l'ordre"* in S.C. Res. 1040 (Jan. 29, 1996), *infra* note 91. In Canada, the Charter of Rights and Freedoms translates "rule of law" as *"la primauté du droit"* Constitution Act 1982 (Can.), Part I, preamble. I am grateful to Gary F. Bell for bringing the latter to my attention.

10   Dicey wrote that "whereas under many foreign constitutions the rights of individuals flow, or appear to flow, from the articles of the constitution, in England the law of the constitution is the result not the source of the rights of individuals." A.V. Dicey, *Lectures Introductory to the Study of the Law of the Constitution* (London: Macmillan, 1885), 294.

relative weight accorded to fundamental rights in civil law as opposed to common law countries, with the United States being a prominent exception.[11]

German scholars typically trace the origins of the *Rechtsstaat* (the law-based State, or constitutional State) to Kant (Kant 1965). Robert von Mohl developed the idea in the 1820s, contrasting it with the aristocratic police State (Mohl 1829). For Hans Kelsen, one of the most influential scholars of twentieth-century legal positivism, the rule of law and the State were essentially synonymous (Kelsen 1967, pp. 318–19). The extent to which the concept of *Rechtsstaat* embodies both substantive aspects, such as the requirement that the State be based on reason, as well as formal requirements of legality, is a recurrent debate in the literature with the slide towards National Socialism providing a troubling political backdrop (Barber 2003; Grote 1999; Kirchheimer 1969; Morin 1992). (Nazi Germany is the most prominent example of a State in which the rule of law was used for pernicious ends, but far from the only one. Apartheid South Africa was another such "wicked" legal system (Dyzenhaus 1991)—a list to which some might add certain aspects of the U.S. legal response to the global war on terror (Chesterman 2011)).

Though the French concept of *État de droit* was originally derived from the German *Rechtsstaat* (Chevallier 1999, p. 11), ideas now centrally connected to the rule of law predate this nineteenth-century translation. Montesquieu's *L'esprit des lois*, anonymously published in 1748, advocated constitutionalism, the separation of powers, and basic civil liberties (Montesquieu 1989). Rousseau's *Social Contract* also affirmed the supremacy of law, but in the form of legislation as the expression of the popular will and therefore not subject to any form of limitation (Rousseau 1923). Thus the 1789 Declaration of the Rights of Man laid crucial foundations for the emergence of human rights more generally, but it was only in 1971 that the Conseil Constitutionnel for the first time invalidated a French law for infringing one of those rights.[12]

---

11   The United States, however, retains the prominent role of the judiciary, epitomized in the landmark decision of *Marbury v. Madison*, in which Chief Justice Marshall insisted that "it is, emphatically, the province of the judicial department to say what the law is." 6 US (1 Cranch) 137 (1803).

12   Conseil Constitutionnel Decision of July 16, 1971 (1972) D.S. Jur. 685 (1971), J.C.P. III No. 16832 (parliamentary law held unconstitutional as violation of fundamental right to freedom of association). The French constitutional scholar Jean Rivero refers to this case as the French *Marbury v. Madison*, though this perhaps understates the significance of the Conseil d'État in checking the power of the executive. See Richard J. Cummins, "Constitutional Protection of Civil Liberties in France," *American Journal of Comparative Law* 33 (1985).

Other Approaches

Though colonialism served to export European law across the various empires to varying degrees, the emergence of laws regulating governmental powers was not, of course, confined to Europe. This was not always well understood. Montesquieu, for example, wrote at length about China as a despotic regime under an emperor with absolute power, regulated not by law but rites that shaped the relationship between emperor and subject, father and son. This overlooked the presence of legal codes dating at least as far back as the sixth century BC (Liu 1998), but is suggestive of the traditional tension between Confucianism and Legalism that emerged between the eighth and the third centuries BC. Confucians held that society should be organized around *li* (rites, or rules of propriety) and that to rely on law was to admit to a failure of virtue. Legalists sought to use *fa* (norms, or law) to regulate society through the possibility of punishment. These debates resonate with the discussion of early Greek approaches described above and may be roughly compared to "rule of man" and "rule by law" (Chen 2000; Liang Chi-Chao [Liang Qichao] 1930; Peerenboom 2002; Thio 2002).

As to the possibility of holding the governing authority itself to account, the legitimacy of imperial rule in China was defended, from the eleventh century BC Zhou Dynasty onwards, by reference to the Mandate of Heaven (*tianming*). This held that a just emperor's rule would be blessed, but that an unwise ruler would lose Heaven's favor so that the mandate will pass to someone else. Interesting echoes can be found in the *Second Treatise* of John Locke, written before but updated and published after the Glorious Revolution and the Bill of Rights Act 1689, where he held that the prerogative powers of a sovereign were not subject to review by earthly powers but only by an "appeal to Heaven." As in the case of the Mandate of Heaven, this ultimate sanction embodies a somewhat circular logic: the illegitimacy of a ruler is proved by the fact of his or her being deposed (Locke 1988, vol. 2, § 168).

In the Arab world, the Code of Hammurabi preceded a rich tradition of Islamic law. Though founded on revelation and scripture rather than secular authority, this tradition embraced a notion of supremacy of law—application of the law to the ruler as well as the ruled, and the independent interpretation of law by scholars—far earlier than its European counterparts. As with the early moves towards the rule of law in Europe, however, theory was not always matched by practice (Bassiouni and Badr 2002; Dokupil 2002; Kamali 2003; Mallat 2004; Mugraby 2003). The term "rule of law" itself does not translate directly into modern Arabic. A common approximation is *siyadat al-qanun*. Literally translated this means "sovereignty of law," a concept more akin to the notion of rule by law (Brown 1997). Many developing and post-colonial States have also embraced law as a means to augment centralized authority rather than to restrain it. Promotion of the rule of law in such States by Western officials has thus sometimes been seen by those officials as a means of advancing human rights and liberal democracy, while their counterparts have seen it as a means of making government more efficient and therefore supporting the legitimacy of the State (Blackton 2003; Ghai 1986).

A Core Definition

The content of the term "rule of law," then, remains contested across both time and geography. Analysis of its content often begins by parsing out formal and substantive understandings (Craig 1997). Those theories that emphasize the formal aspects describe instrumental limitations on the exercise of State authority; they tend to be minimalist, positivist, and are often referred to as "thin" theories—distinguishing them from the "thick" theories that incorporate substantive notions of justice (Peerenboom 2004; Rawls 1972, pp. 235–43). The latter conceive the rule of law more broadly as a set of ideals, whether understood in terms of protection of human rights, specific forms of organized government, or particular economic arrangements such as free market capitalism (Hayek 1944, p. 72; Jennings 1952, p. 47). Ronald Dworkin has referred to the two conceptions as the "rule-book" model and a "rights" model, respectively; (Dworkin 1985, pp. 11–13) Judith Shklar as models of institutional restraint and the "rule of reason" (Shklar 1987, pp. 1–2). David Dyzenhaus casts theorists of the first school, including Shklar, as democratic positivists and those of the second, including Dworkin, as liberal anti-positivists (Dyzenhaus 1999, p. 2).

Such categories are far from stable. Substantive theories are typically built on the back of formal ones, and any "thin" theory must necessarily exist within a political context (Peerenboom 2004, p. 6). Indeed, a common critique of those who claim to articulate "thin" theories is that substantive elements have been included by stealth (Fallon 1997, p. 54). The problem with articulating a "thick" or substantive theory, by contrast, is that it may imply defense of a complete social philosophy and render the rule of law no longer meaningful in its own right (Goodhart 1958, pp. 943–4; Raz 1979, pp. 210–11).

A third way of considering the rule of law, suggested by the approach here of examining its international context, is to look at the function that the rule of law is intended to serve in a society. Rule of law promotion, discussed in the next section, tends to be presented as a form of technical assistance. On its face, this resembles a formal theory looking to the architecture of a legal system rather than the content of its laws. Yet closer examination reveals that rule of law assistance is supported because of perceived outcomes it may achieve in the recipient community: in addition to promoting human rights and providing a stable foundation for economic development, it has also been used to establish non-violent mechanisms for resolving political disputes (Waldron 1999, p. 37). This is incompatible with most substantive theories of the rule of law, however, as those most actively involved in promotion of the rule of law—U.N. officials, donor governments, non-governmental organizations, external advisers, and so on—are outside the legal system in question and, almost literally, above the law. As we shall see, this has troubling implications for the idea of an "international rule of law."

For present purposes, a definition that is applicable and acceptable across cultures and political systems will necessarily be a formal one. This is consistent with *how* the rule of law is articulated in international forums, but not necessarily *why.* The latter question may incorporate aspects of the substantive and functional understandings of the rule of law, but these may be distinguished from the basic norms, institutions, and procedures implied by the term itself.

That being said, what we might term a core definition of the rule of law as it has evolved over time appears to have three elements:

- First, the power of the State may not be exercised arbitrarily. This incorporates the rejection of "rule of man," but does not require that State power be exercised for any particular purpose. It does, however, require that laws be prospective, accessible, and clear.
- Secondly, the law must apply also to the sovereign and instruments of the State, with an independent institution such as a judiciary to apply the law to specific cases. This implies a distinction from "rule by law."
- Thirdly, the law must apply to all persons equally, offering equal protection without prejudicial discrimination. The law should be of general application and consistent implementation; it should be capable of being obeyed. This presumes that the rule of law is more than simply "law in the books" and that these principles also apply to "law in action" (Pound 1910).

These elements of the core definition may be summarized as a government of laws, the supremacy of the law, and equality before the law.

Promotion of the Rule of Law through International Forums

Having adopted a core definition of the rule of law, reflecting what one hopes is a broad understanding of its content, it is possible now to explore the ways in which the domestic rule of law has been used in international forums. This examination of the manner in which the rule of law is deployed will help elaborate how and why the concept may apply to the international level itself.

Through treaties and international organizations, the rule of law has been promoted at the international level for all the functional reasons described earlier: human rights treaties have advocated the rule of law as the foundation of a rights-respecting State; development actors, including donor States, have promoted the rule of law as essential for economic growth; and more recently security actors, notably the U.N. Security Council, have promoted the rule of law as a form of conflict resolution.

It is important to distinguish promotion of the rule of law in the sense used here from specific action to deal with past incidents. "Transitional justice," for example, is frequently used to refer to both prosecution of war criminals and the establishment of a legal system, but it is typically the former that receives the most attention and resources. Demonstrating that leaders who violate the law may themselves be prosecuted is an important part of the core definition outlined earlier, but if accountability depends on the massive international presence that may follow a crisis then it may be seen as the exception rather than the norm. Episodic prosecutions when outside political will and resources are available may do little to establish sustainable institutions (Chesterman 2007).

Similarly, terms such as "human rights" are used in multiple senses in this context. Certain human rights concerning the right to life and freedom of the person, for example, might be seen as essential aspects of a government of laws; non-discrimination may similarly be seen as an essential aspect of equality before the law. Inclusion of such specific rights, however, is distinct from the manner in which the rule of law is argued to be a tool for promoting human rights more generally. It is the latter sense that is intended here.[13]

To be clear, the fact that the rule of law is used to promote what some include within a substantive conception of the rule of law should not be confused with a reversion here to such a substantive understanding. Rather, the rule of law is best understood in the core sense outlined earlier and then examined with reference to the various purposes (including the achievement of specific political ends) to which it is put.

Human Rights

The preamble to the 1948 Universal Declaration of Human Rights states that "it is essential, if man is not to be compelled to have recourse, as a last resort, to rebellion against tyranny and oppression, that human rights should be protected by the rule of law."[14] The Declaration goes on to enumerate specific rights such as prohibiting arbitrary deprivation of liberty, requiring fair trials by independent and impartial tribunals, and protecting equality before the law. These protections broadly correspond to the three aspects of the core definition adopted here, with the qualification that independence of the judiciary is only part of what is implied by supremacy of the law. The rule of law as protected under the Universal Declaration is thus open to an interpretation that is more consonant with what has been described earlier as rule *by* law.

With varying degrees of specificity—in particular concerning the requirements of a fair trial and prohibited forms of discrimination—the Universal Declaration is consistent with most subsequent general human rights treaties.[15] Other documents

---

13   One might also argue that the rule of law is only possible with a certain level of economic development, or basic peace and security within a territory.

14   Universal Declaration of Human Rights, GA Res 217A(III) (1948), U.N. Doc. A/810 (1948), preamble.

15   See, e.g., International Covenant on Civil and Political Rights, Dec. 16, 1966 (*in force* Mar. 23, 1976), 999 UNTS 171; [European] Convention for the Protection of Human Rights and Fundamental Freedoms, done at Rome, Nov. 4, 1950 (*in force* Sept. 3, 1953), 213 UNTS 222; American Convention on Human Rights, Nov. 22, 1969 (*in force* July 18, 1978), 1144 UNTS 123, available at http://www1.umn.edu/humanrts/oasinstr/zoas3con.

provide guidelines on compliance, including codes of conduct for law enforcement officials,[16] principles on the independence of the judiciary,[17] as well as more elaborate regimes on specific types of discrimination.[18]

The 1993 Vienna World Conference on Human Rights recommended that the United Nations should offer technical and financial assistance upon request to "national projects in reforming penal and correctional establishments, education and training of lawyers, judges and security forces in human rights, and any other sphere of activity relevant to the good functioning of the rule of law."[19] This was endorsed in a series of General Assembly resolutions, each citing the rule of law as "an essential factor in the protection of human rights."[20]

Again, this might be seen as consistent with rule by law, though some advances have been made through human rights jurisprudence concerning the right to an effective remedy,[21] which has recently been the subject of a new set of basic principles.[22] In addition, at least since the 1999 *Pinochet* case,[23] the extent of head of State immunity has been substantially reduced. This has been complemented by the rise of international criminal law.

---

htm; African [Banjul] Charter on Human and Peoples' Rights, June 27, 1981 (*in force* Oct. 21, 1986), 21 ILM 58.

16   Code of Conduct for Law Enforcement Officials, GA Res 34/169, U.N. Doc. A/34/46, Annex (1979).

17   Basic Principles on the Independence of the Judiciary, U.N. Doc. A/CONF.121/22/ Rev.1 (1985).

18   See, e.g., International Convention on the Elimination of All Forms of Racial Discrimination, Dec. 21, 1965 (*in force* Jan. 4, 1969), 660 UNTS 195, available at http:// www1.umn.edu/humanrts/instree/d1cerd.htm; Convention on the Elimination of All Forms of Discrimination Against Women, Dec. 18, 1979 (*in force* Sept. 3, 1981), U.N. Doc A/34/46, available at http://www1.umn.edu/humanrts/instree/e1cedaw.htm.

19   Vienna Declaration and Programme of Action, U.N. Doc A/CONF.157/24 (1993), Part I, ch. III, sect. II, para. 69.

20   G.A. Res. 48/132 (1993), preamble. See also G.A. Res. 48/132 (1993); G.A. Res. 49/194 (1994); G.A. Res. 50/179 (1995); G.A. Res. 51/96 (1996); G.A. Res. 52/125 (1997); G.A. Res. 53/142 (1998); G.A. Res. 55/99 (2000); G.A. Res. 55/99 (2000); G.A. Res. 57/221 (2002). Cf G.A. Res. 61/39 (2006) (on "the rule of law at the national and international levels").

21   See, e.g., Castillo Páez v. Peru (1997), 34 Inter-Am. Ct. H.R. (ser. C.) (1997), paras. 82, 83.

22   Basic Principles and Guidelines on the Right to a Remedy and Reparation for Victims of Gross Violations of International Human Rights Law and Serious Violations of International Humanitarian Law, GA Res 60/147, U.N. Doc. A/RES/60/147 (Dec. 16, 2005), available at http://www1.umn.edu/humanrts/instree/res60–147.html.

23   R v. Bow Street Metropolitan Stipendiary Magistrate, *ex parte* Pinochet Ugarte (H.L., 1999), 2 W.L.R. 827 (1999).

Development

As indicated earlier, the rule of law has long been seen as a vehicle for promoting economic development (Boon 2007; Smith 1976, p. 15). In the 1960s, the U.S. Agency for International Development, the Ford Foundation, and other private American donors began an ambitious program to reform the laws and judicial institutions of countries in Africa, Asia, and Latin America. The "law and development" movement, steeped in dependency theory, generated hundreds of reports and articles—yet a decade later leading academic participants and a former official at the Ford Foundation declared it a failure (Gardner 1980; Merryman 1977; Trubek and Galanter 1974). Criticisms included the program's over-reliance on exporting certain aspects of the U.S. legal system, notably strategic litigation and activist judges, that were incompatible with the target countries (Franck 1972; Merryman, et al. 1979, p. 18). Later assessments have been less negative, however, noting that law reform projects take many years to bear fruit and that the rise and fall of the movement may have been more connected to U.S. domestic political issues in the period 1965–75 than with programs on the ground in developing countries (McClymont and Golub 2000; Tamanaha 1995, pp. 472–3).

Subsequent efforts have focused less on exporting a specific national model, but continue to assume a close relationship between the rule of law and economic development (Davis 2004; Ngugi 2005; Upham 2002). One of the difficulties has been in coming up with objective criteria to measure the rule of law. The 1992 Human Development Report, issued by the U.N. Development Program, suggested five possible indicators: fair and public hearings in criminal cases; a competent, independent, and impartial judiciary; the availability of legal counsel; provision for review of convictions in criminal cases; and whether government officials or pro-government forces are prosecuted when they violate the rights and freedoms of other persons.[24] The World Bank has defined rule of law for these purposes as "the extent to which agents have confidence in and abide by the rules of society, and in particular the quality of contract enforcement, the police, and the courts, as well as the likelihood of crime and violence" and uses aggregate indicators from a basket of other sources to measure the rule of law in more than 200 countries and territories.[25]

From around 1997, the development community began using the more general term "good governance" to refer to a set of activities that embraced participation,

---

[24]   U.N. Development Program, Human Development Report 1992: Global Dimensions of Human Development (UNDP, New York, 1992), available at http://hdr.undp.org/reports, 31.

[25]   World Bank, A Decade of Measuring the Quality of Governance: Governance Matters 2006 (World Bank, Washington, DC, 2006), available at http://www.worldbank.org, 3. On a scale from −2.5 to +2.5, the 2005 statistics range from Somalia (−2.36) to Iceland (+2.10). *See* statistics available at http://info.worldbank.org/governance/kkz2005/indicator_report.asp?indicatorid=5.

transparency, and accountability in government—specifically including the rule of law.[26] The term "governance" itself had emerged within the development discourse in the 1990s as a means of expanding the prescriptions of donors to embrace not merely projects and structural adjustment but government policies. Though intergovernmental organizations like the World Bank and the International Monetary Fund are technically constrained from referring to political processes as such, "governance" provides a convenient euphemism for precisely that (Hyden 1999; Munck 2003).

Developing States themselves have embraced the rule of law, acknowledging in the 2005 World Summit Outcome Document that "good governance and the rule of law at the national and international levels are essential for sustained economic growth, sustainable development and the eradication of poverty and hunger."[27]

Peace and Security

The U.N. Charter refers to domestic law only in the context of trust territories, the last of which became independent in 1994.[28] Article 2(7) of the Charter specifically excludes matters "essentially within the domestic jurisdiction" from U.N. interference, except when the Security Council exercises its coercive powers to maintain international peace and security under Chapter VII. Since the mid-1990s, these powers have increasingly been used to support, supplant, or replace domestic legal systems.

Apart from a preambular reference in relation to the deterioration of law and order in the Congo in 1961,[29] the Council first used the words "rule of law" in the operative paragraph of resolution 1040 (1996), where it expressed its support for the Secretary-General's efforts to promote "national reconciliation, democracy, security and the rule of law in Burundi."[30] (It is noteworthy that the French text rendered rule of law as "*le rétablissement de l'ordre.*")[31] Many peace operations have subsequently had important rule of law components, such as those in

---

26   U.N. Development Programme, Governance for Sustainable Human Development (UNDP, New York, Jan. 1997), available at http://magnet.undp.org/policy.

27   World Summit Outcome Document, para. 11. See also para. 21, 24(b).

28   U.N. Charter, art. 84.

29   S.C. Res. 161B (Feb. 21, 1961), preamble ("*Noting with deep regret and concern* the systematic violations of human rights and fundamental freedoms and the general absence of the rule of law in the Congo"; the relevant French text was "*l'absence générale de légalité au Congo*").

30   S.C. Res. 1040 (Jan. 29, 1996), para. 2.

31   "The reestablishment of order." S.C. Res. 1040 (Jan. 29, 1996), para. 2 (French text available at documents.un.org).

Guatemala (1997),[32] Liberia (2003–),[33] Côte d'Ivoire (2004–),[34] Haiti (2004–),[35] and the Democratic Republic of the Congo (2007–).[36] The mandates for such missions tend to be broad, calling for the "re-establishment" or "restoration and maintenance" of the rule of law, without formally articulating what this might entail. In practice, the dominant activities have tended to be training of personnel, assisting institution-building, advising on law reform issues, and monitoring, with the emphasis on criminal law processes (O'Connor 2006). Less attention has been paid, for example, to land law (Fitzpatrick 2002).

In two situations, Kosovo (1999–) and East Timor/Timor-Leste (1999–2002), the United Nations has had direct responsibility for the administration of justice, including control of police and prison services. Similar powers were exercised in Bosnia and Herzegovina through the Office of the High Representative from 1996 (Chesterman 2004, pp. 154–82). Though created as temporary operations, each was challenged on the extent to which the rule of law applied to international officials who enjoyed personal or functional immunity from legal process, were unaccountable to the local population through any kind of political process, and who exercised "all legislative and executive authority ... including the administration

---

32   U.N. Verification Mission in Guatemala (MINUGUA).

33   U.N. Mission in Liberia (UNMIL).

34   S.C. Res. 1528 (Feb. 27, 2004), para. 6(q) (authorizing the U.N. Operation in Côte d'Ivoire (UNOCI) to "assist the Government of National Reconciliation in conjunction with ECOWAS and other international organizations in re-establishing the authority of the judiciary and the rule of law throughout Côte d'Ivoire").

35   S.C. Res. 1542 (Apr. 30, 2004), para. 7(I)(d) (authorizing the U.N. Stabilization Mission in Haiti (MINUSTAH) "to assist with the restoration and maintenance of the rule of law, public safety and public order in Haiti through the provision *inter alia* of operational support to the Haitian National Police and the Haitian Coast Guard, as well as with their institutional strengthening, including the re-establishment of the corrections system"). The U.N. Observer Mission in El Salvador (ONUSAL, 1991–95) had a rule of law component within its human rights division.

36   S.C. Res. 1756 (May 15, 2007), para. 3 ("decid[ing] that the U.N. Organization Mission in the Democratic Republic of the Congo (MONUC) "will also have the mandate, in close cooperation with the Congolese authorities, the United Nations country team and donors, to support the strengthening of democratic institutions and the rule of law in the Democratic Republic of the Congo and, to that end, to ... (c) Assist in the promotion and protection of human rights, with particular attention to women, children and vulnerable persons, investigate human rights violations with a view to putting an end to impunity, assist in the development and implementation of a transitional justice strategy, and cooperate in national and international efforts to bring to justice perpetrators of grave violations of human rights and international humanitarian law ... (e) Assist in the establishment of a secure and peaceful environment for the holding of free and transparent elections; (f) Contribute to the promotion of good governance and respect for the principle of accountability").

of the judiciary."[37] Such powers, recalling the provisions of military occupation, became harder to justify as months became years and the disjunction between what international officials said and what they did continued.[38]

In addition to supporting or supplanting domestic rule of law institutions, the Security Council has created International Criminal Tribunals to replace domestic processes for trials arising from the former Yugoslavia (1991–)[39] and Rwanda (1994).[40] These tribunals were explicitly created as part of an effort to bring peace to war-torn territories, though they have been criticized for spending significant resources in order to prosecute few individuals with little lasting impact on the judicial institutions of the territory concerned. Hybrid tribunals, such as the Special Court for Sierra Leone[41] and the Extraordinary Chambers in the Courts of Cambodia,[42] were intended to blend international supervision with development of national capacity but have had limited success.

The International Criminal Court (I.C.C.) exercises complementary rather than primary jurisdiction:[43] this may encourage national prosecution where possible, suggesting a desire to bolster national courts as well as protect State sovereignty. Nevertheless, the Security Council retains the power to defer prosecutions for a renewable period of one year. This reflects ongoing tension between the

---

37   UNMIK Regulation 1999/1 (July 25, 1999), On the Authority of the Interim Administration in Kosovo, § 1.

38   See, e.g., Ombudsperson Institution in Kosovo, Second Annual Report 2001–2002 (July 10, 2002), available at http://www.ombudspersonkosovo.org (noting that "UNMIK is not structured according to democratic principles, does not function in accordance with the rule of law, and does not respect important international human rights norms. The people of Kosovo are therefore deprived of protection of their basic rights and freedoms three years after the end of the conflict by the very entity set up to guarantee them.").

39   S.C. Res. 827 (1993). Unlike the International Criminal Tribunal for Rwanda, which has jurisdiction over incidents within the period Jan. 1 – Dec. 31, 1994, the International Criminal Tribunal for the former Yugoslavia has jurisdiction to prosecute persons responsible for crimes committed "since 1991." Statute of the International Criminal Tribunal for the former Yugoslavia, S.C. Res. 827 (1993), Annex, art. 1. Though no formal end to this temporal jurisdiction has been defined, in practice it is likely to be 1999, given the decision to cease new prosecutions.

40   S.C. Res. 955 (1994).

41   Agreement Between the United Nations and the Government of Sierra Leone on the Establishment of a Special Court for Sierra Leone, completed at Freetown, Jan. 16, 2002.

42   Agreement Between the United Nations and the Royal Government of Cambodia Concerning the Prosecution Under Cambodian Law of Crimes Committed During the Period of Democratic Kampuchea, completed at Phnom Penh, June 6, 2003, available at http://www.eccc.gov.kh.

43   Statute of the International Criminal Court (Rome Statute), U.N. Doc. A/Conf.183/9 (July 17, 1998), available at http://www.icc-cpi.int/library/about/officialjournal/Rome_Statute_120704-EN.pdf, art. 1.

international interest in promoting justice or securing peace (Bergsmo and Pejic 1999; Chesterman 2001; Stahn 2002).

The Rule of Law within International Organizations

Though the rule of law has been promoted strongly through international forums, it has been less clear what relevance it has to the conduct of international affairs itself. This is in part because, as we have seen, the historic challenge for the rule of law has been its relationship to the sovereign. In a domestic legal order, the sovereign exists in a vertical hierarchy with other subjects of law; at the international level, sovereignty tends to be conceived of as remaining with States, at least nominally existing in a horizontal plane of sovereign equality. This section considers how the rule of law might apply to the internal operations of organizations constituted by those States, before turning in the following section to the rule of law as it would apply to States and other actors on the international plane more generally.

The United Nations

The United Nations is a creature of treaty. Its legal personality was recognized in the 1949 *Reparations* advisory opinion of the International Court of Justice (I.C.J.) as implicit in the decision of 50 States to create the organization;[44] today that intention to create legal personality is often included explicitly in the text of a treaty.[45]

Referring back to the core definition of the rule of law, the United Nations operates through legal mechanisms, though these are not always free from arbitrariness. Here a distinction must be made between the exercise of discretion formally provided for in the constituent document of the organization and the arbitrary exercise of the powers that it grants. Both may be illustrated by actions of the Security Council. Originally designed as an archetypically political body, it is entirely proper that members of the Council should determine whether, for example, to send peacekeepers to a specific crisis. The moves from 1999 to use targeted sanctions to limit financing of terrorist operations, by contrast, have been criticized for the manner in which individuals may be listed and have their assets frozen without either transparency or the possibility of formal review (Chesterman 2006, pp. 1109–20). In 2005, Member States called upon the Security Council to adopt "fair and clear procedures" for listing and delisting;[46] this led to the creation of a focal point within the U.N. Secretariat to receive requests for delisting, but

---

44   Reparation for Injuries Suffered in the Service of the United Nations (Advisory Opinion, 1949) I.C.J. Rep. 174 (1949).

45   See, e.g., Rome Statute, art. 4(1) ("The Court shall have international legal personality.").

46   World Summit Outcome Document, para. 109.

left the decision to unfreeze assets at the absolute discretion of the members of the Council.[47] Such concerns may be contrasted with the elaborate protections established when the Council created the International Criminal Tribunals for the former Yugoslavia and Rwanda.

On the question of applying the law to the United Nations itself,[48] there is a surprising degree of uncertainty as to whether the organization is bound by, for example, the human rights treaties for which it has been the primary vehicle. The United Nations is not a party to the human rights treaties negotiated under its auspices or monitored through its agencies. In part this reflects the traditional view that only States properly enter into such treaties, a view based on the understanding that it is primarily States that violate or protect human rights. As the United Nations has assumed State-like functions, however—including administrations that ran entire territories—the question of whether the United Nations is required to abide by basic human rights standards has become more pressing. In a series of cases arising from the use of targeted financial sanctions, the European Court of First Instance has held that Security Council decisions, by virtue of the U.N. Charter's primacy clause in Article 103, are constrained only by norms of *jus cogens*.[49] This

---

47   S.C. Res. 1730 (Dec. 19, 2006), Annex. Decisions by the committee administering the sanctions are by consensus; in the absence of consensus a matter may be referred to the Council proper, where the veto power of the permanent five members would apply. See Security Council Committee Established Pursuant to Resolution 1267 (1999) Concerning Al-Qaida and the Taliban and Associated Individuals and Entities, Guidelines of the Committee for the Conduct of Its Work (as amended) (New York, Nov. 7, 2002), available at http://www.un.org/Docs/sc/committees/1267/1267_guidelines.pdf.

48   For disputes within the organization, the U.N. Administrative Tribunal (UNAT) was established by the General Assembly through resolution 351A(IV) (1949). It is an independent organ competent to hear and pass judgment upon applications alleging non-observance of contracts or terms of employment by staff members of the U.N. Secretariat. See, e.g., *Qiu, Zhou, and Yao v. Secretary-General of the United Nations* (United Nations Administrative Tribunal Judgement No. 482, May 25, 1990), U.N. Doc. AT/DEC/482 (1990) (The Chinese Translators Case).

49   Ahmed Ali Yusuf and Al Barakaat International Foundation v. Council of the European Union and Commission of the European Communities (Court of First Instance of the European Communities, Case T-306/01, Sept. 21, 2005) (2005), available at http://curia.eu.int, para. 277 ("the Court is empowered to check, indirectly, the lawfulness of the resolutions of the Security Council in question with regard to *jus cogens*, understood as a body of higher rules of public international law binding on all subjects of international law, including the bodies of the United Nations, and from which no derogation is possible"). See also Yassin Abdullah Kadi v. Council of the European Union and Commission of the European Communities (Court of First Instance of the European Communities, Case T-315/01, Sept. 21, 2005) (2005), available at http://curia.eu.int; Faraj Hassan v. Council of the European Union and Commission of the European Communities (Court of First Instance of the European Communities, Case T 49/04, July 12, 2006) (2006), available at http://curia.eu.int; Chafiq Ayadi v. Council of the European Union (Court of First Instance

is one of only a few cases in which a tribunal has reviewed, even indirectly, the validity of Council action.[50]

Similarly, in 1952 a committee of the American Society of International Law expressed doubts that international humanitarian law was fully applicable to U.N. forces, concluding that the United Nations should "select such of the laws of war as may seem to fit its purposes." (Bivens et al. 1952, p. 220) It has been assumed by most writers that States involved in U.N.-authorized enforcement actions nevertheless remain bound by their individual obligations under the *jus in bello* (Bowett 1964, pp. 503–6). This would be true for actions authorized by the U.N. Security Council, but it would be less clear if the Council deployed forces made available to it under Article 43 agreements—a hypothetical proposition since no such agreements have been concluded (Greenwood 1996; Peck 1995). Remaining doubts about the applicability of international humanitarian law to the United Nations have been removed by the issuance of an administrative order by the Secretary-General.[51]

The United Nations lacks a formal process to establish the *vires* of its organs as the question of interpreting the Charter powers of each was quite consciously left to the organs themselves.[52] The I.C.J. does not exercise the functions of a constitutional court, though an organ may choose to submit a relevant question to it for an advisory opinion.[53] In the *Lockerbie* case, a direct clash loomed between the Security Council and the Court when both were seized of issues arising from the bombing of Pan Am Flight 103 on December 21, 1988 over Lockerbie, in Scotland. The Court declined to rule on the merits in provisional measures and

---

of the European Communities, Case T-253/02, July 12, 2006) (2006), available at http://curia.eu.int.

50   See also Legal Consequences for States of the Continued Presence of South Africa in Namibia (South-West Africa) Notwithstanding Security Council Resolution 276 (1970) (Advisory Opinion, 1971) I.C.J. Rep. 16, 54 (1971), para. 118 (referring to "a situation which the Court has found to have been *validly* declared illegal" by the Security Council (emphasis added)); Prosecutor v. Tadic (ICTY Appeals Chamber, Appeal on Jurisdiction, Oct. 2, 1995) Case No. IT-94-1-AR72 (1995), available at http://www.un.org/icty, paras. 28–30 ("neither the text nor the spirit of the Charter conceives of the Security Council as *legibus solutus* (unbound by law)").

51   Secretary-General's Bulletin: Observance by United Nations Forces of International Humanitarian Law, U.N. Doc. ST/SGB/1999/13 (Aug. 6, 1999), available at http://www.un.org/Docs/journal/asp/ws.asp?m=ST/SGB/1999/13. See also Conditions of Application of Humanitarian Rules of Armed Conflict to Hostilities in Which United Nations Forces May Be Engaged (1971 Zagreb Resolution) (Institut de Droit international, Zagreb, First Commission, Rapporteur: Mr. Paul de Visscher, Sept. 3, 1971), available at http://www.idi-iil.org/idiE/resolutionsE/1971_zag_03_en.pdf.

52   Statement of Committee IV/2 of the San Francisco Conference, Report of Committee IV/2 of the United Nations Conference on International Organization, San Francisco, June 12, 1945, UNCIO Doc. 933, IV/2/42(2), p.7; 13 UNCIO Documents, 703, at 709–10.

53   U.N. Charter, art. 96.

preliminary objections proceedings in 1992 and 1998, but even as it affirmed the discretion of the Security Council the Court implicitly asserted its own power to determine the limits of that discretion.[54] The case has been likened to *Marbury v. Madison*[55] in which the U.S. Supreme Court asserted the ultimate power to determine whether the political branch had acted constitutionally—though this is premised on a reading that focuses more on what the Court did *not* say rather than what it did (Franck 1992).

Turning to the notion of equality before the law, the United Nations is based upon the principle of the sovereign equality of its members,[56] though the structure of the Security Council establishes that some—with permanent positions on the Council and a veto over its decisions—are more equal than others. This has been an issue in the context of quasi-legislative resolutions adopted by the Council on matters such as counter-terrorism and proliferation of weapons of mass destruction (Alvarez 2003). Criticisms that such resolutions inappropriately use what may be understood as the Council's "emergency" powers under Chapter VII (Schott 2007) to establish abstract rules of general application stress either the limits on the Council's powers under the Charter or its relative legitimacy as opposed to, say, the General Assembly. The former argument draws upon rule-of-law-type arguments to constrain the powers of the Council; the latter appears to assume that the General Assembly is more "democratic" than the Council and therefore more legitimate, both dubious assumptions (Talmon 2005, p. 179).

Other International Organizations

It is questionable whether the United Nations may properly be said to embody the rule of law in a meaningful way, in large part due to the peace and security powers given to or asserted by its Security Council and the unusual relationship to other international legal regimes due to Article 103 of the U.N. Charter. Other institutions created to foster economic development or protect human rights tend to be more constrained by rules in the exercise of their delegated authority.

The World Trade Organization (WTO), for example, was established by treaty in 1995 with rules, institutions, and procedures for the liberalization of trade (Weiler 2001). In the human rights sphere the various treaty bodies have

---

54   Questions of Interpretation and Application of the 1971 Montreal Convention Arising from the Aerial Incident at Lockerbie (Libya v. U.S.) (International Court of Justice, Request for the Indication of Provisional Measures, Apr. 14, 1992) (1992), available at http://www.icj-cij.org; Questions of Interpretation and Application of the 1971 Montreal Convention Arising from the Aerial Incident at Lockerbie (Libya v. U.S.) (International Court of Justice, Preliminary Objections, Feb. 27, 1998) (1998), available at http://www.icj-cij.org.

55   Marbury v. Madison (1803), 5 US (1 Cranch) 137 (1803).

56   U.N. Charter, art. 2(1).

jurisdiction limited by the consent of States but generally operate in accordance with a clear normative regime, with independent institutions to determine compliance with the law and process guarantees. The I.C.C., to pick a prominent recent creation, is established as a legal person constrained by its statute. It has an elaborate, independent procedure for the determination of compliance with that statute and protections of the procedural rights of persons brought before it. Both organizations operate through laws and are bound by them.

The limits of such analysis, however, are that the WTO, the I.C.C., and indeed the United Nations, do not exist as autonomous and complete jurisdictions in a manner comparable to the national legal systems that gave rise to the concept of rule of law. Though analogies may be made, examination of such institutions in isolation begs the larger question of whether the rule of law is a coherent concept at the international or, perhaps, global level.

An International Rule of Law?

What, then, might the rule of law mean at the international level? It is helpful here to distinguish between three possible meanings. First, the "international rule of law" may be understood as the application of rule of law principles to relations between States and other subjects of international law. Secondly, the "rule of international law" could privilege international law over national law, establishing, for example, the primacy of human rights covenants over domestic legal arrangements. Thirdly, a "global rule of law" might denote the emergence of a normative regime that touches individuals directly without formal mediation through existing national institutions.

The first sense is how the rule of law is typically understood in this context and as it will be applied here (Bishop 1961). The second may be relevant to certain regional organizations, notably the European Union, but such regimes are exceptional and, with the aggregation of power, resemble State-like institutions rather than international organizations in the strict sense of the word (Kumm 2003). The third approach accurately reflects the rise of quasi-administrative regimes that fall outside traditional domestic and international legal categories, but remains at an early stage of development (Chesterman 2008; Kingsbury, et al. 2005). It is possible that justice will one day be sought through global law, but at the present time it is most likely to be pursued through the global organization of well-ordered States.

Though the U.N. Charter has been compared to a kind of constitution for the modern international order (Franck 2003), its language concerning international law is hortatory rather than declaratory. The preamble expresses determination "*to establish conditions* under which justice and respect for the obligations arising from treaties and other sources of international law can be maintained"; its principles include peaceful resolution of disputes that may threaten the peace "in conformity with the principles of justice and international law"—though the latter phrase does not qualify the related goal of suppressing breaches and preventing or removing threats.[57] An important role of the General Assembly is "encouraging the progressive development of international law and its codification."[58]

Similarly, documents such as the Declaration on Friendly Relations refer to the "promotion of the rule of law among nations."[59] Thirty years later, in the Millennium Declaration, Member States resolved to "strengthen respect for the rule of law in international as in national affairs and, in particular, to ensure compliance by Member States with the decisions of the International Court of Justice, in compliance with the Charter of the United Nations, in cases to which they are parties."[60]

These cautious endorsements of the rule of law reflect the primitive nature of international law as a legal system. If the rule of law is understood in the core, formal sense used here, it might be questioned whether the process of international rule-making can itself be said to be governed by laws (Hart 1994, pp. 213–37). Those judicial institutions that exist are limited to essentially voluntary jurisdiction,[61] and sovereign equality may be the founding myth of the international legal order but remains a myth nonetheless.[62] Such an account might conclude that there is

---

57   U.N. Charter, art. 1(1).

58   U.N. Charter, art. 13(1)(a).

59   Declaration on Principles of International Law Concerning Friendly Relations and Co-operation Among States in Accordance with the Charter of the United Nations (Declaration on Friendly Relations), 25 GAOR, Supp (No 28), U.N. Doc. A/5217 (1970), preamble.

60   Millennium Declaration, GA Res 55/2, U.N. Doc. A/RES/55/2 (2000), available at http://www.un.org/millennium/declaration/ares552e.htm, para. 9.

61   See, e.g., Statute of the International Court of Justice, art. 36.

62   Sovereign equality in its traditional conception made sense when most laws were derived from natural law; as the consent-based notion of international law evolved and positivism took hold, it came to be understood literally as the consent of each and every State to general norms rather than the presumed universal applicability of certain rules to all. (There are rare examples of norms being imposed against the will of persistent objector States, such as the prohibition of apartheid over the objections of South Africa and the U.N. Charter provisions on the applicability of its peace and security provisions to non-members: U.N. Charter, art 2(6).) This was only possible because for centuries international law tended to avoid the hardest questions that might undermine the principle: on the one hand, by not attempting to regulate such areas of activity as recourse to war; on the other, by excluding from consideration relations with those deemed outside the law, such as those subject to colonialism. Assumptions today that international law meaningfully constrains States even in the use of force and sets the smallest and poorest States on an equal footing with the largest and richest has led some—typically the larger and richer—to question whether freedom from jurisdiction and consent in law-making processes should continue to apply equally to all. Michel Cosnard, "Sovereign Equality: "the *Wimbledon* Sails on"", in *United States Hegemony and the Foundations of International Law*, eds. Michael Byers and Georg Nolte (Cambridge: Cambridge University Press, 2003); Nico Krisch, "More Equal than the Rest? Hierarchy, Equality and US Predominance in International Law," in

presently no such thing as the international rule of law, or at least that international law has yet to achieve a certain normative or institutional threshold to justify use of the term. This may in turn be understood as a subset of the larger ongoing debates over whether international law is "law" in any strict sense of the word, a largely sterile inquiry due to the dearth of strong theories of international law and the abundance of practice accepting its legality nonetheless.[63]

The problem is the uncritical assumption that domestic legal principles can be translated directly to the international sphere. As Martti Koskenniemi has shown, since at least the middle of the eighteenth century, jurists have included the rule of law among these principles (Koskenniemi 1990). This fails to take account of structural differences between international law and domestic law—the horizontal organization of sovereign and quasi-sovereign entities as opposed to the vertical hierarchy of subjects under a sovereign—but also of the historical and political context within which the rule of law was developed.

That history of the rule of law is a tale of kings and judges, of revolutions and bills of rights. One might conceive the creation of the League of Nations and the United Nations in such a context, but a more persuasive account can be made of the modern political context within which the rule of law is promoted: as a tool with which to protect human rights, promote development, and sustain peace. This functionalist understanding of how and why the rule of law is *used*—as distinct from the formal understanding of what it *means*—matches more closely the manner in which the rule of law is articulated at the international level; it also offers some suggestions as to how the core definition used here may apply to the international legal system.

The first aspect, government of laws, requires non-arbitrariness in the exercise of power (Waldron 1989, pp. 82–4). This is embodied in the foundational concept of *pacta sunt servanda*,[64] but is also evident in efforts to establish international protections for human rights, formal regimes to govern international trade, and international security institutions such as the Security Council. Moves towards the rule of law in this area include the further codification of the content of international

---

United States Hegemony and the Foundations of International Law, ed. Michael Byers and Georg Nolte (Cambridge: Cambridge University Press, 2003).

63   Dicey, for example, suggested that international law consisted of "rules of public ethics, which are miscalled international law." Dicey, *Law of the Constitution*, 23. International law has long endured a tension between the realist understanding of law as an instrument of policy and the legalist view of law as a constraint on policy. It is possible to distinguish further between the political realist critique that the rule of law cannot be achieved internationally because the institutions necessary to make and enforce law do not exist at that level, and the legal realist critique that the rule of law is conceptually impossible because law is always an instrument of policy at any level. Benedict Kingsbury, "The Concept of Compliance as a Function of Competing Conceptions of International Law," *Michigan Journal of International Law* 19 (1998); Terry Nardin, "Theorizing the International Rule of Law," *Review of International Studies* 34 (2008), 385–401.

64   Agreements are to be kept.

law as well as the manner in which it is created; rule of law concepts such as clarity are undermined by fragmentation of the legal order (Koskenniemi and Leino 2002) and assertions that legally indeterminate categories of "legitimacy" exist alongside determinations of legality (Chesterman 2002; Franck 1990).

The second aspect, supremacy of the law, distinguishes the rule of law from rule *by* law. This distinction is less applicable to the international legal system, however, where the primary question is not the relationship between subject and sovereign but between subject and subject. In such a regime the relevance of concepts such as separation of powers is less important than the possibility of determinative answers to legal questions. Rule of law advances would include greater acceptance of the compulsory jurisdiction of the I.C.J. and other independent tribunals, and confirmation that international law applies to international organizations in general and to the U.N. Security Council in particular.

The third aspect of the core definition, equality before the law, raises the question of who the true subject of law is. Equality of individual human beings before the law is a formal constraint on the exercise of public power by State institutions; it has a very different meaning in the context of sovereign equality of States. The individual's relationship to the State is defined by its coerciveness: one does not normally choose the State to the laws of which one is subject. Legal systems frequently treat juridical persons, such as corporations, differently from natural persons; it therefore seems unnecessary to overemphasize the formal equality of States as such. Steps towards an international rule of law in this area would include more general and consistent application of international law to States and other entities; it might also entail amelioration of structural irregularities such as the veto power over Security Council decisions presently enjoyed by the victors of the Second World War.

These are all, in essence, political challenges. Recognizing the rule of law as a political ideal at the international level, rather than asserting it as a normative reality, properly locates the conduct of most of international affairs in the political rather than the strictly legal sphere. Over time this may change, but in the efforts to achieve human rights, development, and peace, the international rule of law presently offers a means rather than an end (Koskenniemi 1989; Nagel 2005).

Conclusion

The rule of law, as Judith Shklar ultimately acknowledged in her provocative chapter on the topic, is more than mere ruling-class chatter. But assertions that the rule of law is a meaningful concept at the international level depend on a coherent meaning at the national level, and the applicability of the term to power relations between States as well as within them. Neither should be taken for granted.

Through examining the evolution of the term, this chapter has sought to establish a core definition of "rule of law" that properly reflects what is distinctive about the term and is applicable across cultures. The price of clarity is abandoning the additional role that the rule of law sometimes plays as a Trojan horse to import other political goals such as democracy, human rights, and specific economic policies. It is a price worth paying, however, as these substantive goals may properly be seen as distinct from the rule of law—folding them into its robes reduces it to a rhetorical device at best, a disingenuous ideological tool at worst. In this core sense the rule of law reflects the history of efforts to restrain sovereign power that continue in many States today, including some established liberal democracies confronting what the modern sovereign claims are emergencies requiring ever-greater claims to executive authority (Dyzenhaus 2006; Gross and Ní Aoláin 2006).

At the international level anything resembling even this limited idea of the rule of law remains an aspiration. Yet seeing the rule of law as a means rather than an end, as serving a function rather than defining a status, more accurately reflects how the rule of law developed and has been imported or imposed around the world. And for international law, this understanding appropriately highlights the political work that must be done if power is to be channeled through law.

References

2005 World Summit Outcome Document, UN Doc A/RES/60/1, September 16, 2005, available at www.un.org/summit2005.

Adams, John 1775. Novanglus No. 7 (January 1775), available at douglassarchives. org/adam_a50.htm.

Alvarez, José (2003). "Hegemonic International Law Revisited," *American Journal of International Law* 97, 873–88.

Aristotle (350 BC). *The Politics*. Translated by Benjamin Jowett. Boston, MA: MIT Internet Classics Archive.

Barber, N.W. (2003). "The Rechtsstaat and the Rule of Law," *University of Toronto Law Journal* 53, 443–54.

Bassiouni, M. Cherif, and Gamal M. Badr (2002). "The Shari'ah: Sources, Interpretation, and Rule-Making," *UCLA Journal of Islamic and Near Eastern Law* 1, 135–81.

Bergsmo, Morten, and Jelena Pejic (1999). "Article 16: Deferral of Investigation or Prosecution." In *Commentary on the Rome Statute of the International Criminal Court*, ed. Otto Triffterer. Baden-Baden: Nomos, 373–82.

Bishop, William W., 59 Mich L Rev 553 (1961) (1961). "The International Rule of Law," *Michigan Law Review* 59, 553–74.

Bivens, William J., Clyde Eagleton, Leland M. Goodrich, Hans Kelsen, Josef L. Kunz, and Louis B. Sohn (1952). "Report of Committee on the Study of the Legal Problems of the United Nations, Should the Laws of War Apply to United Nations Enforcement Action?," *American Society of International Law Proceedings* 46, 216–20.

Blackton, John Stuart (2003). "Democracy Lite: Arab Judicial Reform," Arab *Reform Bulletin* 1, no. 4.

Boon, Kristen E. (2007). ""Open for Business": International Financial Institutions, Post-Conflict Economic Reform, and the Rule of Law," New York University *Journal of International Law and Politics* 39, 513–81.

Bowett, Derek W. (1964). *United Nations Forces: A Legal Study of United Nations Practice*. London: Stevens.

Boyer, Allen D. (ed. (2004). *Law, Liberty, and Parliament: Selected Essays on the Writings of Sir Edward Coke*. Indianapolis: Liberty Fund, 2004.

Bracton, Henry de (1968). *De legibus et consuetudinibus Angliae*. Translated by Samuel E. Thorne. Cambridge, MA: Belknap Press.

Brown, Nathan J. (1997). *The Rule of Law in the Arab World: Courts in Egypt and the Gulf*. Cambridge: Cambridge University Press.

Chen, Albert H.Y. (2000). "Toward a Legal Enlightenment: Discussion in Contemporary China on the Rule of Law," *UCLA Pacific Basin Law Journal* 17, 125–65.

Chesterman, Simon (2001). "No Justice Without Peace? International Criminal Law and the Decision to Prosecute." In *Civilians in War*, ed. Simon Chesterman. Boulder, CO: Lynne Rienner, 145–63.

Chesterman, Simon (2002). "Legality Versus Legitimacy: Humanitarian Intervention, the Security Council, and the Rule of Law," *Security Dialogue* 33, 293–307.

Chesterman, Simon (2004). *You, The People: The United Nations, Transitional Administration, and State-Building*. Oxford: Oxford University Press.

Chesterman, Simon (2006). "The Spy Who Came in from the Cold War: Intelligence and International Law," *Michigan Journal of International Law* 27, 1071–1130.

Chesterman, Simon (2007). "Ownership in Theory and in Practice: Transfer of Authority in UN Stateuilding Operations," J*ournal of Intervention and Statebuilding* 1, no. 1, 3–26.

Chesterman, Simon (2008). "Globalization Rules: Accountability, Power, and the Prospects for Global Administrative Law," *Global Governance* 14, 39–52.

Chesterman, Simon (2011). *One Nation Under Surveillance: A New Social Contract to Defend Freedom Without Sacrificing Liberty*. Oxford: Oxford University Press.

Chevallier, Jacques (1999). *L'État de droit*. 3rd edn. Paris: Montchrestien.

Cosnard, Michel (2003). "Sovereign Equality: 'The *Wimbledon* Sails on'." In *United States Hegemony and the Foundations of International Law*, ed. Michael Byers and Georg Nolte. Cambridge: Cambridge University Press, 117–34.

Craig, Paul (1997). "Formal and Substantive Conceptions of the Rule of Law: An Analytical Framework," *Public Law*, 467–87.

Cummins, Richard J. (1985). "Constitutional Protection of Civil Liberties in France," *American Journal of Comparative Law* 33, 721–32.

Davis, Kevin E. (2004). "What Can the Rule of Law Variable Tell Us about Rule of Law Reforms?," *Michigan Journal of International Law* 26, 141–62.

Dicey, A.V. (1885). *Lectures Introductory to the Study of the Law of the Constitution*. London: Macmillan.

Dokupil, Susanna (2002). "The Separation of Mosque and State: Islam and Democracy in Modern Turkey," *West Virginia Law Review* 105, 53–129.

Dworkin, Ronald (1985). *A Matter of Principle*. Cambridge, MA: Harvard University Press.

Dyzenhaus, David (1991). *Hard Cases in Wicked Legal Systems: South African Law in the Perspective of Legal Philosophy*. Oxford: Clarendon Press.

Dyzenhaus, David (2001). "Hobbes and the Legitimacy of Law," *Law and Philosophy* 20, 461–98.

Dyzenhaus, David (2006). *The Constitution of Law: Legality in a Time of Emergency*. Cambridge: Cambridge University Press.

Dyzenhaus, David (ed. (1999). *Recrafting the Rule of Law: The Limits of Legal Order*. Oxford: Hart Publishing, 1999.

Fallon, Richard H., Jr. (1997). "'The Rule of Law' as a Concept in Constitutional Discourse," *Columbia Law Review* 97, 1–56.

Fitzpatrick, Daniel 2002. Land Policy in Post-Conflict Circumstances: Some Lessons from East Timor (Evaluation and Policy Analysis Unit, United Nations High Commissioner for Refugees, Geneva, February 2002), available at www.unhcr.ch/cgi-bin/texis/vtx/research/opendoc.pdf?tbl=RESEARCH&id=3c8399e14.

Franck, Thomas M. (1972). "The New Development: Can American Law and Legal Institutions Help Developing Countries?," *Wisconsin Law Review* 3, 767–801.

Franck, Thomas M. (1990). *The Power of Legitimacy Among Nations*. Oxford: Oxford University Press.

Franck, Thomas M. (1992). "The 'Powers of Application': Who Is the Ultimate Guardian of UN Legality?," *American Journal of International Law* 86, 519–23.

Franck, Thomas M. (2003). "Is the UN Charter a Constitution?" In *Verhandeln für den Frieden—Negotiating for Peace: Liber Amicorum Tono Eitel*, ed. Jochen Abr Frowein, et al. Berlin: Springer, 95–106.

Gardner, James (1980). *Legal Imperialism: American Lawyers and Foreign Aid in Latin America*. Madison: University of Wisconsin Press.

Ghai, Yash (1986). "The Rule of Law, Legitimacy, and Governance," *International Journal of the Sociology of Law* 14, 179–208.

Goodhart, Arthur L. (1958). "The Rule of Law and Absolute Sovereignty," *University of Pennsylvania Law Review* 106, 943–63.

Greenwood, Christopher (1996). "Protection of Peacekeepers: The Legal Regime," *Duke Journal of Comparative and International Law* 7, 185–208.

Gross, Oren, and Fionnuala Ní Aoláin (2006). *Law in Times of Crisis: Emergency Powers in Theory and Practice*. Cambridge: Cambridge University Press.

Grote, Rainer (1999). "Rule of Law, Rechtsstaat, and 'Etat de droit'." In *Constitutionalism, Universalism and Democracy: A Comparative Analysis*, ed. Christian Starck. Baden-Baden: Nomos, 269–306.

Hart, H.L.A. (1994). *The Concept of Law*. 2nd edn. Oxford: Clarendon Press.

Hayek, Friedrich (1944). *The Road to Serfdom.* Chicago: Chicago University Press.

Hayek, Friedrich (1960). *The Constitution of Liberty.* Chicago: University of Chicago Press.

Hobbes, Thomas (1914). *Leviathan.* London: Dent.

Hyden, Goran (1999). "Governance and the Reconstitution of Political Order." In *State, Conflict and Democracy in Africa,* ed. Richard Joseph. Boulder, CO: Lynne Rienner, 179–95.

Jennings, W. Ivor (1952). *The Law and the Constitution.* 4th edn. London: University of London Press.

Kamali, Mohammad Hashim (2003). *Principles of Islamic Jurisprudence.* 3rd edn. Cambridge: Islamic Texts Society.

Kant, Immanuel (1965). *The Metaphysical Elements of Justice: Part I of The Metaphysics of Morals.* Translated by John Ladd. Indianapolis: Bobbs-Merrill.

Kelsen, Hans (1967). *Pure Theory of Law.* Translated by Max Knight. 2nd edn. Berkeley: University of California Press.

Kingsbury, Benedict (1998). "The Concept of Compliance as a Function of Competing Conceptions of International Law," *Michigan Journal of International Law* 19, 345–72.

Kingsbury, Benedict, Nico Krisch, and Richard B. Stewart (2005). "The Emergence of Global Administrative Law," *Law and Contemporary Problems* 68, 15–61.

Kirchheimer, Otto (1969). "The Rechtsstaat as Magic Wall." In *Politics, Law, and Social Change: Selected Essays of Otto Kirchheimer,* ed. Frederic S. Burin and Kurt L. Shell. New York: Columbia University Press, 429–52.

Koskenniemi, Martti (1989). *From Apologia to Utopia: The Structure of International Legal Argument.* Helsinki: Lakimiesliiton Kustannus.

Koskenniemi, Martti (1990). "The Politics of International Law," *European Journal of International Law* 1, 4–32.

Koskenniemi, Martti, and Päivi Leino (2002). "Fragmentation of International Law. Postmodern Anxieties?," *Leiden Journal of International Law* 15, 553–79.

Krisch, Nico (2003). "More Equal than the Rest? Hierarchy, Equality and US Predominance in International Law." In *United States Hegemony and the Foundations of International Law,* eds Michael Byers and Georg Nolte. Cambridge: Cambridge University Press, 135–75.

Kumm, Mattias (2003). "International Law Before National Courts: The International Rule of Law and the Limits of the Internationalist Model," *Virginia Journal of International Law* 44, 19–32.

Liang Chi-Chao [Liang Qichao] (1930). *History of Chinese Political Thought During the Early Tsin Period.* New York: Harcourt Brace.

Liu, Yongping (1998). *Origins of Chinese Law: Penal and Administrative Law in Its Early Development.* Oxford: Oxford University Press.

Locke, John (1988). *Two Treatises of Government.* Cambridge: Cambridge University Press.

Mallat, Chibli (2004). "From Islamic to Middle Eastern Law: A Restatement of the Field (Part II)," American Journal of Comparative Law 52, 209–86.

McClymont, Mary, and Stephen Golub (eds) (2000). *Many Roads to Justice: The Law-Related Work of Ford Foundation Grantees Around the World*. New York: Ford Foundation, 2000.

Merryman, John Henry, David S. Clark, and Lawrence Friedman (1979). *Law and Social Change in Mediterranean Europe and Latin America: A Handbook of Legal Indicators for Comparative Study*. Stanford, CA.: Stanford Studies in Law and Development.

Merryman, John. H. (1977). "Comparative Law and Social Change: On the Origins, Style, Decline & Revival of the Law and Development Movement," American Journal of Comparative Law 25, 457–83.

Mohl, Robert von (1829). *Das Staatsrecht des Königreichs Württemberg*. Tubingen: Laupp.

Montesquieu, Charles de Secondat (1989). *The Spirit of the Laws*. Translated by Anne M. Cohler, Basia Carolyn Miller and Harold Samuel Stone. Cambridge: Cambridge University Press.

Morin, Jacques-Yvan (1992). "The Rule of Law and the Rechtsstaat Concept: A Comparison." In *Federalism-in-the-Making: Contemporary Canadian and German Constitutionalism, National and Transnational*, ed. Edward Mcwhinney, Jerald Zaslove and Werner Wolf. Dordrecht: Kluwer, 60–85.

Mugraby, Muhamad (2003). "Some Impediments to the Rule of Law," Fordham International Law Journal 26, 771–84.

Munck, Gerardo L. 2003. Measures of Democracy, Governance and Rule of Law: An Overview of Cross-National Data Sets (World Bank, Washington, DC, 15–July 17, 2003), available at siteresources.worldbank.org/INTMOVOUTPOV/Resources/2104215–1148063363276/071503_Munck.pdf.

Nagel, Thomas (2005). "The Problem of Global Justice," Philosophy & Public Affairs 33, no. 2, 113–47.

Nardin, Terry (2008). "Theorizing the International Rule of Law," Review of International Studies 34, 385–401.

Ngugi, Joel M. (2005). "Policing Neo-Liberal Reforms: The Rule of Law as an Enabling and Restrictive Discourse," University of Pennsylvania Journal of International Economic Law 26, 513–99.

O'Connor, Vivienne (2006). "Rule of Law and Human Rights Protections Through Criminal Law Reform: Model Codes for Post-conflict Criminal Justice," International Peacekeeping 13, no. 4, 517–30.

Peck, Julianne (1995). "The UN and the Laws of War: How Can the World's Peacekeepers Be Held Accountable?," Syracuse Journal of International Law and Commerce 21, 283–310.

Peerenboom, Randall (2002). *China's Long March Toward Rule of Law*. Cambridge: Cambridge University Press.

Peerenboom, Randall (2004). "Varieties of Rule of Law." In *Asian Discourses of Rule of Law: Theories and Implementation of Rule of Law in Twelve Asian Countries, France and the US*, ed. Randall Peerenboom. New York: RoutledgeCurzon, 1–55.

Plato (1892). *The Republic*. Translated by Benjamin Jowett. Oxford: Clarendon Press.

Pound, Roscoe (1910). "Law in Books and Law in Action," A*merican Law Review* 44, 12–36.

Rawls, John (1972). *A Theory of Justice*. Oxford: Clarendon Press.

Raz, Joseph (1979). *The Authority of Law: Essays on Law and Morality*. Oxford: Clarendon Press.

Raz, Joseph (1990). "The Politics of the Rule of Law," *Ratio Juris* 3, 331–9.

Reid, John Phillip (2004). *Rule of Law: The Jurisprudence of Liberty in the Seventeenth and Eighteenth Centuries*. DeKalb, IL: Northern Illinois University Press.

Rousseau, Jean-Jacques (1923). *The Social Contract*. Translated by G.D.H. Cole. London: J.M. Dent.

Rutherford, Samuel (1644). *Lex, Rex, or the Law and the Prince: A Dispute for the Just Prerogative of King and People*. London: John Field.

Saunders, Cheryl, and Katherine Le Roy (eds) (2003). *The Rule of Law*. Sydney: Federation Press, 2003.

Schott, Jared (2007). "Chapter VII as Exception: Security Council Action and the Regulative Ideal of Emergency," *Northwestern University Journal of International Human Rights* 6, 24–38.

Shklar, Judith (1987). "Political Theory and the Rule of Law." In *The Rule of Law: Ideal or Ideology*, ed. Allan C. Hutchinson and Patrick Monahan. Toronto: Carswell, 1–16.

Smith, Adam (1976). *An Inquiry into the Nature and Causes of the Wealth of Nations*. Chicago: University of Chicago Press.

Stahn, Carsten (2002). "The Ambiguities of Security Council Resolution 1422 (2002)," *European Journal of International Law* 4, 85–104.

Stephenson, Matthew 2001. The Rule of Law as a Goal of Development Policy (World Bank, Washington, DC, 2001), available at www1.worldbank.org/publicsector/legal/ruleoflaw2.htm.

Talmon, Stefan A. (2005). "The Security Council as World Legislature," *American Journal of International Law* 99, 175–93.

Tamanaha, Brian Z. (1995). "The Lessons of Law-and-Development Studies," *American Journal of International Law* 89, 470–86.

Thio, Li-Ann (2002). "Lex Rex or Rex Lex? Competing Conceptions of the Rule of Law in Singapore," *UCLA Pacific Basin Law Journal* 20, 1–76.

Thompson, E.P. (1977). *Whigs and Hunters: The Origin of the Black Act*. Harmondsworth: Penguin.

Trubek, David M., and Marc Galanter (1974). "Scholars in Self-Estrangement: Some Reflections on the Crisis in Law and Development," *Wisconsin Law Review* 4, 1062–1101.

Upham, Frank 2002. Mythmaking in the Rule of Law Orthodoxy (Carnegie Endowment for International Peace, Washington, DC, 2002), available at www.carnegieendowment.org/files/wp30.pdf.

Viel, H.-Dieter (2005). *The Complete Code of Hammurabi.* Munich: Lincom Europa.

Waldron, Jeremy (1989). "The Rule of Law in Contemporary Liberal Theory," *Ratio Juris* 2, 79–96.

Waldron, Jeremy (1999). *The Dignity of Legislation.* Cambridge: Cambridge University Press.

Weiler, J.H.H. (2001). "The Rule of Lawyers and the Ethos of Diplomats: Reflections on the Internal and External Legitimacy of WTO Dispute Settlement," *Journal of World Trade* 35, no. 2, 191–207.

Chapter 3

'Thin Theories' of the Domestic and International Rule of Law

Charles Sampford

Introduction

I have written at length on the Rule of Law in both domestic[1] and international affairs[2] as well as applying it to public law, legal ethics, protection of civilians, and failed states. In this chapter, I will summarize some of the key points concerning the various definitions and interpretations of the 'Rule of Law' as they apply to this volume and the project of which it forms a part.

Central to what I have written over the last 12 years is a narrative which sees the Rule of Law as an ideal within sovereign states (the 'domestic' Rule of Law) that then emerges as an ideal in relations between sovereign states (the 'international' Rule of Law). I first outlined this narrative when I was invited to open the final plenary session of the world congress on legal and social philosophy in 1999 on the topic 'sovereignty and intervention'. At that time, I argued that the United States should be complimented on its work in developing the Rule of Law and other liberal democratic values within the domestic sphere but should seek to extend the same principles into the international sphere. During the last decade the developed world has tended to emphasize the importance of the former while the developing world, stung by American led interventions in Kosovo and Iraq, has emphasized the international Rule of Law. My own view has been that we needed both. Each reinforces the other and a failure in one may undermine the achievement of the other. In 2005 at the United Nations World Summit, developed and developing nations unanimously reached a historic, appropriate and highly laudable 'compromise' – that they should endorse both – i.e. the need

---

1   'Review of Walker's *The Rule of Law*', shorter version of the above 1990 Public Law 581 and 'The Rule of Law', *Oxford Companion to Australian Politics*, Oxford: Oxford University Press, 2007.

2   'Sovereignty and Intervention', in Campbell and Leiser (eds), *Human Rights in Theory and Practice*, Aldershot: Ashgate, 2001, and 'Reconceiving the Rule of Law for a Globalizing World', in J. Zifcak (ed.), *Reconceiving the Rule of Law*, London: Routledge, 2005.

for 'universal adherence to and implementation of the rule of law at both the national and international levels'.[3]

The compromise does not lie in lacking a full and ringing endorsement of both ideals. The real compromise is in the lack of commitment to its realization and implementation. An excuse often offered is an uncertainty about the meaning of the Rule of Law, the suggestions that it has different meanings within different cultures, and its meaning and applicability in the international sphere. Indeed, the UN Rule of Law unit was established because it appeared that each of nine UN agencies with a claim to involvement in the Rule of Law had a different definition.

This chapter will commence with the above-mentioned narrative, and discuss some of the interpretations of the concept 'Rule of Law' in domestic settings and international settings. In doing this, I will emphasize the variety of mutually supporting interpretations of the Rule of Law – fundamental governance value, an ethics for officials, a basic principle of constitutionalism, and a set of institutions that supports its attainment. I will dwell mostly on the first and will repeat[4] my suggestion that a 'thin' theory of the Rule of Law is the most appropriate concept in domestic affairs. I will then argue that such a theory can and should be applied internationally, and can withstand the criticisms of those who doubt that the Rule of Law can be effectively applied to international affairs.

A Narrative: From Liberal Democratic Values for Sovereign States to Global Values for a Global Order

The Rise of the Sovereign States

Strong sovereign nation states emerged in seventeenth-century Europe. A medieval patchwork of feudal cities, principalities and a weakening 'Empire' – together with guilds and the Church – had governed European life for a millennium. This patchwork was placed under severe stress by economic forces and religious schism. Glimpses of chaos in England and France were followed by the horror of the Thirty Years War and the near breakdown of English society in the Civil War. After the Treaty of Westphalia ended the Thirty Years War in 1648, '[a]n international structure composed of a hierarchy of emperor, kings, princes, and cities was replaced with one composed of many formally-independent and formally-equal states'.[5]

Although these nation states were highly authoritarian, their theoretical champions – writers like Jean Bodin, Jean-Jacques Burlamaqui, Thomas Hobbes,

---

3   UN General Assembly A/g0/L.1 15 September 2005 clause 134.

4   'Flesh out' hardly seems an appropriate metaphor in this context!

5   J. Kurth, 'The Protestant Deformation and American Foreign Policy', paper presented to The Philadelphia Society 37th National Meeting (22 April 2001) available at http://www.townhall.com/phillysoc/Kurth%20Speech.htm.

and Samuel Pufendorf – applauded and justified them for that very reason. When life was 'solitary, poor, nasty, brutish and short'[6] due to civil war, banditry or religious zealotry, rational men[7] would happily choose to submit to a government strong enough to keep the peace by whatever means necessary. Modest and minimalist as it was, the Westphalian bargain was observed within Europe – both 'horizontally' among different nations' governments, and 'vertically' between each government and its citizens – for almost three centuries.[8]

However, the Treaty of Westphalia was in many senses a tyrants' charter – an agreement of tyrants, made by tyrants, for tyrants[9] (some may prefer the term 'absolutist rulers')[10]. It recognized a set of formally independent and equal states whose sovereigns were recognized on the basis of their ability to effectively control the territory of a state. Their brutal suppression of the former rulers they displaced and others who did not accept their right to rule was an indication of sovereignty rather than a disqualification from it (a point of disagreement between traditional tyrants like Libya's Gaddafi, doing what tyrants do, and the UN endorsed 'responsibility to protect').

Enlightenment Governance Values

Once life and civil peace were secure, citizens began to expect more from their states. In the eighteenth-century North Atlantic Enlightenment,[11] *philosophes*, lawyers and

---

6   'In such condition there is no place for industry, because the fruit thereof is uncertain: and consequently … no navigation … no commodious building … no arts; no letters; no society; and which is worst of all, continual fear, and danger of violent death; and the life of man, solitary, poor, nasty, brutish, and short'. T. Hobbes, *Leviathan*, Cambridge: Cambridge University Press, 1991, chapter 13, 'Of the Natural Condition of Mankind as Concerning Their Felicity and Misery', p. 89.

7   The fact that only rational men were considered was not because the philosophers thought that rational women would not.

8   Europeans did not extend the same respect to non-European nations until Westphalia's 300th anniversary, but that extension was generally seen as the logical application of Westphalia rather than its contradiction.

9   With apologies to Abraham Lincoln's Gettysburg Address.

10   I choose the pejorative term for good reason. When tyrants reigned in Ancient Greece, the term *tyrannos* referred to an absolute ruler who ruled without legal restriction. This gained a pejorative meaning based on their behaviour in office and the justifiably bad press given by Greek philosophers writing during the period of Athenian democracy. The *philosophes* gave absolute rulers a bad press for similar reasons.

11   I call this the 'North Atlantic' Enlightenment – not merely to honour those American institutions who have been my hosts and benefactors over the last three years (including the Fulbright Commission, Harvard, Columbia and the Council on Foreign Relations), but to emphasize the way philosophical and institutional ideas flowed back and forth across the Atlantic, growing in strength with each passage. In particular, this term recognizes North America's breakthrough in contributing crucial thinking about the *institutional* methods of securing the Enlightenment's goals.

revolutionaries sought to civilize these authoritarian states by holding them to a set of more refined and ambitious values – notably liberty, equality, citizenship, human rights, democracy and the Rule of Law. These values were necessary, not for bare survival, but for comfortable, civilized and dignified existence.

This process started with Locke's reaction to Hobbes' social contract.[12] The parties to Hobbes' social contract were individuals in the lawless state of nature. The sovereign was established by the social contract, but was not party to it. The sovereign's will would rule and, although it was prudent to express this will in the form of laws proclaimed for the subjects, the law did not bind the sovereign himself. Hobbes' conception of the law as command left no room for the commander being bound. Locke, however, subsequently insisted that the sovereign was also a party to the contract, and also bound by laws made under it. For him, the supreme ruler was 'bound to govern by established standing laws, promulgated and known to the people'.[13] A sovereign who broke the agreement could be brought to account by his or her subjects, through the people's right to revolt. The enforcement mechanism was much cruder and lacked the sophistication of later means of securing accountability (namely the courts and ballot-box). Nevertheless, it did offer a means of ensuring that government officials, right up to the sovereign itself, obeyed the law (or at least did not flagrantly disregard it).

By the end of the eighteenth century, other Enlightenment values had been asserted. Some of them demanded that the content of the laws secure individual liberty, equality and the 'Rights of Man'.[14] Enlightenment thinkers also re-examined who should make the laws (namely a democratic assembly) and, most important of all, who comprised the state (all citizens). These largely superseded Locke's right to revolt because it enabled the people to rid themselves of oppressive laws and rulers by lawful, peaceful and orderly means. It also produced what I have advisedly called the Enlightenment's 'great leap forward' – a revolutionary Feuerbachian reversal of the relationship between the state and its people.[15] Individuals no longer had to justify themselves to the state as loyal and obedient subjects of their sovereigns. Rather, the governments of sovereign states had to justify themselves to their citizens.

---

12   See J. Locke, 'An Essay Concerning the True Original, Extent and End of Civil Government', in *Social Contract: Essays by Locke, Hume and Rousseau*, London: Oxford University Press, 1947, chapter 9, §131, 'Of the Ends of Political Society and Government'.

13   Ibid.

14   As I have argued elsewhere (e.g., in 'The Four Dimensions of Rights and Their Means of Protection', in Galligan and Sampford (eds), *Rethinking Human Rights*, Sydney: Federation Press, 1997), the process has continued, with the exposition of values on the environment and group rights being first asserted in the nineteenth century and given greater emphasis and clarity during the twentieth.

15   Feuerbach said that Christians imagined that God created man in His own image but that it was rather more likely that man had created God in his own image.

Nineteenth-century thinkers extended the range of rights championed, for example, adding concern for environment and for practical and social equality. By the mid twentieth century, disputes had moved on to the interpretation and ranking of those rights – especially between civil and political rights and social and economic rights.[16]

Of all these values, the Rule of Law is primary.[17]

Institutionalizing Those Values

Ideals are not self-implementing – especially ideals that aim for a better society; they require institutions to realize them. If the font of new ideas was located in the Atlantic nations of Scotland and France, the centre of gravity for institutional innovation was the eastern seaboard of the United States. Initially, the early European *philosophes* – apart from a few who wanted to copy English constitutionalism – simply proposed institutions modelled on the monarchical states most familiar to them.[18] Enlightened despotism, of course, requires a despot, so *philosophes* like Voltaire and Diderot pinned their hopes in turn on Frederick the Great in Prussia, then Peter and Catherine the Great in Russia, and finally Napoleon in France. But this was never a promising strategy and Voltaire left in disgust. In term, these despots and their institutions, too, eventually dissolved into chaos and violence.[19]

While superficially the US Constitution may seem simply to have 'frozen' key elements of the 1776–87 British Constitution[20] (as famously misdescribed by Montesquieu)[21] its most distinctive features – federalism, a constitutionally

---

16   See C. Sampford (1997) 'The Four Dimensions of Rights', in Galligan and Sampford, *Rethinking Human Rights*, pp. 50–71.

17   In the sense that, although the Rule of Law alone is not sufficient, it is almost certainly a *necessary* precondition for those other features that, while external to the Rule of Law, are necessary for a decent society (see below).

18   Voltaire, Diderot and Helvétius were all attracted for a time to enlightened despotism. See, for example, T. Munck, *The Enlightenment: A Comparative Social History 1721–1794*, London: Arnold, 2000.

19   This is not to deny that institutions bequeathed by these despots have endured, e.g., the *Code Napoleon*.

20   Notably: an executive completely separate from the legislature (not even Cabinet members were to be legislators); impeachment as the only way for the legislature to remove executive officials; the copying, with some undesirable variations of the UK 1689 Bill of Rights' 'right to bear arms'; and, as we shall see, much broader and less reviewable powers vested in the Head of State to act outside the nation's boundaries.

21   Montesquieu's image of it involving a three-way separation of powers was deeply flawed as a description, or even an interpretation, of the British Constitution. It is one of history's great ironies that Montesquieu's description was most accurate under William III and George III, because parliamentary control over the executive was largely achieved between those monarchs' reigns but disappeared with the loss of the American colonies. The

entrenched court, a states' upper house, legislative ratification of treaties, and various other 'checks and balances' – were important innovations, and have often been copied. It was only in the nineteenth century that Europe began generating institutional innovations of its own: responsible parliamentary government, the start of the welfare state, and accountability mechanisms such as the administrative tribunal and the ombudsman.

Globalization's Challenge to Liberal Democratic Values

However, a series of recent trends over the last 20 years, popularly labelled 'globalization', have challenged these values, primarily by challenging the power of nation state institutions which are currently the only feasible means for upholding these values. I eschew the two most common responses – (1) abandoning whatever values cannot be realized by global or transnational institutions, and (2) clinging to the nation state as the only possible way of preserving these values. For the last dozen years, I have suggested a third way, namely reconceiving liberal democratic values, and re-institutionalizing them for a global world – something that would involve nothing less than a new Enlightenment. Such a global Enlightenment should aim to civilize the increasingly harsh global economy, just as the eighteenth-century Enlightenment began the process of civilizing the absolutist post-Westphalian states. Such a 'global' enlightenment would not be a 'northern' or 'Western' phenomenon – least of all one limited to the transatlantic dialogue. It would need to be built on governance values found in a range of cultures, all of which appear to have values that reflect similarly enlightened responses to the problems of government which are consistent (I like to use the term 'congruent') with liberal democratic values. Of course, all cultures also have authoritarian strains – not least the West, which managed to produce Nazism and Bolshevism in a single century. The point is not that some cultures are authoritarian and some are liberal. All of them have both tendencies. Dialogue can strengthen the liberal elements in all, as well as help us devise new 'global' values that can civilize the globalizing world, in the same way as liberal- and social-democracy civilized the West. Over the last decade the centres I have led have promoted this dialogue

---

Americans created a strong head of state wielding full executive power – the very thing they had rebelled against, and the British were rejecting. More importantly, one chief American objection to British rule was that they did not have the same rights as Englishmen because the Crown had more power, with fewer constraints, outside the shores of England than on home soil. Despite their objection to this feature of the British Constitution, they gave the presidency a similarly great and largely unfettered power to act outside the United States – one of the reasons why George W. Bush (ironically George III of America) sought to detain and try prisoners outside US soil, thereby claiming properly legislative and judicial powers without constitutional constraint.

through a series of dialogues on the Rule of Law, democracy, citizenship, equality, human rights and the environment.[22]

This project seeks to go beyond debating values, to examining the way that such values can be institutionalized. Just as the dialogues commenced in 2000 with one on the Rule of Law, so the first of the 'institutionalizing' projects looks at the international Rule of Law.

The 'Domestic' Rule of Law

A Contested Concept with Multiple Dimensions

The Rule of Law is a majestic phrase with many largely reinforcing and supportive meanings. It stands for a fundamental value or ideal, an ethic for lawyers and officials, the basic principles of constitutionalism, and a set of institutions that supports its attainment. While these multiple meanings and dimensions may occasionally serve to confuse, each of them are vital in achieving the others. The partial achievement of each supports the fuller achievement of all.

Some of the most popular definitions mix an expression of the normative ideal with the institutional prerequisites for the achievement of that ideal. Developing ideas found in Hayek,[23] Fuller[24] and others, Joseph Raz listed eight basic principles discussed below. (Normatively laws should be prospective, open and clear, relatively stable; made under clear and general rules. Institutionally independent and relatively accessible courts should provide natural justice and have review powers).[25]

The rule of law as a fundamental governance value
The Rule of Law is now seen as one of the fundamental values underlying modern states – along with human rights, democracy and the famous trinity of *liberté, egalité, fraternité* – values that were imposed on the previously authoritarian sovereign states that emerged after Westphalia (see narrative above). The Rule of Law was the first of these values to emerge, and many states were substantially *Rechsstaats* long before they saw even a modicum of democracy and human

---

22   Sampford and Connors (formerly Sampford and Patapan) (general editors), Challenges of Globalization series, London: Routledge.

23   F.A. Hayek, *The Constitution of Liberty*, Chicago: University of Chicago Press, 1960 [** exact cite is in Raz].

24   L.L. Fuller, *The Morality of Law*, New Haven and London: Yale University Press, 1964 (1969), p. 39ff.

25   J. Raz, *The Authority of Law: Essays on Law and Morality*, Oxford: Clarendon Press, 1979; Chesterman summarizes these eight principles into three broad principles: S. Chesterman, 'An International Rule of Law?', *The American Journal of Comparative Law* 56, 331, 2008, 342. See also M. Aronson and B. Dyer, *Judicial Review of Administrative Action*, 2nd edn, NSW: LBC Information Services, 2000, chapter 1.

rights. The Rule of Law is not only the longest-standing of Enlightenment values; it is generally the least controversial and is arguably the most fundamental. This is the sense in which the Rule of Law is most discussed by legal philosophers, so I will deal with this in the next section.

The rule of law as an ethic for officials

The Rule of Law is a central ethical principle for judges and the legal profession more generally. The profession's central goal is the effective operation of law so that official power is exercised predictably and according to predetermined rules. The Rule of Law is also central to most public officials, including civil servants, the military and, at root, elected officials – power is held in trust to be used only to the extent permitted and for the purposes authorized.

The Rule of Law has an illustrious history in Europe, the US and many Commonwealth countries. The recent lack of support by the US and the United Kingdom may cause concern for some but it is important to recognize that the US, similar to most P5 members, has a very high degree of compliance with treaties and has been pressing for an enforceable rules-based system in global trade and largely got it with the WTO. While more politicians openly argue that the US should ignore international law in the use of force, the legality of American interventions were strongly asserted by presidents Clinton in Kosovo and Bush in Iraq and the amounting of a ferocious attack on Kofi Anan[26] – indicating that they seem to think that this is important politically and in the court of public opinion. While I would emphatically assert that more than lip service is required, the perceived need lip service is promising – along with the embarrassment of hypocrisy when found out.

The rule of law as a basic constitutional principle

The Rule of Law underlies and is supported by basic constitutional principles such as constitutional rule and the separation of powers. However, it does not require a formal or written constitution and the concept clearly pre-dates such instruments. What the Rule of Law does seem to require is a separation of judicial power from legislative and executive power, and a means of determining what texts are recognized as laws.

The rule of law as a set of institutions

Those who value the Rule of Law recognize that it can never operate effectively as a purely normative phenomenon (be it value, ethic or principle). It requires institutions to make it effective.

1.	If we are to know what law must rule, it is necessary to have an institution or set of institutions that are sources for authoritative texts. Legislatures are

---

26	David Sands, 'Powell rebukes Annan on Iraq', *Washington Times*, 17 September 2004 (citing US, UK and Australian government representatives.

the most common but *grundnorms* can, and generally do, recognize other sources.
2. There is a need for an institution that provides authoritative interpretations of the meaning of those texts in particular circumstances.

Other institutions that can reinforce the Rule of Law include an independent bar, independent prosecutorial services and, to an extent, police forces. Institutions such as the ombudsmen and independent commissions against corruption can make the laws more effective and ensure that powers are used for the purposes for which they are entrusted.

The rule of law and nascent integrity systems

Since the late 1990s, it has become increasingly accepted that to avoid corruption and other abuses of power requires an 'integrity system' – a set of norms (formal and informal), institutions, and practices that serve to promote integrity and inhibit corruption. All effective integrity systems involve some basic institutional arrangements associated with the Rule of Law – especially courts and a legal profession that are not indebted to the holders of political power and that can review the actions of powerful institutions to determine whether or not they are acting within their legitimate power. These institutions are the oldest and longest standing elements of the integrity systems of Western states.

These meanings are now well developed, widely supported and generally achieved in the domestic affairs of most modern democracies and several autocracies from the seventeenth-century Prussian *Rechsstaat* onwards. They are also mutually supportive, so that the partial achievement of each supports the fuller achievement of all. However, they are far less developed in international affairs, and face obstacles that lead some to doubt the possibility of an international Rule of Law or international law itself.

The Domestic Rule of Law as Fundamental Governance Value

'Rule of Laws, not Men'

One of the simplest and most enduring versions of the idea of the Rule of Law centres on an evocative but impossible ideal: 'the rule [or government] of law[s], not the rule of men' (or of women, or indeed of any fallible mortals).[27] Taken

---

27 The term appears to have first been used by the English republican writer James Harrington, in his tracts *The Prerogative of Popular Government* (1657) and *The Commonwealth of Oceana* (1656), in slightly different terms: 'an empire of laws and not of men'. The revised version is widely used: cf., for example, J. Toohey, 'A Government of Laws, and Not of Men?', Paper presented to the 'Constitutional Change in the 1990s'

literally, this is nonsense.[28] Sovereign authorities rule through human beings, but the Rule of Law ensures that the process is, as far as possible, channelled through the means of rule-making and attempts at faithful rule implementation. In other words, it ensures that individual citizens have a fair warning before they break a law and a fair hearing afterwards. They are not simply punished without any (or with insufficient) regard to the laws at the time they acted.

Joseph Raz thought that this was crucial to the nature of law itself.[29] He saw law as a two-stage decision-making process, where rules are first made by the legislature and then interpreted by the executive and judiciary. Ideally, the officials applying the law at both stages view themselves as part of an enterprise in which the state has attempted to make rules that guide citizens; therefore, officials conscientiously seek to draw their own reasons for decision from these rules. There are, of course, imperfections in the way rules are made and interpreted, but those who are involved in both stages of the process still endeavour to be true to their function. This idea is linked to Raz's 'sources' thesis – that all legal rules have sources, and it is at the source of each that the first stage of decision-making occurs. This offers a more realistic revision of the 'Rule of Laws, not men' formulation: the law comes from a source outside the officials who are applying it. It need not be Divine or natural or otherwise superhuman in origin; it is enough that those who enforce the rules are not the same people that make them.

Another recent re-formulation of this enduring ideal is Ronald Cass's idea of 'fidelity' to rules,[30] building on Dworkin's view of 'Law as Integrity', which calls on officials, especially judges, to make every statute and common-law rule the 'best it can be'.[31]

Fleshing out the Epigram – the 'Thin Theory' of the Rule of Law

Despite various attempts to define and elucidate 'Rule of Law', many prominent theorists – notably Cass, Hayek, Raz and Fuller[32] – seem to converge upon the same basic core.

What I refer to as Raz's 'thin theory' of the Rule of Law involved eight desiderata. The first three reflect most of Fuller's virtues:[33]

Conference, Darwin (6 October, 1993), reprinted in *Public Law Review*, vol. 4, no. 3, pp. 158–74.

28   See chapter 7 of C. Sampford, *Retrospectivity and the Rule of Law*, Oxford: Oxford University Press, 2006.

29   Raz, *The Authority of Law*.

30   R.A. Cass, *The Rule of Law in America*, Baltimore: Johns Hopkins University Press, 2001.

31   R.M. Dworkin, *Law's Empire*, London: Duckworth, 1986, p. 379.

32   See discussion in Sampford, 'Reconceiving the Rule of Law for a Globalizing World', in Zifcak, *Reconceiving the Rule of Law*.

33   Fuller, *The Morality of Law*, pp. 39ff.; Raz, *The Authority of Law*, pp. 214–19. Raz does not specifically mention consistency and generality. Generality, however, would be

1. laws should be prospective, open and clear;
2. laws should be relatively stable;
3. law-making should be guided by open, stable, clear and general rules.

The next five prevent enforcement machinery being distorted to undermine the first three – and reflect some of the other, more institutional, meanings of the Rule of Law:

4. independence of the judiciary must be guaranteed;
5. principles of natural justice should be observed;
6. courts should have review powers;
7. courts should be easily accessible;
8. discretion of crime-policing agencies should not be perverted.

The combination of the last six emphasize a core element of the 'Rule of Laws not men' idea. No one is above the law in two senses. First, the law applies to all – including those who hold official power. Secondly, power-holders only exercise power that has been granted to them by law and must use it in ways that are determined by law and for the purposes for which it is given – matters which are not determined by them but are subject to the determination of others. Raz emphasized that this is a limited concept of the Rule of Law.[34] For him, it is essentially a negative value insofar as it is directed at preventing some of the harms that could be done by those wielding power. It does not, however, eliminate all harms, and might even exacerbate others.

The Rule of Law, so conceived, makes law a more effective tool. Officials would enforce rules uniformly and those subject to it would modify their behaviour in the light of those rules (to realize the benefits it provided or avoid the harm it could do to them). This made the law more effective and, for most people, self-enforcing. In Raz's famous analogy, the Rule of Law is good law in the same sense as a knife is good. Whether harm results depends on what the law, like the knife, is used for.

This limited concept of the Rule of Law does not seek to incorporate the other Enlightenment values of democracy, citizenship and human rights. It does not eschew these values but allows them to be defined more independently, and allows their presence or absence to be determined more reliably. This does not mean that the other values cannot be embraced wholeheartedly. Rather, it means that there are a number of values for assessing the worth of a legal order, of which the Rule of Law is one. The lack of one or more of the other values might well justify us in overthrowing a legal order that had the one virtue of exhibiting the Rule of Law. The lack of democracy, for example, will generally justify the replacing of that

---

affected by differences between individuals deemed sufficient to support legal distinctions, while the procedural safeguards Raz advocates would guarantee relative consistency.

34   Raz, *The Authority of Law*.

order with a democratic one – although a democracy with no Rule of Law may generate at least as much misery as an autocracy with the Rule of Law.

A good legal order needs more than one virtue. As Raz argues, it is better to identify separately, the various virtues we would wish legal orders to demonstrate rather than to roll them all into a single virtue. Theories that do not seek to incorporate other Enlightenment values I call 'thin theories' of the Rule of Law. In contrast, theories that add other values (enlightened or otherwise) I call 'thick theories' of the Rule of Law.

Broader Definitions – 'Thick Theories' of the Rule of Law

Fuller's listing of Rule of Law virtues has tempted many to add other desiderata to the list. (The International Commission of Jurists added 'social, economic, educational and cultural conditions'.[35] Others have included legitimacy, accountability and respect for human rights). Herein we see a tendency to add many of the later Enlightenment values (particularly democracy and rights) as well as some of the institutional mechanisms thought to be most effective in realizing those values, to the minimalist early Enlightenment value of the Rule of Law.

It seems prima facie hard to argue with these broader definitions, the 'extra' values being widely shared. If we can secure their acceptance from everyone who claims to believe in the Rule of Law by showing that they are necessarily inherent within the Rule of Law, then why not do so? Surely this would spare us the need to expend political capital fighting these battles later to secure values we thought we had already won? I think, however, that we should restrain ourselves from this temptation and opt for a narrower conception – a 'thin theory' of the Rule of Law.[36]

There are various reasons for preferring a thin theory of the Rule of Law (several of which are discussed in more detail in my 2005 essay).[37] Firstly, one must be cautious about the 'imperialism of values'. If we view democracy, liberty, or the Rule of Law as good things, we are tempted to include most of the (political) things that the author considers to be good within the relevant concept. Consequently, the different values tend to lose their sharp focus, with a number

---

35   Clause 1 of the Committee I of the International Congress of Jurists at New Delhi, 1959 cited in ibid., p. 211. Raz is critical of extending the doctrine of the Rule of Law to include such desiderata, referring to it as a 'perversion'. He writes that the report of the committee 'goes on to mention or refer to just about every political ideal which has found support in any part of the globe during the post-war years' (ibid., pp. 211 and 210).

36   John Rawls famously outlined 'thick' and 'thin' theories of 'the good' (*A Theory of Justice*, Massachusetts: Harvard University Press, 1971, pp. 118–42). I am proposing a similar distinction for the Rule of Law. However, the reason for thinning out the Rule of Law is not the controversial nature of some of the other additions.

37   'Reconceiving the Rule of Law for a Globalizing World', in Zifcak, *Reconceiving the Rule of Law*.

of undesirable ideological consequences. Different, potentially conflicting values are incorporated into the one value.[38] Further, as some of the values added become controversial, it will weaken support for the concept of the Rule of Law – there is a spectrum, not a clear break, between 'widely-accepted' and 'controversial' values. An expanded list is also far less likely to fit within an overarching concept and central organizing idea such as those discussed in the previous section, and the more we build positive values into law before it is called a law, the more difficulty we will have in overtly criticizing that law. The more positive values that must be respected before the Rule of Law is seen to exist, the more difficulty there will be in questioning it through the prism of other values.

Extending the Reach of the Rule of Law

As illustrated, some writers have sought to extend the concept of the Rule of Law to incorporate a wide set of important but contestable values. However, the Rule of Law, at least in its traditional, more limited sense, has also been extended recently in another way. One of the greatest developments of this century is that the institutional mechanisms for implementing the Rule of Law have extended to other than judicial officials. It has been applied to members of the executive with increasing fervour. For a long time it has been accepted that they should only act according to law.[39] The problem was that there were few means of determining whether they had. For this reason, administrative action has been increasingly open to scrutiny not only through monitoring bodies and appeal mechanisms, but also through the twin requirements of having to provide reasons and relevant documents – both features of judicial review. The courts have had a central role in the development of these requirements and they have made legal success against resistant administrators more possible while reducing the need to resort to formal legal action.

There has been a parallel struggle with those other wielders of great organizational power – corporate executives. The move to establish corporate governance has been about setting rules and goals for the use of corporate power – in part by governments and in part by shareholders. Both attempts have been resisted and criticized along lines that are surprisingly familiar to anyone who observed the former attempts

---

38 The most common conflation over the last 50 years is that of human rights and democracy. Political liberty is a prerequisite for democracy. However, the entrenchment of rights against democratic legislatures is a restriction of democracy. Some such entrenchment is, in this author's view, justified. But it is justified as a restriction of democracy rather than as a part of over-expansive concept of the Rule of Law.

39 Indeed, some lawyers are surprised to see the extent to which traditional public servants are knowledgeable of, and sticklers for, the laws under which their departments operate.

of public service mandarins to preserve their power and shield its exercise from public scrutiny.[40]

This reflects an aspect of the widespread appeal of the Rule of Law. When the concept was originally outlined, the greatest source of power was the sovereign state. Sovereigns claimed absolute and paramount power. They had just fought for supremacy over other sources of power within their territories: the Church, the aristocracy and foreign states. Sovereigns had sought to reduce the power of feudal lords who had previously claimed a right to autonomously control their territory. They sought to bring churches to heal in a variety of ways – from choosing the bishops to choosing the official religion. The Treaty of Westphalia itself involved a formal agreement to forbear from interfering in the internal affairs of other nations.

However, this should not blind us (as it sometimes did Enlightenment thinkers) to other sources of power that can arbitrarily restrict our capacities to make and carry out life plans. The *philosophes* were aware of the continuing power of the aristocracy and the Church. Their solution was to continue the sovereignty project and subject them to the state and the state to the people. However, they generally did not foresee the power of modern corporations and unions (although Adam Smith's concerns about corporations and monopolies would count as honourable exceptions to this generalization). More reprehensibly, few appreciated that the women, servants and slaves in their own households generally had much more to fear from the ever-present *philosophe* than they had from a remote absolute monarch! One of the features of the last 300 years is the appreciation of these other sources of power and the belief that those who hold such power are responsible for its exercise and should not do so in an arbitrary fashion. Sometimes this has manifested itself in demands that the law extend into what might otherwise have been considered the 'private sphere'.[41] However, another manifestation lies in the demands that shareholders, employees and other 'stakeholders' whose lives are affected by the decisions of large organizations that those who make those decisions are bound by, and act within, rules set by those organizations.[42]

The Rule of Law deals with the way that wielders of state power use that power. However, similar arguments apply to wielders of other kinds of strong organizational power. The Rule of Law for a more global world is not just about international law or about the application of universal rules to sovereign states. It is about the idea that, for all forms of institutional power, there should be rules that are made subject to the Raz criteria. The sources will be different and the means of interpretation must be different. But in each case, there should be impartial arbitrators to determine whether or not the rules have been followed in letter and spirit.

---

40   I sometimes think that Sir Humphrey's skills live on in much of corporate management. A new series of 'Yes CEO' might be a useful sequel!

41   F. Olsen, 'The Family and the Market', 96 *Harvard Law Review* 1497 (1983) at p. 1510.

42   R. Edward Freeman, *Strategic Management: A Stakeholder Approach*, Cambridge: Cambridge University Press, 2010, originally published by Pitman, 1984.

The Value Placed on the 'Thin Theory'

Even though the 'thin theory' might not seem as attractive as full-blown 'thick theories', many positive claims may be made about this more limited sense of the Rule of Law –

- Citizens must plan for their lives because the behaviour of state officials is predictable.[43]
- The Rule of Law promotes stability.
- The Rule of Law avoids a number of important procedural injustices of the kind Fuller indicated. This amounts to a kind of 'formal' justice.
- As Raz argues, where rulers are prepared to be bound by their rules, it makes the law a more effective tool. Indeed, if the rulers do not tie the sanctions they apply to the rules they have established in advance, then people will be less likely to follow the rules they apply.
- One of the most famous and impassioned defences of the Rule of Law was in a deeply flawed legal regime – that of eighteenth-century England. At that time, democracy, rights, substantive equality and other liberal democratic values were not only not supported, but their advocacy could lead to prosecution and transportation. Nevertheless, E.P. Thomson praised the Rule of Law because the imposition of effective restraints on power and the defence of the citizen from power's 'all-intrusive claims' seemed to him 'an unqualified human good'.[44]

It is rare for an 'instrumental' good to be unqualified and I would never make that assertion. As Raz points out, the Rule of Law makes laws more effective, whether we value or abhor the relevant rule. Although elements of the Rule of Law, especially the requirement of publicity, may be inconvenient for 'bad' laws in most societies, it is no guarantee against them. One can imagine a government passing racist or xenophobic laws to gain favour from a population with a tradition of racism. Nevertheless, this is not a reason to abandon the Rule of Law, merely to pursue other values of human rights as well.

Reasons for Preferring 'Thin' Theories

I can understand why many would prefer a 'thick' theory of the Rule of Law to a 'thin' theory. The added values of democracy and rights are admirable and I fully endorse them. I also fully accept that the value of the Rule of Law is enhanced

---

43   Of course, planning requires much else besides – including the resources to carry out plans. Furthermore, there are other sources of power which may be exercised capriciously and unpredictably, most noticeably corporate and economic power.

44   E.P. Thomson, *Whigs and Hunters: The Origin of the Black Act*, London: Penguin, 1990.

if the law is made democratically and with a desire to protect and further human rights (as rights and democracy are enhanced by the Rule of Law). The Rule of Law, democracy, rights (along with citizenship, liberty, equality and the natural environment in which all this takes place) are a mutually supporting package of Enlightenment values which are compromised and sometimes negated in the absence of each other.

Nevertheless, like Raz, I prefer to use a narrower concept of the Rule of Law – as one value among other values, that is not determinative of action or preference. In general, I like to unpack the package of Enlightenment values for a number of reasons:

- If separated conceptually, they can be understood more effectively.
- Many of them are subject to competing definitions and a variety of nuances and subtleties. If other values are included within the Rule of Law, then one cannot know whether the Rule of Law is in place unless one has settled the meaning of, say, 'democracy'. Those who adopt a different conception of democracy may deny the existence of the Rule of Law – or may put off its application until the other conditions are met.
- The values can have independent, even if diminished, worth.[45]
- It may not be possible to introduce all the relevant values simultaneously, so that it appears as if no progress is being made and no praise can be given for that progress.

One of the potential reasons for preferring thick theories is the concern that fundamentally inadequate laws will receive the cachet and legitimacy of the word 'law' and be supported by 'Rule of Law' values. Only laws that reflect values such as 'democracy' and 'rights' should receive the honour of being called 'laws' and the legitimacy that word generates. For me, this is the right answer to an unnecessary question. Because a particular form of words can be identified as a 'law' does not mean that one has to be bound by it. One can never surrender one's conscience to an outside power. The fact that something is a law does not mean that it must be unequivocally obeyed. I am attracted to the inclinations of British positivists from Bentham onwards.[46] If law is seen as arising out of social facts, then one can fix it as a phenomenon for praise or blame. If law has to meet certain criteria of justice before being called law, it is harder to criticize it.

45　See Thompson's plea, ibid.

46　Bentham, *Introduction to Principles of Morals and Legislation*, 1781; John Austin, *The Province of Jurisprudence Determined* (1831): 'The existence of law is one thing; its merit or demerit is another', Lecture 5, p. 157.

The International Rule of Law as a Governance Value

Differences between Domestic and International Law and Their Relevance to the Rule of Law

The development of the domestic Rule of Law offers some important parallels and contrasts for contemporary international Rule of Law. In the late seventeenth century, philosophers like Hobbes were devising creation myths about social contract states.[47] Ironically, states really were contracting among themselves to avoid a state of nature. Such international law as existed was a matter of contract and custom rather than binding law. The Treaty of Westphalia was a pact between independent and equal states who recognized themselves as such (and, in one of its most important provisions, recognized the United Dutch Provinces). It also provided one of the key foundations of customary international law.[48]

The content of these treaties was limited to the few matters on which trans-state agreement could be reached. As a result, international law was even more minimalist and incomplete than the minimal states that are today's neoliberal ideal and were the early Enlightenment reality. They did not set up any sovereign to police them nor did they create enforcement mechanisms to replace self-help (one of the factors Hobbes saw as contributing to the state of nature). Further, the bargaining positions of states were fundamentally different to those of individuals in a state of nature. As H.L.A. Hart emphasized, there was the general absence of the third condition Hume identified for the establishment of laws (relative scarcity of resources, limited altruism and mutual vulnerability of individual humans)[49]. There is much variation from state to state on the first and third. Some states are all but immune from interference by all but the strongest and most unlikely of coalitions. In an important sense, the state is not mortal and is not as vulnerable to 'dying'. 'Life', for states at war, is rarely 'nasty, brutish and short' but nasty, brutish and *prolonged*. As a state does not perish when its soldiers die it can, unfortunately, remain at war for years, and the complete collapse of a state through military defeat is extremely uncommon.

However, the relative vulnerability of states and the normal inability of any one (between Rome and post-Cold War USA) to dominate the rest was a critical factor in the development of such international law. Had one of these states

---

47   Hobbes, *Leviathan*.

48   One striking feature of the Westphalia Treaty is how many of its Articles were devoted to specifying, in minute detail, the titles, lands, compensation, and other privileges due to princely rulers dispossessed in the religious wars. On the other hand several Articles (see fn 3) guaranteed rights for individual citizens, such as freedom of private religious worship.

49   H.L.A. Hart, *The Concept of Law*, Oxford: Clarendon Press, 1961, pp. 189–95. See also Runciman, 'A Bear Armed with a Gun', 25(7) *London Review of Books* (2 April 2003).

possessed enough power to establish dominion over the others, a different system would have emerged – one of Empire. But none did prevail so that Europe had the benefits (and detriments) of a system of nominally equal sovereign states subject to weak international law. In Hobbes' day, one power did indeed claim the nominal title of Empire; and an alliance with Spain, enriched by its new colonies, gave the Holy Roman Empire a chance to give the title real power. But the defeat of that alliance (before Italian-inspired fortifications were built by the Dutch) led Spain and the Emperor to accept the Westphalian settlement.[50] The carnage of twentieth century wars led to the development of international laws attempting to cover armed conflict, and the United Nations was generated by the sense of universal vulnerability to the kind of war just ended and, even more, the kind of war in prospect at the time of its foundation.

The fact that international law emerges via different means and has a radically different extent may lead some to say that international law is not law. If this is so, there can be no 'Rule of Law'. Such claims are receding into the past as various forms of international law grow in strength. Nonetheless, there are some important differences between international law and domestic law that should be borne in mind when constructing a conception of the Rule of Law in a globalizing society:

1. There is no body that claims a monopoly on the use of force in the way that sovereign states do within their territory. This contrast can be overstated. No sovereign state really has a monopoly on the use of force within its territory, and their claim to a monopoly of the legitimate use of force may not be shared by all or even a majority. All states allow citizens the use of force in self-defence. The US revels in that permission, raising it to a right to bear arms. Internationally, there is a right to use force in self-defence but, as a matter of international law, only the United Nations Security Council has the power to authorize the use of force for other reasons. Like all laws, such prohibitions may be breached, but the number and extent of such breaches since the Second World War are very few. The biggest difference is that, in the classic image of the modern sovereign state, there are no domestic players who could breach such laws with the same degree of impunity as superpowers can breach international law. I emphasize the 'classic image' of states. Pre-Westphalian 'states' were plagued by 'over-mighty subjects' to which the assertion and acquisition of central coercive power was a response. Some current states are over-mighty 'subjects' of international law, able to act with impunity in which their economic or para-military clout give them effective impunity when they act to further core interests. Nevertheless, there remains a difference – not about whether

---

50 Napoleon, the next who sought to establish an empire across Europe, felt it necessary to abolish the last vestiges of the Holy Roman Empire so that he could claim the Imperial title for himself. It was only after his defeat that 'Empire' came to mean simply one more, unusually powerful, state among states.

there are monopolies of force at domestic or international level, but the fact that the disproportion in force between sovereign and subject within states is reversed when it comes to international law.

2. Where sovereign states claim jurisdiction over all matters occurring within their borders, the subject matters which international law seeks to regulate are far more limited. However, this is not so different to what happens in states that are weak by design (like confederations) or practice (weak and failed/failing states).

3. An important issue in the domestic Rule of Law is the 'closure rule'. Domestic jurisdictions have two contrasting closure rules to resolve legal doubts. For officials exercising power in that capacity, anything not legally authorized is prohibited, but for private individuals, anything not legally prohibited is permitted. In international law, the latter closure rule has applied to states, NGOs and corporations. To the extent that it is relevant, the former applies to international institutions. However, it could rightly be argued that, when someone is claiming to enforce the Rule of Law, they are claiming for themselves the mantle of an official of international law – a police officer. Accordingly they should apply the domestic closure rule – of only acting when they are legally empowered to do so under international law.

4. For many, the main problem for international law and its rule is not so much one of content but of commitment. Low expectations about the effectiveness of international law may undermine its perceived legitimacy and the willingness of international actors to take it seriously. In particular, concern is expressed about the commitment of the US and its allies to international law over the last 20 years. Despite recent aberrations, Australia and the US have long been supporters of a rules-based international system on a bi-partisan basis. The quotation from President Eisenhower, referred to in my later chapter in this volume, is more representative of the long-term views of Australians and Americans than the 24 years from Reagan's repudiation of the ICJ to the electorate's repudiation of George W. Bush. Even during those 24 years, the US claimed to act in conformity to international law and some of us have argued that it is in their interests to do so. With the greater realization of the limits of American military and economic power, unilateral action in contravention of international law may become more difficult and less attractive. The alternate view is that the US should seek to rebuild and then strengthen international law as insurance for the time when their military power is equalled or surpassed.

The differences listed above are sometimes overstated. However, the differences between international and domestic law are legion and substantial. The real question is whether these differences mean that the Rule of Law is not an important ideal within international law. In general, I would argue that none of them vitiate the elements of the thin version of the Rule of Law as a potential central global governance value.

International law should be prospective, open and relatively stable (it generally is). It should also be clear – something which is hampered by deliberate ambiguity in drafting and the rarity of judicial interpretation. Its creation should be by open, stable, clear and general rules (treaty making and much UN procedure generally is – though some of the paths for its creation such as state practice are not). The other principles including natural justice, judicial review by independent and accessible judges and invidious policing are all vital to the credibility of international law and institutions. They are all possible even if undesirably rare. Above all no states should be above the law or seek to exercise power other than according to law – and those who claim to enforce international law should be bound by international law. The law must apply to those who profess to be good as well as those they accuse of being bad – and who is good or bad must be determined by independent bodies applying clear rules established in advance. Those independent courts are there and states and UNSC alike could, and should, be prepared to subject their actions to those courts.

To the extent that there are gaps and shortcomings in international law, those omissions and shortcomings just provide an argument for closing the gaps and addressing the shortcomings. To the extent that courts are not used, they should be used more. To the extent that the powers of the relevant actors are limited they should still be exercised only when given by international law – and used for the purposes given according to the principles of natural justice. The limited power of parking inspectors are expected to be exercised according to the Rule of Law – as should any supposedly limited powers of the UNSC or those acting under their mandate. If they cannot do that, they will not, and should not, be entrusted with any further powers. To me, it would seem that most of the arguments in favour of the domestic Rule of Law run to international law. It is capable of achieving most of the virtues of a 'thin' version of the Rule of Law within a domestic polity: predictability, stability and effectiveness – if those who hold and wield power recognize the Rule of Law abide by it, and are willing to subject their own behaviour to existing independent judicial institutions.

The International Rule of Law: Other Dimensions

Just as the domestic Rule of Law has a number of mutually supportive dimensions, an effective international Rule of Law is likely to need similar dimensions – the realization of which may involve significant challenges.

Ethics for Officials

The problems of commitment to the international Rule of Law that I have mentioned lessen the likelihood that international law will be at the forefront of the ethical considerations of lawyers and officials. Lawyer's ethics, formed around the laws and institutions of nation states, may not show the same respect for international law as domestic law. Indeed, Anglo-Saxon systems of legal ethics are based on the duties to courts.[51] Where that domestic law reflects and advances other important ideals, lawyers may have much greater attachment to domestic law.

There are relatively few international officials. The main actors are not individual officials, such as the UN Secretary-General, but states. Many officials within key institutions (like the UNSC) explicitly act as directed by the states from which they come rather than as public officials exercising power for the purposes for which it is granted.

Constitutional Principles

The limited reach and scope of international law mean that some may doubt the applicability of familiar constitutional principles on the UN. This aspect is reinforced by the lack of familiar institutions such as legislatures and executives and the fact that the institutions that operate internationally are often hybrids, compromises and historical oddities.

The Limitations of International Law

International law emerges via different means (there is no real equivalent to a legislature), applies to states rather than citizens, has a radically different extent and lacks an all-powerful sovereign body to enforce it. However, most international law is followed most of the time despite the lack of a sovereign power with the monopoly of legitimate force. In fact, all laws are followed for a number of reasons – of which the nature and certainty of sanctions for breach is but one, and for most actors not the primary one.

Institutions

The largest problems for the international Rule of Law lie in the lack of institutions that create, interpret and enforce international law. Most international law is not made by 'legislatures' (e.g., the UN General Assembly) or courts, but

---

51   While duties to clients are important, both kinds of duties are determined by courts, and a lawyer's ethical duties are based on being 'officers of the court'. As the duty to client is ultimately determined by the court, it is not surprising duties to court take priority over duties to clients to the extent that there is a conflict. To me, there should be no conflict if the relevant duties are properly construed. In my view, the duty to the client is part of the lawyer's duty to courts and the administration of justice. Lawyers representing clients in an adversary system are doing their duty to the court by ensuring that justice is done via a vigorous contestation of issues in front of that court. See C. Sampford and C. Parker, 'Legal Ethics: Legal Regulation, Ethical Standard Setting and Institutional Design', in S. Parker and C. Sampford (eds), *Legal Ethics and Legal Practice: Contemporary Issues*, Oxford: Oxford University Press, 1995.

by contract (i.e., treaties) among nation states. From the point of view of most liberal democratic constitutionalists, there are some severe institutional limitations in international law. There is no tripartite division of legislative, executive and judiciary. Indeed, the UN Security Council is a potentially dangerous combination of all three with no formal legal checks and balances. There is no central body charged with enforcement of international law. Enforcement is generally left up to the signatories and is generally only enforced by the stronger party.

This lack of effective institutionalization inhibits the development of the Rule of Law in its other senses. The lack of a legislature is not a fundamental problem for the Rule of Law. It makes change difficult but all that is needed is a set of clearly agreed sources, the means by which those sources generate authoritative legal texts, and the hierarchy of sources in cases of conflict.

However, there is a court which can provide authoritative interpretations of those texts and of any conflicts between them. What is more, the ICJ is harder to stack than the highest courts of any other jurisdiction in the world. The problem is, of course, the lack of compulsory jurisdiction and the limited number of cases that can therefore be heard before it.[52] This makes it much harder for the law to give clear guidance to those who want to be bound. The lack of an effective court that sits regularly also makes it difficult to develop and enforce ethical codes for international lawyers.

Objections to the International Rule of Law

I will consider a number of potential arguments against extending the Rule of Law from domestic to international affairs. These fall into two categories – International versions of the arguments against the domestic Rule of Law, and arguments against the international Rule of Law *per se*.

International Versions of the Arguments against the Domestic Rule of Law

- The Rule of Law serves the strong and those who have made the law. The Rule of Law has hegemonic and legitimating effects. Further, formal equality masks substantive injustice. The strong might be seen as even stronger in international law.

  Answer: The requirement of consensus makes it more difficult for the strong to get their way in passing new laws that suit them. As in many polities, the problem is that they will prevent new laws being passed that do not suit them.

---

52   If States do not agree to be bound by the ICJ, then the ICJ has no jurisdiction even over crimes such as genocide.

- International law cannot, realistically, be effectively enforced against the strongest nations. In domestic law, 'over-mighty subjects' like Mafia bosses can use more legal tricks than the average person, but ultimately Al Capone and John Gotti went to jail. But no 'international policeman' can possibly 'arrest' the United States or the People's Republic of China – unless in the future either superpower drastically declined, in which case other, more powerful rivals might become the chief 'culprits' instead. One would hope that an avowedly constitutionalist democracy like the USA would voluntarily exhibit 'a decent Respect to the Opinions of Mankind.'[53]

Answers: There are several answers to this argument. The first points out that it is in the interests of the powerful to follow the Rule of Law.[54] There is a temptation to ignore the Rule of Law but this is a false choice because if you do not stick to rules, others will not know how to behave (the latter is one of the reasons why Australian forces have been so successful peacekeeping and US forces have not). The second points out that the bulk of law is not criminal but enabling. The third points out that the experience of the US in wars in which it has ignored international law (and, indeed, international opinion) has not been good. The fourth points out that the US needs international cooperation to secure the things it wants – copyright protection and the fight against terrorism[55] and free trade deals (sometime, somebody might start to ask why a rational agent would sign a free trade agreement with somebody who openly flouts international law). Finally, a leadership which ignores the Rule of Law internationally might start to ignore the Rule of Law domestically.

- The Rule of Law is only one of a series of goods – and if you cannot have the other goods, it may be a bad thing. For example, the Rule of Law in a liberal democracy will be good, usually, because it means the laws enforced will be democratic in their origin and liberal in their content. But in a repressive theocracy or one-party state, the Rule of Law will not secure religious freedom or dignity. Indeed, if it means zealous judges cannot be swayed by bribes or by mercy, it would make such a regime worse.

Answer: It is fully accepted that the Rule of Law is not the only good in international law as domestic law. Indeed, I have argued that one can never

---

53   *Declaration of Independence of the Thirteen United States of America*, Second Continental Congress (4 July 1776), preamble.

54   C. Sampford, 'Challenges to the Concepts of "Sovereignty" and "Intervention"', in B.M. Leiser, and T.D. Campbell (eds), *Human Rights in Theory and Practice*, Aldershot: Ashgate, 2001.

55   Ibid.

surrender one's conscience to any law, domestic or international.[56] That does not mean that it is not a good and a potentially powerful good. The argument has to be why it should be ignored in a particular case.

- Some prefer democracy before the Rule of Law and would prefer to wait for the former before accepting the latter. This is sometimes related to an unwillingness to give any credence to non-democratic law. A similar argument would seek the democratization of international institutions before enforcing the international Rule of Law.

  Answer: My response to this argument in international is the same as my response to its common domestic variety: The Rule of Law has tended to precede democracy; democracies need the Rule of Law to determine what bodies can determine laws and policy 'democratically'; and the Rule of Law would have to involve the exercise of judicial power to determine and interpret international law. This would stimulate 'legislative' activity – creating treaties and securing General Assembly decisions where parties did not like the decisions reached by courts.

- The most powerful – international business and international agencies – are not constrained. The only constraints are on individual sovereign states, especially those struggling for democracy. Business activities that were subject not only to the Rule of Law but the Rule of Law of democratically elected regimes, are either controlled by unelected bodies themselves controlled by one or two states (e.g., WTO) or not controlled at all.

  Answer: The most appropriate response is not to abandon the Rule of Law but to extend it to these subjects.

Arguments against the International Rule of Law per se

- It might be argued that the international Rule of Law is no good if it is limited, i.e., if, for example, there are rules against intervention but not against ethnic cleansing. International Law is very different from domestic laws because it covers so few areas of life. It does not cover many of the areas that Hart has listed as the 'minimum content of natural law' – laws allocating property and its transfer (and hence prohibiting forceful transfers outside this provision), and laws protecting human life. Whether or not this is conceived as 'natural law' or not, they are a minimum list of what might be adequate. In the absence of such laws, it is not possible for individuals to make and carry out life plans, the ultimate justification of the Rule of Law. Furthermore, it could be argued that, while international law is insufficiently

---

56   See C. Sampford, 'Get New Lawyers', in 6 *Legal Ethics* 85, at p. 93.

complete to allow ordinary individuals to make the kinds of plans that the Rule of Law is intended to permit, it does allow those who are bent on evil to plan their evil deeds because they are secure in the knowledge that no one can touch them (or, a version of this, because a sympathetic permanent member of the Security Council will veto any action against them).

It could be argued that international law, as the law of states, covers issues of violence (the international use of force), property (at least the vital 'real' property of sovereign territory) and its taking (invasion). However, international law is now much more than the law of states. By trying individuals for war crimes, the Nuremberg trials made individuals the subject of international law.[57] The human rights provisions of that UN Charter and the Declarations and Covenants that followed, indicated that individual human beings could be the beneficiaries of international law. The treatment of individuals by sovereign states was once more a matter of international concern and provided for by international law.

Answer: The issue is not whether international law covers these issues but the differential enforceability of the requirements of states to respect human rights and the requirements of states to respect each other's borders. This returns us to the point that it does not allow individuals to make meaningful life plans – or even plan on living! This kind of argument may be seen as making the value of the international Rule of Law weaker and more easily trumped by other considerations – most notably the human rights violations mentioned. Alternatively, it may be seen as an argument that is more likely to trump the value of the Rule of Law in such cases. In either case, it does not suggest that the Rule of Law is not valuable and it does not mean that it will always be trumped. Caution needs to be taken in this case because it is only the powerful states that can do the trumping and their motives may be less than pure.

• Sovereignty – historically and, still, ideologically – is an argument against the international Rule of Law. Sovereignty as defined by Austin, makes a point of this.[58] The existence of an 'independent political community' largely free of outside direction is an essential requirement of sovereignty. Enlightenment values imposed the check of the Rule of Law, then of institutional checks and balances, and then of democracy. For a long time the concept of sovereignty was a barrier to the introduction of similar

---

57   B.A. Bozcek, *Dictionary of International Law*, Scarecrow Press 2005, see definition and references p. 75.

58   In the *Province of Jurisprudence Determined*, the 'sovereign' is defined as a person (or determinate body of persons) who receives habitual obedience from the bulk of the population, but who does not habitually obey any other (earthly) person or institution.

checks and balances in international law. For those who are proud of their legal traditions, there is a danger in giving in to other laws – especially when there is a perceived democratic deficit in the making of international law. From an Anglo-American perspective, international law seems very imperfect on all the criteria by which they would seek to judge themselves and seek to be judged – democratic legitimacy, comprehensiveness, impartial judicial interpretation and judicially sanctioned enforcement, and so on. However, sovereignty is breaking down. Separation of constitutional law and international law is breaking down.[59] Once that happens, there can be no doubting that traditional public law concepts (most notably the Rule of Law) will gain a new lease of life in international law.

Answer: The problem with strong theories of sovereignty is that they do not have room for international law. Indeed, international law is only defined through the eyes of domestic constitutional law. Sovereignty was, in fact, asserted against transnational laws and institutions (or rather laws and institutions that were only seen as transnational after the assertion of sovereignty and nationhood). It was resistance to the power of the Catholic Church within the borders of the emerging states of Europe that led to initial conflict and local compromises concerning the appointment of bishops. What impelled England's break with Rome was King Henry VIII's refusal to accept Roman diktats. However immoral this Tudor Clinton may have been, it is salutary to remember that his father-in-law was in effective occupation of Rome – something that made the dispensation to allow Henry to marry his dead brother's wife in breach of Church law easy, and the dispensation to divorce her impossible.

- Governments involve more than legislators to make laws and courts to interpret them. They need a range of other institutions that the international system does not possess.

  Answer: This may well be true. However, the whole point of the Rule of Law in a domestic system is that it can be of real value even where the state is weak or limited. Indeed, many are suggesting that it is the first thing that is needed.[60]

- Comparisons of the package in current circumstances present international law as seemingly weak and inadequate compared with the full-blown state

---

59   See Sampford, 'Challenges to the Concepts of "Sovereignty" and "Intervention"', chapter 16.

60   See M. Plunkett, 'Rebuilding the Rule of Law', in W. Maley, C. Sampford and R. Thakur (eds), *From Civil Strife to Civil Society: Civil and Military Responsibilities in Disrupted States*, Tokyo: United Nations University Press, 2003, pp. 207–28.

systems we are used to (i.e., why should the Americans, with the version of democracy that so many admire – with its checks and balances, culture, supreme court, etc. – bow to a set of laws with no legislature, no proper police force, a lesser judiciary?).

Answer: It has to be admitted that no set of institutions is perfect – international law is far from so. But domestic institutions have their weaknesses as well. Secondly, there will virtually never be a conflict between domestic and international law and, if there is, it is almost always because of a treaty entered into by the democratically elected government according to its Constitution (and in the US ratified by the Senate). Third, and most fundamentally, other nations and other peoples do not vote in US elections. Accordingly, there is no way that American democracy trumps the international Rule of Law. From the point of view of a non-American who suffers from an illegal act of a democracy or a dictatorship: they do not have a vote in it. It is better that they are protected by the Rule of Law than by nothing – just as citizens in pre-democratic countries were generally better off if their rulers at least subjected their own demands to the Rule of Law. It might be argued that a democracy will flout international law and the interests of other citizens less frequently. That is almost certainly true. However, it is not an argument against the international Rule of Law, it is an argument that the international Rule of Law should rarely pose a problem for a well-ordered democracy.

- Some might see the 'Rule of Law' as culturally grounded. It is sometimes argued that the Rule of Law only flourishes in a particular cultural setting. When it is pointed out that virtually all societies, Western and non-Western, possess concepts akin to the Rule of Law, the criticism may vary. The need is for support within the domestic culture of the relevant sovereign state.

Answer: The Rule of Law translates well enough into most cultures, is found within most of the relevant international treaties, and is the necessary basis for international trade. I can see no difficulty in the acceptance of the Rule of Law by the international community. It is those who want to flout the law who have the most difficulty with it!

- The great powers would not have signed on to international treaties and institutions, if they had realized that they would have been enforced. This may well be true empirically.

Answer: This is a subsequent assertion of bad faith that they should be stopped from making. Of course, they might argue that, in a democracy, they cannot bind their successors – this has important resonances for some of the parliamentary sovereignty cases that so concerned UK and

Commonwealth countries.[61] It could be argued that they changed the law so that, for some issues, it was necessary to do other things in order to get certain kinds of laws changed. In any case, those cases, apart from being rooted in one limited legal culture, are only relevant to the jurisdiction concerned. It may well be internally that the courts do not recognize the obligations the nation has undertaken. However, this does not mean that an international court will not recognize those obligations.

Conclusion

These considerations remind us that we cannot hope for as much in the international Rule of Law as we can from the Rule of Law in well-ordered liberal democracies. The limitations of international law mean that we cannot expect to find and insist that international law conform to a 'thick theory' of the Rule of Law. However, the Rule of Law according to the 'thin theory' remains a meaningful ideal that has broad support across cultures and into the international sphere.

If it could be achieved, it would not be an 'unqualified good' – I am sceptical of any such claims for individual liberal democratic values because liberal democratic values tend to both support and qualify each other and they cannot, *pace* Rawls, be placed in lexical order.

However, the idea that power be subject to effective inhibitions and the defence of the citizen from power's all intrusive claims, is certainly of value and is much missed by the victims of the use of illegal and brute force in international relations. Some of the institutional means by which an international Rule of Law might be advanced have been suggested in an earlier paper.[62] The project of which this is a part is an attempt to find those means.

This is broadly consistent with Chesterman's approach. He set out three possible meanings of the international Rule of Law – the application of Rule of Law principles to states and other subjects of international law, priority of international law over other forms of law, and the direct application of international law to individuals.[63] He prefers the first and this is closest to the one suggested by me – though I note that, in his chapter, he suggests that the theory should be so 'thin' as to be anorexic.

---

61   E.g., *Attorney-General (New South Wales) v Trethowan* (1932) 47 CLR 97.

62   Sampford, 'Challenges to the Concepts of "Sovereignty" and "Intervention"', chapter 16.

63   S. Chesterman, 'An International Rule of Law?', *The American Journal of Comparative Law* 56, 331, 2008, 342.

Chapter 4

Reflections on the Rule of Law: Its Scope and Significance for Partners in Development

John Barker[1]

Introduction

In the past decade or so, multilateral and bilateral development agencies have sought to articulate and support the rule of law in host States as part of a wider strategy to promote stability, good governance and development.[2] While the rule of law may have been overestimated[3] as a mechanism for resolving political conflict,[4] corruption and poverty, there has been a tendency to oversimplify its meaning in a manner that unduly restricts its application and influence.

---

1   The author has served as a consultant to multilateral and bilateral development organisations in the design, implementation and evaluation of justice sector programmes in west and southern Africa over the course of some 20 years. He would like to acknowledge with gratitude the insights of many colleagues whose views and experiences have helped to shape these observations; however, responsibility remains solely with the author.

2   It is revealing to compare the evolving definitions and strategies employed by the World Bank, UNDP and the EU, as well as bilateral donors and NGOs such as the International Commission of Jurists and the International Crisis Group. See also Stephen Humphreys, *Theatre of the Rule of Law: Transnational Legal Intervention in Theory and Practice* (Cambridge University Press, 2011) and *Guide to Rule of Law Country Analysis*, USAID, 2010. For a history of the subject, see Brian Z. Tamanaha, *On the Rule of Law* (Cambridge University Press, 2004), 9. For observations about the importance of the security sector, see Mark Schneider, 'Placing Security and Rule of Law on the Development Agenda', Development Outreach, The World Bank Institute (Washington, 2009), accessible at: http://siteresources.worldbank.org/WBI/Resources/213798-1253552326261/do-oct09-schneider.pdf (accessed 16 December 2012).

3   The Commission on Legal Empowerment of the Poor correctly drew attention to the need for legal empowerment but is characterized as being overly optimistic about its impact and possibly harmful in excessive legal formalization. Humpreys, *Theatre of the Rule of Law*, 211ff.

4   Jeremy Farrall, 'Impossible Expectations? The UN Security Council's Promotion of the Rule of Law after Conflict', in *The Role of International Law in Rebuilding Societies after Conflict*, ed. Brett Bowden, Hilary Charlesworth and Jeremy Farrall (Cambridge University Press, 2009), 135.

Differences in institutional mandates, skill sets and agendas have shaped agencies' understanding of the rule of law. This in turn has had considerable bearing on their strategies and areas of focus. The result has been a rather limited understanding and inadequate approach to promoting the rule of law with consequences for public decision-making and the level of development achieved.[5]

This chapter seeks to explain some of the theoretical underpinnings of the rule of law concept as well as their implications. The practical observations contained here are based on field experience in the design and implementation of projects in support of the rule of law in the context of development.[6] The purpose here is not to provide a comprehensive survey or a formulaic definition of the rule of law,[7] but rather to offer some empirical lessons and draw attention to available opportunities to deepen and widen strategies for its effective promotion.

The first part of this chapter sets out a conceptual framework that seeks to illuminate important foundational concepts, before drawing attention in the second part to some salient lessons that flow from the way we think about the rule of law which in turn may help to facilitate more effective programming. It will be argued that, for the rule of law to be realized, law formation must be insulated by democratic processes from self-serving political forces that sacrifice the interests of citizens to enrich and/or entrench economic and political elites.

It will also be argued that an understanding of the rule of law that emphasizes enforcement cannot serve the complex legal, social, political and economic needs of society or permit law to play its full role as a transformational force in development. There has been a tendency in the past to confine justice sector programming efforts to the administration of justice (meaning courts and tribunals, Ministries of Justice, law reform and human rights bodies, the practising bar, police, prisons, and anti-corruption agencies) or to narrow it down further

---

5   See Kevin E. Davis and Michael J. Trebilcock, 'The Relationship between Law and Development: Optimists versus Skeptics', *American Journal of Comparative Law*, 56, no. 4 (2008); NYU Law School, Public Law Research Paper No. 08-14; NYU Law and Economics Research Paper No. 08-24, available at SSRN: http://ssrn.com/abstract=1124045 (accessed 16 December 2012). See also Michael Trebilcock, 'The Rule of Law and Development: In Search of the Holy Grail', in *The World Bank Legal Review (vol. 3), International Financial Institutions and Global Legal Governance*, ed. Hassane Cissé, Daniel D. Bradlow and Benedict Kingsbury (World Bank 2012), 207–39. See also *The World Bank Legal Review (vol. 4) 'Legal Innovation and Empowerment for Development'*, ed. Hassane Cissé, Sam Muller, Chantal Thomas and Chenguang Wang (World Bank, 2013), at http://issuu.com/world.bank.publications/docs/9780821395066 (accessed 7 February 2013).

6   The author was involved with the design of justice sector support programmes developed by the European Union, the UNDP, the Office of the High Commissioner for Human Rights, the UK Department for International Development, the Canadian International Development Agency, British Council and various NGOs.

7   For an invaluable repository of available literature on the rule of law and other governance materials, see Governance and Social Development Resource Centre www.gsdrc.org (accessed 16 December 2012).

to the criminal/juvenile justice sector.[8] Such interventions may be essential but are hardly sufficient, bearing in mind that there is no sphere or department of government, including the legislative branch, that lies beyond the reach of an extensive web of legal imperatives[9] in which legal rules, information, advice and training play a fundamental role in optimizing decision-making outcomes, the holy grail of good governance.

Another fundamental aspect of the rule of law often overlooked is its implicit structuring of decision-making in all parts of government. One example is the strictures of administrative justice which confront capricious decisions tainted by bias or arbitrary considerations. Arguably, the citizens of all nations have a right to *responsible* decision-making in the sense that public decisions should be structured (bound by rules that promote reasonableness and procedural justice), accountable, evidence-based, strategic, ethical and directed to promoting the public interest. While the individual elements of responsible decision-making are reasonably well understood, the knowledge is specialist in nature and dispersed across many disciplines. More work is needed to integrate this knowledge into a unified discipline as a part of its practical realization.

A further aspect of the rule of law, frequently overlooked but closely bound to the most pressing interests of citizens, is economic justice. Ideological confrontation coupled with difficulties inherent in reconciling market forces with fairness have meant that economic justice has not been well served. Although regulatory mechanisms, competition laws and consumer law are meant to level the playing field and promote wider access to opportunities, goods and services, many economies are feeling the crippling effects of failure to regulate markets effectively. This is a rule of law problem because it is the rules and on whose behalf they are written that determine how the goods of society are allocated.

Finally, when societies are critically examined through the lens of rule of law and especially good governance, the distinction between 'developed' and 'developing' fades as the limitations and needs of more developed economies come more clearly into view. Accordingly, we need to work respectfully and innovatively together as partners to find solutions that address similar and increasingly urgent structural problems confronting both sides of the North–South divide.

---

8   See, for example, the narrow scope of The United Nations Rule of Law Indicators: Implementation Guide and Project Tools, 2011 at http://www.un.org/en/events/peacekeepersday/2011/publications/un_rule_of_law_indicators.pdf (accessed 16 December 2012).

9   Legal requirements imposed upon officials throughout government include rules proscribing the receiving of benefits and other obligations arising from administrative law, for example, discussed below in 'Practical Lessons'.

Conceptual Framework

Rule of Law as Principle

The rule of law[10] occupies a key position in the firmament of interconnected concepts and principles that contribute to good governance, recognized in the Declaration of Millennium Goals[11] to be a precondition of development. Examples of other constitutive principles of good governance include legitimacy,[12] constitutionalism,[13] legality,[14] accountability,[15]

10   For an excellent discourse on the rule of law, see Tom Bingham, *The Rule of Law* (Allen Lane, 2010).

11   Some key documents on the UN and the rule of law are: United Nations Millennium Declaration (A/RES/55/2); 'The Brahimi Report': Comprehensive review of the whole question of peacekeeping operations in all their aspects (A/55/305); 2005 World Summit Outcome (A/RES/60/1); Secretary-General's Report 'In Larger Freedom: Towards Development, Security and Human Rights for All' (A/59/2005); Secretary-General's Report 'The Rule of Law and Transitional Justice in Conflict and Post-Conflict Societies' (S/2004/616); Secretary-General's Report 'Uniting Our Strengths: Enhancing United Nations Support for the Rule of Law' (A/61/636); Secretary-General's Report 'Strengthening and Coordinating United Nations Rule of Law Activities' (A/63/226); Secretary-General's Report 'Annual report on strengthening and coordinating United Nations Rule of Law Activities' (A/64/298).

12   Legitimacy is a complex and pervasive concept that is more far-reaching than legality, capturing the notion that authority claimed or exercised is duly constituted and maintained over time in both form and substance, reflecting a politically or socially acceptable level of support or consensus. See Michel Rosenfeld, 'The Rule of Law and the Legitimacy of Constitutional Democracy', *Southern California Law Review* 74 (2001), available at SSRN: http://ssrn.com/abstract=262350 or http://dx.doi.org/10.2139/ssrn.262350 (accessed 16 December 2012); Thomas M. Franck, 'Democracy, Legitimacy and the Rule of Law: Linkages', NYU Law School, Public Law and Legal Theory Working Paper No. 2 (1999), available at SSRN: http://ssrn.com/abstract=201054 or http://dx.doi.org/10.2139/ssrn.201054 (accessed 16 December 2012). See also Lukas Meyer, *Legitimacy, Justice and Public International Law* (Cambridge University Press, 2009).

13   Constitutionalism establishes, structures, legitimizes and limits the exercise of public authority through a stable, paramount framework of laws and conventions that configure key institutions and their respective mandates and powers, as well as the processes by which laws are made and amended.

14   Legality refers to the principle that actions must be duly authorized and in conformity with legal requirements. A more technical understanding includes notions of legal clarity and non-retrospectivity. See discussion under 'Legal Regularity' below. See also Kenneth S. Gallant, *The Principle of Legality in International and Comparative Criminal Law* (Cambridge University Press, 2009), 15–19, 23.

15   Accountability can take many forms including political accountability, legal accountability, financial accountability, functional accountability for employment and contractual services, professional accountability, collegial accountability to peers, moral accountability to faith communities and familial accountability to family and clan. These

effectiveness,[16] separation of powers,[17] participatory democratic processes, good faith, fairness,[18] justice[19] and respect for human rights.[20] A definition offered by the Office of the UN Secretary-General illustrates the aggregation of concepts and the difficulty of providing a standalone definition that is not influenced by context:

> The rule of law refers to a principle of governance in which all persons, institutions and entities, public and private, including the State itself, are accountable to laws that are publicly promulgated, equally enforced and independently adjudicated, and which are consistent with international human rights norms and standards. It requires, as well, measures to ensure adherence to the principles of supremacy of law, equality before the law, accountability to the law, fairness in the application of the law, separation of powers, participation in decision-making, legal certainty, avoidance of arbitrariness and procedural and legal transparency.[21]

This seeming jumble of concepts, aspirations and norms serves as important organizing principles for delivering justice. They manifest themselves through rules and institutional arrangements at every level, including customary

---

tend to have strong moral and ethical dimensions. Accountability is often in tension with independence of action. In many offices of State and independent bodies such as judicial officers, police chiefs, prosecution agencies, anti-corruption agencies, human rights commissions, ombudsman functions, complaints commissions, central banking functions, regulatory bodies, etc., the challenge is to balance mechanisms that maximize public accountability and minimize political interference, a significant indicator of the quality of the rule of law.

16 Effectiveness is particularly relevant to public service delivery and requires capability. It is the foundation upon which the State entities make a claim to public revenues and in respect of which the legitimacy of many States is now severely tested. This includes the provision of support and protection to citizens from security arrangements to health, social services, education, infrastructure and regulatory frameworks.

17 See Latimer House Guidelines, http://www.thecommonwealth.org/shared_ asp_files/uploadedfiles/%7BACC9270A-E929–4AE0-AEF9-4AAFEC68479C%7D_ Latimer%20House%20Booklet%20130504.pdf (accessed 16 December 2012).

18 Thomas M. Franck, *Fairness in International Law and Institutions* (Clarendon Press, 1995), 7ff.

19 The distinction between fairness and justice is the subject of debate, but justice is taken here to be more closely anchored to the normative and institutional recognition of legal obligations and entitlements.

20 Brian Z. Tamanaha, 'A Concise Guide to the Rule of Law', in *Florence Workshop on the Rule of Law*, ed. Neil Walker and Gianluigi Palombella, St. John's Legal Studies Research Paper No. 07-0082 (Hart Publishing Company, 2007). Available at SSRN: http://ssrn.com/abstract=1012051 (accessed 16 December 2012).

21 (S/2004/616) Report of the Secretary-General on the Rule of Law and Transitional Justice in Conflict and Post-Conflict Societies: www.un.org/en/ruleoflaw/ (accessed 16 December 2012).

international law, international conventions, bilateral treaties, constitutional instruments, statutes, regulations, decrees, policies, and decisions of courts and tribunals. They may be informal or formal, directive[22] or mandatory, permeating professional codes and best practice and mediating a wide range of relationships at the interstate level, among the three branches of government and between State and citizen. They also inform the rules of engagement between the State, the private sector, the not-for-profit sector and at the interface between national institutions and the international community.[23]

The principles that shape the rules and institutional arrangements referred to above are not themselves laws and therefore are not legally binding *per se*. This is not a weakness, for they are arguably more influential than formal laws by virtue of their import, stability and universality, informing and guiding the pursuit of justice in its more tangible forms. Occupying loftier realms of shared human aspiration, they are independent of particular legal and political systems and beyond the reach of trade-offs and compromised ideals that breed injustice in how they are applied in practice. While often ignored or overridden in the pursuit of self-interested goals, history and daily experience are full of evidence that a yearning for an inclusive, fair society still burns brightly in the collective consciousness of humanity and in articulated aspiration.

Constitutive Elements of the Rule of Law

Considerable resources have been invested in the promotion of the rule of law, based upon a quite rudimentary understanding of its meaning. These investments have not lived up to expectation,[24] raising the question of whether the traditional emphasis on supporting the supply side of legal service delivery is deficient as a strategy and, at a more basic level, whether the rule of law is more of an outcome than a tool. It is submitted that, although the rule of law is the resultant of many political, cultural and resource-driven forces often hidden from view, a failure to grasp its scope and potential has led to missed opportunities to use some of its elements to greater effect as levers.[25]

---

22   Directive is meant here in the constitutional sense of not having direct binding legal effect but indirect influence as an aid to interpretation.

23   See discussion at p. 96, below, on the need for the international community to incorporate principles of good governance in the manner in which it engages with developing countries.

24   Thomas Carothers, 'Promoting the Rule of Law Abroad', Carnegie Endowment for International Peace, *Rule of Law Series*, no. 34 (January, 2003), 3. For a discussion of the promotion of the rule of law and the Law in Development movement, see Gordon Barron, 'World Bank and Rule of Law Reforms', in *LSE Working Paper Series* no. 05-70 (2005) accessible at: www2.lse.ac.uk/internationalDevelopment/pdf/WP70.pdf (accessed 17 December 2012).

25   See, for example, Rachel Kleinfeld, *Advancing the Rule of Law Abroad: Next Generation Reform* (Carnegie Endowment for International Peace, 2012).

In exploring this question, it is illuminating to consider constituent layers of the rule of law separately – although they are more blended in practice. These layers are considered below under the rubric of law and order, legal regularity, procedural justice, institutional capacity and substantive rights.

Law and Order

At its most basic, the rule of law is contrasted with a state of lawlessness where order breaks down and citizens take the law into their own hands. Conversely, where the rule of law prevails, laws are observed and enforced, people are safeguarded, contract and property rights are respected and offenders are punished. Keeping the peace is generally regarded as the first order of business of the State. The importance of maintaining order is starkly illustrated in stabilization and post-conflict situations, which allow little room for development while human security is under threat.[26]

This understanding is far from complete, however. First, conflating enforcement and compliance tends to emphasize coercive measures. This can be highly counterproductive. Second, it does not distinguish between forms of illegality fatal to socioeconomic ordering and forms of law-breaking routinely managed by legal systems. Third, it does not address the problem of *who* determines the content of the law and in whose interest. In many nations, one of the greatest challenges of our time is preventing those entrusted with power from preying on their own populations and public goods. Fourth, it does not do justice to the rich spectrum of dispute resolution mechanisms that serve to prevent as well as to settle disputes and promote harmony, trust and productive relations.

The rule of law has a strategic role to play well beyond the application of coercive enforcement measures to keep order. A regime that imposes itself merely to restore or maintain law and order is difficult to distinguish from other rent-seeking protection rackets – and one that invites competition from others as local populations apprehend the extent to which their own development is being held back. It is in this context that undemocratic, weak and failed States are most prone to State capture by narrow interests.[27]

---

26 See also World Bank survey Voices of the Poor, Deepa Narayan et al., *Can Anyone Hear Us? Voices from 47 Countries*, (1999) which highlighted security as a priority need articulated by the poor. http://siteresources.worldbank.org/INTPOVERTY/Resources/335642-1124115102975/1555199-1124115187705/vol1.pdf (accessed 16 December 2012).

27 http://www.foreignpolicy.com/articles/2011/06/17/2011_failed_states_index_interactive_map_and_rankings (accessed 19 January 2013).

Legal Regularity

A more technically rigorous understanding of the rule of law includes a grasp of qualities that distinguish law from other normative imperatives over and above the manner of their enforcement. These qualities emphasize legal regularity and predictability to guide the conduct of those subject to the law.[28] Such qualities include public promulgation, clarity, prospectivity, relative stability,[29] generality[30] and equality in their application. There is also an emphasis on law guiding and limiting the discretion of public officials.[31] These elements introduce an indispensable manifestation of justice wherein citizens have due notice of their obligations and derive significant social and economic benefits from legal continuity and protection from arbitrary decision-making.

Procedural Justice

More ambitious formulations of the rule of law seek to ensure procedural fairness[32] by reference to principles of natural justice and due process.[33] These are potent

---

28   This view is represented by writers such as Joseph Raz, in 'The Rule of Law and its Virtue', in *The Law Quarterly Review* 93 (1977), 195.

29   These four are among the eight characteristics of a viable legal system postulated by Fuller, including rules-based coherence, being free from contradiction, implementation being possible and congruence between law and the actions of those enforcing law are cited in Lon Fuller, *The Morality of Law* (Yale University Press, 1969).

30   This means directed at the community as a whole and not at particular persons. Sometimes referred to as 'laws of attainder', *ad hominem* statutes were also considered a breach of separation of powers and of due process requirements. Peter Gerangelos, 'The Separation of Powers and Legislative Interference with Judicial Functions in Pending Cases', *Federal Law Review* 30, no. 1 (2002).

31   'The rule of law does not require that official or judicial decisionmakers should be deprived of all discretion, but it does require that no discretion should be unconstrained so as to be potentially arbitrary. No discretion may be legally unfettered.' Bingham, *The Rule of Law*, 54.

32   Many civil and political rights are protected and realized through procedural requirements. In criminal cases these include the presumption of innocence, the right to be represented, the right of the accused to know the case to be answered, the right to be heard and the right to cross-examine witnesses.

33   Due process appeared in the 1326 version of the Magna Carta. The phrase 'natural justice' is used in the United Kingdom in preference to 'due process' which in American law involves additional procedural and substantive safeguards, or 'fundamental justice' which appears in Canadian law. Constitutional differences between the US and UK impeded the development in the UK of judicial review processes, particularly the sovereignty of Parliament doctrine which, until membership in the EU and accession to numerous human rights conventions, was treated as carte blanche for members of Parliament. It is still regularly employed by political elites in many countries to legislate as they see fit even in cases where there are major constitutional constraints. The fact that Members of Parliament

forces for good. There is a tendency to underrate the impact of procedural rules on substantive outcomes, yet procedural justice forms a central pillar of justice by virtue of its capacity to introduce structure, discipline and accountability to public decision-making that so often determines in practice the realization of rights. By providing a useful framework to guide State officials and traditional authorities such as chiefs through complex decision-making processes, procedural justice represents an important pathway to substantive fairness.[34]

Institutional Capacity

Some definitions incorporate institutional requirements that the justice sector provide a basic level and quality of service delivery.[35] An independent judiciary[36] is seen by many as an integral part of the rule of law in order to assure impartiality in deciding cases and mediating disputes.[37] Some go further, requiring threshold levels of competence, access and resourcing throughout the sector in order to function effectively in enforcing or realizing rights. Problems of access include geographical, financial and linguistic barriers, rights awareness, rule complexity, standing and representation, abuse of process and delay. Rights that can be claimed through the courts have a different character from those which can only be realized

---

are elected is, by some logic that remains mysterious, treated by some parliamentarians as a modern day version of the divine right of kings, contrary to the rule of law. This is what the Magna Carta itself sought to address in relation to the sovereigns of the day.

34   See 'The Judge over your Shoulder' provided to the UK civil service at http://www. tsol.gov.uk/Publications/Scheme_Publications/judge.pdf (accessed 16 December 2012).

See also Bingham *The Rule of Law*, chapter 6. The Office of the President and Cabinet in Malawi has incorporated similar training into its programme for civil servants in all departments. See Christopher Forsyth and Steve D. Matenje, 'Some Reflections on Administrative Justice in Malawi: Practical Steps', *Acta Juridica: Comparing Administrative Justice across the Commonwealth* (2006): 389–404 (ISSN: 00651346). In addition, the EU funded a South African motivational training programme for judges and magistrates in Malawi that focused on the close relationship between ethical framework, motivation, morale and productivity.

35   The World Justice Project defines the rule of law by four principles: (a) the government and its officials and agents are accountable under the law; (b) the laws are clear, publicized, stable, and fair, and protect fundamental rights, including the security of persons and property; (c) the process by which the laws are enacted, administered, and enforced is accessible, fair, and efficient; and (d) access to justice is provided by competent, independent, and ethical adjudicators, attorneys or representatives, and judicial officers who are of sufficient number, have adequate resources, and reflect the makeup of the communities they serve. See http://worldjusticeproject.org/what-rule-law (accessed 16 December 2012).

36   Raz, *The Rule of Law and its Virtue*, 195.

37   Specialist tribunals and alternative dispute resolution (ADR) facilities including ombudsman functions are increasingly recognized as important tools supplementary to courts in addressing access to justice concerns.

through long-term investment of public resources to build service delivery, not only in the justice sector but in many non-justice subject areas as well. For this reason, a more holistic approach to the reach of law is required, explored further in the second part, below. Sadly, in many countries there is an inverse relationship between resources committed and level of greatest contact between the justice system and the citizen.

Substantive Rights

While more positivist definitions may include elements of procedural justice and institutional functionality, they stop short of positing justice or fairness as matters of substantive entitlement.[38] By contrast, there is a growing awareness that the rule of law cannot fully be realized if it cannot distinguish between laws that subjugate people and those that empower them. Without substantive norms such as human rights, law is too easily used as a tool of oppression, particularly of minorities and vulnerable groups.[39]

Definitions aside, the fact is that national and international societies make complex demands on legal systems and their subjects. This demand comes from the commercial sector and through substantive human rights standards incorporated into legal instruments at every level, as illustrated by many socioeconomic rights. Few legal theorists, practitioners, politicians or citizens would suggest that goals such as the promotion of human rights, dignity and well-being are not compelling social and legal objectives, even if unjust laws happen to be on the books or are consistent with restricted academic definitions of the rule of law.[40] For many, injustice and rule

---

38   See Raz, *The Rule of Law and its Virtue*, 195. Note, however, that too much attention to a purely formal definition is somewhat artificial because in practice virtually every element exists in all legal systems and the presence of repugnant laws merely indicates that the rule of law is not a condition in a binary system. Moreover, imposing legal stability brings about a certain kind of empowerment of citizens through a reduction of risks normally associated with reliance on relative strangers.

39   According to the Universal Declaration of Human Rights, 'human rights should be protected by the rule of law', G.A. Res. 217A (III), U.N. Doc. A/810, Preamble (3) (1948). One of the most ambitious projects to articulate principles governing the rule of law was undertaken by the International Commission of Jurists in 1956. This initiative led to the Declaration of Delhi which includes socioeconomic rights as well as civil rights. The most recent survey-based project led to the Rule of Law Index of the World Justice Project based on nine qualities: limited government powers, absence of corruption, order and security, fundamental rights, open government, effective regulatory enforcement, access to civil justice, effective criminal justice and informal justice.

40   In fact there are many reasons why justice may be compromised, including juridical reasons. Law often serves two masters, namely the public as a whole and individuals in their unique circumstances. It is difficult to achieve in any given instance a result that does justice to all, whether in legislation or in court rulings.

of law involves a logical contradiction, especially if one takes as axiomatic that the intended beneficiaries[41] of the political-legal-economic system are citizens.

Many deplorable practices, such as the mutilation and trafficking of children and women, cannot be justified by cultural relativity and often involve serious criminal offences that already form part of the penal laws of most countries. A further risk associated with naive deference to many traditional systems is a perpetuation of gender-bias and other injustices inherent in some traditional power structures. The challenge can also come, however, from limited institutional capacity and resources to confront entrenched positions and sensitize communities.

Importing, if not imposing, a growing array of substantive norms is not without cost, however. The more inclusive and prescriptive the rule of law is, the harder it is to reconcile such imperatives with the values of other cultures, also reflected in their formal and informal legal systems.[42] These external values need a chance to root organically within a culture. The price of imposing norms can be active resistance or backlash, impaired long-term buy-in, and a weakening of any claim to universality and even legitimacy.[43] Moreover, other important rights can be eclipsed and undermined when the rights system is politicized and targeted. Nor is a cavalier attitude on the part of more developed countries conducive to self-examination and identification of notable deficiencies within their own political, legal and economic systems.

While not denying the global importance or constitutional nature of the principal global conventions and *jus cogens* norms, it is not easy to prescribe how far to press substantive human rights norms that are embodied in some regions but opposed in others.[44] This requires considerable care and a level of local knowledge that many international organizations and observers do not possess, seek or build into their programmes at an early formulation stage.

Arguably, a more effective approach would be to focus on the procedural aspects of decision-making, such as legal presumptions and principles of natural

---

41 By 'principal beneficiary' is meant the reference point for any measure of efficacy.

42 See John Reitz, 'Export of the Rule of Law', *Transnational Law and Contemporary Problems* 13 (2003): 429; Randall Peerenboom, 'Varieties of the Rule of Law: An Introduction and Provision Conclusion', in *Asian Discourses on Rule of Law*, ed. Randall Peerenboom (Routledge Curzon, 2004). Inclusionary definitions have to be more flexible in their interpretation of how relative, context or resource-dependent certain rights, especially the socioeconomic rights, are. See also Simon Chesterman, 'An International Rule of Law?' *American Journal of Comparative Law* 56 (2008): 331–61. The more prescriptive the normative content, the more one must determine how flexible and responsive it can be without being weakened or compromised in some fundamental way.

43 See Humphreys, *Theatre of the Rule of Law*, 224.

44 As gay rights campaigns in parts of Africa demonstrate, stark fault lines are reflected in confrontations over substantive rights. Unfortunately, for many in Africa the concept of minority rights has, as a result, become restricted and taken on a pejorative meaning. Moreover, sharp differences in cultural values have thrown a political lifeline to moribund dictatorships in several African States.

justice, since they can strongly influence substantive outcomes without undue external interference. This is especially useful when engaging with traditional leaders who are responsible for dispute resolution and resource management at community level. This approach may facilitate a more harmonious and authentic evolution of public perceptions and cultural practices, especially in countries such as in the Middle and Far East where the subject of human rights is perceived as excessively confrontational and threatening to traditional values.

The above is no more than a tentative conceptual framework that separates key aspects of the rule of law and presents them as progressive layers intended to underpin and frame the observations that follow.

Practical Lessons

Rule of Law and Democratic Lawmaking Processes

Aristotle's 'law should govern'[45] reflects an aspiration down the ages for limits to be placed on the predatory, arbitrary and irrational exercise of power that has caused immeasurable human suffering.[46] The assertion that 'no one is above the law'[47] has far-reaching implications for democratic processes and the pursuit of justice. It is in fact a highly *political* formula that reverses power and replaces the empty 'people's' rhetoric of aging dictatorships and faded revolutions with something rather more genuine. In this formulation, leaders are in every sense trustees,[48] bound to serve the citizen and to derive only such benefits as are prescribed by rules that ultimately should lie beyond their powers.[49]

---

45   'Politics, Book 3', ed. Jonathan Barnes, *The Complete Works of Aristotle*, The Revised Oxford Translation (Princeton University Press, 1984).

46   See the first rule of law principle of the World Justice Project, p. 85, footnote 35, above.

47   Albert V. Dicey, *An Introduction to the Study of the Law of the Constitution*, 5th edn (Macmillan, 1897). First published in 1885, Dicey popularized the term 'rule of law', describing it as 'a trait common to every civilised and orderly state', p. 180. According to Dicey, not being above the law requires an equality of all persons in relation to enforcement mechanisms as well: 'every man, whatever be his rank or condition, is subject to the ordinary law of the realm and amenable to the jurisdiction of the ordinary tribunals', p. 185. Being 'ruled by law' means that one can be 'punished for a breach of law, but he can be punished for nothing else', p. 194.

48   This is made explicit in s. 12(ii) of the 1994 Malawi Constitution 'All persons responsible for the exercise of powers of State do so on trust'.

49   This can be understood as a variation on the concept of a veil of ignorance. See John Harsanyi, 'Cardinal Welfare, Individualistic Ethics, and Interpersonal Comparisons of Utility', *The Journal of Political Economy* 63, no. 4 (August 1955): 309–21 at 316. See also John Rawls, *A Theory of Justice* (Belknap Press, 1971), 60.

Virtually all political leaders purport to rule on behalf of all citizens in accordance with the wishes of the people. However far apart theory and practice are, there is virtual unanimity in principle as to the identity of the intended beneficiaries of the political, legal and economic systems. This precept is essentially political in nature, presenting law as something other than a self-interested command.[50] Any 'insulating' process therefore must protect and take as its reference point the wishes and interests of citizens. There is no guarantee that their wishes and long-term best interests will coincide but consultative and open democratic processes provide the safest space for public and expert opinion to be shared and reconciled in an open and informed manner.[51] Equally important is a vigilant and well-informed press and civil society as part of a wider matrix of accountability that includes the legitimate concerns of the wider international community.

Unfortunately, legal constraints upon those in power are often weak and easily circumvented. Where legislatures are overly compliant or where informed public scrutiny is lacking, laws are too malleable in the hands of ruling elites[52] to conform in reality with the principle that 'no one is above the law'.[53] The rule of law must engage all aspects of lawmaking processes to ensure that its very essence is not to be undermined. Programmes that strengthen electoral and legislative processes have an important role to play,[54] but must be accompanied by strategies to promote access to information, a politically literate population, a vigilant media, procedural mechanisms such as ring-fenced constitutional provisions, and

---

50   See Austin's command backed by threats. John Austin, 'The Province of Jurisprudence Determined', ed. Wilfrid Rumble (Cambridge University Press, 1995, first published 1832); John Austin, *Lectures on Jurisprudence, or The Philosophy of Positive Law*, two vols (1879), ed. Robert Campbell, 4th edn, rev. (London: John Murray, Bristol: Thoemmes Press reprint, 2002).

51   The measure of risk (nuclear energy, genetically modified organisms, carbon emissions) may call for expertise but acceptance of exposure to significant risk requires legitimate public processes to provide the equivalent of informed consent. For a discussion of conditions for informed consent, see K.S. Shrader-Frechette, *Risk and Rationality: Philosophical Foundations for Populist Reforms* (University of California Press, 1991), 206–207.

52   Attempts by leaders or their supporters to remove presidential term limits illustrate the point – Russia, Colombia, Mexico, Sri Lanka, the Palestinian authority, Malawi, Zimbabwe, DRC and Somaliland are examples.

53   Essential qualities of law, such as predictability, stability and/or generality of application are also weakened. The effect of rule by decree creates a zone of impunity antithetical to the essence of the rule of law.

54   The crafting of standing orders and the strengthening of oversight responsibilities of Parliamentary committees are examples of important processes that are addressed by parliamentary support programmes. See, for example, *Strengthening Parliamentary Accountability, Citizen Engagement and Access to Information: A Global Survey of Parliamentary Monitoring Organizations*, World Bank Institute and NDI, 2011.

adequate consultative and deliberative processes.[55] All help to insulate the content of the law from the manipulations of ruling elites.[56]

If too narrow a definition of law is used by those designing programmes in support of the rule of law, there is a risk of losing important opportunities to challenge illegitimate political processes and related problems that can circumvent and undermine the legal system itself. Confining efforts and resources to courts and the formal machinery of justice is not enough. Support must be provided to other key ministries such as those that are confronted by child trafficking, internally displaced persons, refugees, domestic violence and violations of international humanitarian law. Such design shortcomings can be found even in sector-wide programmes and are due to a combination of unfamiliarity with the subject, risk aversion,[57] and assumptions that the design features of other specialist programmes have the reach to deploy the wide range of specialist skills required.[58] Unfortunately, this assumption seldom proves correct. Unless those responsible for programme design in the justice sector ensure essential linkages with democratic process and wider socioeconomic rights, law will continue to be used as a tool to serve the narrow interests of ruling interests at the expense of citizens.

Structured, Accountable Decision-making: An Emerging Right?

As with good governance, the rule of law is generally understood and promoted by focusing on the normative framework (especially the legal framework), on institutional structures, including processes and accountability mechanisms, and on building specialist legal skills within the sector.[59] These are indispensable; however, there is an unspoken assumption that they are sufficient to bring decision-making up to a desired standard. The international development community's limited impact over many decades, even where substantial investments have been made, challenges this assumption. The measure of success must be more than contributing to an overall functional objective, as the overworked term 'strengthens' conveys in the context of capacity-building. This is not ambitious enough.

---

55   See, for example, Jurgen Habermas, *Between Facts and Norms: Contributions to a Discourse Theory of Law and Democracy*, trans. William Rehg (Polity Press, 1996), ch. 7.

56   See Larry Diamond, *The Spirit of Democracy* (Times Books, 2008).

57   Institutional risk-aversion is not compatible with work in this subject area. It requires skill and experience for external agencies to avoid being caught in political crossfire.

58   Support for the Clerk of Parliament, provision of legal reference materials, joined up training across the sector and public interest advocacy are often weak and fall between categories of programmes.

59   Other factors sometimes considered are: institutional culture, motivation and incentive systems, clan-based loyalty demands, and accountability to taxpayers and voters.

Humanity has paid a heavy price for the disastrous choices of the past, many of them unrecorded and hidden from view.[60] How many more losses will be incurred and opportunities squandered in the decades ahead from chronic sub-optimal decision-making at virtually every level of every public institution in every town, city, state and capital of the world? In the ordering of human society, unless the target is considerably more ambitious and efforts more carefully directed to *optimize* public decision-making, humanity risks being undermined by social and other forces it can no longer control. Decision-making must not be left to chance but must develop into a more inclusive and integrated discipline in its own right – one that embraces norms (including professional codes of conduct as well as legal rights and duties), structures, processes, critical thinking methodology, policy formation, strategic planning, institutional culture, psychology, sociology and even brain physiology.[61] This will lead to a more powerful understanding of the many forces that act upon a decision-maker from outside and from within. As the discipline becomes more developed and refined, more effective programming will become possible, both in terms of what is being promoted and how.

One of the most potent yet underutilized elements of the rule of law is the public law framework of administrative justice that provides a framework to challenge and correct capricious and arbitrary decision-making.[62] This is achieved through a coherent body of rules and principles that place duties upon those exercising public authority, including in the exercise of seemingly wide discretionary powers. Examples include requirements of impartiality and non-discrimination, allowing affected parties to be heard, a prohibition on disproportionate harm, requirements to direct one's mind actively to the matter at hand taking relevant factors into account and excluding irrelevant factors, obligations of good faith and not to prejudge issues before they are heard, thresholds of fairness and reasonableness,[63] avoidance of conflict of interest and abuse of power, including not exceeding powers

---

60   See Norman Dixon, *On The Psychology of Military Incompetence* (Jonathan Cape, 1976).

61   Interesting medical research is pointing to significant changes in brain physiology among those who wield power. See *Proceedings of the Royal Society of Medicine, London*, 9 October 2012.

62   Malcolm Russell-Einhorn and Howard Fenton, *Administrative Law Tools and Concepts to Strengthen USAID Programming* (USAID, 2008). For a domestic law source widely cited in common law jurisdictions, see W. Wade and C. Forsyth, *Administrative Law* (OUP, 2009). For an example of a more eclectic regional approach, see The Administrative Law Training Guidelines, EJTN Working Group Programmes' Administrative Law Sub-Working Group, 2012 at http://www.ejtn.net/Documents/Resources/EJTN_Administrative_Law_Training_Guidelines_2012.pdf.

63   In the UK, these are embodied in the so-called Wednesbury rules under which the decision-maker 'must call his own attention to the matters which he is bound to consider', and 'exclude from his consideration matters which are irrelevant to what he has to consider'. A third requirement adds a more generalized reasonableness test excluding 'absurd' outcomes. See *Associated Provincial Picture Houses v. Wednesbury Corporation*

or exercising them for purposes not intended. These obligations are recognizable in a variety of legal systems although they may be expressed differently. Where decisions are taken that violate these fundamental requirements of decision-making in circumstances where there are no effective legal mechanisms to identify and correct errors, the rule of law is undermined.

It is instructive to understand decision-making not only as bounded by external rules but as the result of a multitude of forces acting upon a decision-maker from many directions to determine decision-making outcomes. External forces may be constructive – the formal rules, policies, guidelines, professional codes of conduct, inspiring leadership and effective accountability structures, or they can be negative in the form of overbearing clan loyalty demands, conflicts of interest, political interference, intimidation or offers of illicit benefits.

More difficult to programme but highly influential are *internal* positive forces. These include honesty and integrity, respect for the law, a sense of civic duty, internalization of professional identity, a desire to follow and set examples of good leadership, a strong skills base, and vigilance in recognizing and avoiding potential conflicts of interest at an early stage. Negative internal forces, quite apart from the inverse of those just listed, include a range of vulnerabilities, fears and even clinical disorders.

By mapping these positive forces and negative influences, it may be possible to develop strategies to change for the better their relative impact. Such strategies have enormous potential in many spheres of public decision-making, since even small changes in routine decision-making practices effected on a global scale could be transformative, unlocking resources and benefits that otherwise never materialize, better equipping mankind to face the challenges of the future.

It is submitted that optimized, responsible decision-making is emerging not only as a coalescing discipline but as a composite right shaped by distinctive correlative obligations on the part of duty bearers. This would have the benefit of sharpening the focus upon attainable elements of sound decision-making and integrating demand and supply side in a practical way that both sides can understand. Is it not appropriate for citizens of all nations to expect and demand of their leaders fully responsible decision-making in their interest? Shouldn't all national assets be managed optimally and sustainably for the benefit of present and future generations? Can mankind afford not to make decision-making itself the focus of future collective endeavour?

Drawing upon a wide range of disciplines would sharpen the focus on how human beings make choices, affording greater prominence to strategies that work best. The evidence to date suggests that there is a genuine thirst for practical decision-making tools and that these can be transformational in terms of morale,

---

[1947] EWCA Civ 1, [1948] 1 K.B. 223, CA (England and Wales). In the US, decisions are subject to similar challenge if they are 'arbitrary and capricious'.

efficiency, reduction of conflict and cost savings.[64] There are also encouraging signs that emerging technologies are now making it possible to crowdsource and map relevant information more accurately and comprehensively. This will not only strengthen the evidence-base but give greater voice to the demand side of the service delivery equation and promote accountability.[65]

Economic Justice and Abuse of Power

Perhaps one of the greatest challenges to sustainable development and economic justice is the lack of alignment of political choices with the needs of populations, especially in the allocation of resources and 'rules of the game' that largely determine how wealth is distributed in society. Many practical obstacles stand in the way of this alignment, including the dissociation of actions and consequences inherent in market systems and a general lack of economic literacy on the part of citizens, legislators and the media. As a result, the negative impact of political and economic choices are often too remote to trace. However, few obstacles are as toxic to democratic processes and citizen well-being as the debts owed by politicians to those who deliver votes and provide access to office.[66] This structural conflict of interest on the part of political leaders combined with a lack of true accountability[67] is a direct challenge to the rule of law and democratic legitimacy.

---

64   The EU supported a pilot course in administrative law, which had such a positive impact that it was integrated into routine civil service training in Malawi. See footnote 34, above.

65   Knowledge-based requirements will be better served in future by new educational tools that will increase lifelong access, including remote access, to knowledge and skills certification. See, for example, Cathy N. Davidson and David T. Goldberg, *The Future of Thinking: Learning Institutions in a Digital Age* (MIT Press, 2010).

66   Whether influence derives from military backing, 'king-making' media moguls, wealthy business interests that fund political campaigns, or organized lobbies, dangerously distorted national and/or foreign policy is not an uncommon outcome. The elephant in the room is the conflict of interest that results from dependence on any group interposing itself between citizens and their leaders. While this problem goes well beyond economic justice, the problem has become especially acute in relation to how the economy is managed, and specifically for whose benefit. There are clear winners and losers. The pendulum has swung so far in favour of protected positions through deregulation, poor protection against cartel behaviour and abuse of intellectual property rights and monopoly positions that wealth creation is being superseded by cost externalization from government to citizens and wealth transfers from citizens to financial elites. For a cogent analysis of the impact of predatory practices in financial services on middle-class families, see Teresa Sullivan, Elizabeth Warren and Jay Westbrook, *The Fragile Middle Class: Americans in Debt* (New Haven: Yale University Press, 2001).

67   In the past, there has been little accounting for decisions beyond being voted out of office for unpopular policies, not unsound ones. True democracy takes place through continuous citizen engagement. Otherwise, elections are little more than a periodic squabble among elites over whose turn it is to govern and/or plunder the nation. Factors such as the

The distorting impact upon domestic and foreign policy and its consequences cannot be overstated.

The spawning of unhealthy interdependencies between business, the media and politics undermine the delicate but important balance between power, wealth, how votes are delivered and access to the goods of society. A lack of transparency and appropriate boundaries in these relationships has led to excessively protected positions in the marketplace, generating extreme rewards that have induced sociopathic corporate behaviour and commercial recklessness.[68] As with corruption, the inducements may be relatively small in relation to the size of the stakes but the behaviour induced is the truly costly element, often many orders of magnitude greater, costing impoverished governments millions of dollars.

Citizens have become easy prey as governments have permitted legal conditions and corporate cultures to prevail where there is considered nothing wrong about pricing based on monopoly or cartel driven value rather than true market value.[69] When economic gain is more directly linked to political and/or military power, it creates even higher stakes winner-take-all competition that leads to greater abuses of office and, in more extreme cases, forms of State capture. This is especially problematic because correction from within is unlikely.[70]

These problems are evident in many countries including our own liberal democracies. A loss of confidence in the good faith and *bona fides* of political leadership is producing a profound and incendiary breakdown in public trust in many parts of the world. It is evidenced by widespread protests at what is perceived to be a betrayal of a social contract/consensus that has undermined significant elements of the population. This marginalized and disenchanted group includes an increasingly aware and networked generation that is just reaching working

---

war on corruption, war crimes trials and progressive empowerment and engagement of communities are progressively but slowly transforming the accountability of political leaders.

68   For the impact on gaps between rich and poor in society, see Richard Wilkinson and Kate Pickett, *The Spirit Level: Why More Equal Societies Almost Always Do Better* (Allen Lane, 2009).

See also www.equalitytrust.org.uk (accessed 16 December 2012) and the Oxfam Report on the effects of inequality: http://oxfamilibrary.openrepository.com/oxfam/bitstream/10546/266321/1/mb-cost-of-inequality-180113-en.pdf (accessed 21 January 2013).

69   Society benefits far more from environments where competition drives prices toward cost and innovation drives cost down. Mere wealth transfer or concentration is not wealth creation and to equate cost externalization with cost saving is also a dangerous illusion.

70   Legal authority and efficacy tend to shrink as political power increases. While politically driven abuses of authority by government officials may be challenged in the courts, they can lead to serious confrontations between legal and political institutions which can weaken the legal system. See Latimer House Guidelines: http://www.thecommonwealth.org/Templates/Internal.asp?NodeID=37744 (accessed 16 December 2012). See also Wade and Forsyth, Administrative Law, 2009. For an interesting rebuttal by Sir Stephen Sedley on the separation of powers, see London Review of Books, 34, no. 4. 23 (February 2012), 15–16.

age when economies are shrinking and failing to accommodate them. As trust and social cohesion break down, the use of coercion to maintain order (and the political status quo) serves to raise suspicions, inflame public opinion and further erode public confidence. This opens up space for opportunistic forces in the form of fierce ethnic competition, criminality and attempts to seize political power, territory and natural resources.[71]

When there is a resort to fear as a means of ordering society, there are negative economic implications as well as more direct human consequences. Information is the lifeblood of the economy and of society as a whole. Fear and excessive centralization of knowledge suppresses the normal and essential flow of information and opinion at all levels. Information gaps and blind-spots heighten commercial and political risk, and stifle initiative and investment. Instead of meritorious appointments, patronage and politicized board-level decision-making exert economically irrational influences upon important decisions that businesses must take to be successful. Rule of law deficiencies can therefore have far-reaching economic implications, while economic turmoil and exclusion unleash forces that undermine the rule of law and reinforce a downward spiral.

The Rule of Law in the Context of North–South Partnerships

Promoting the rule of law is heavily knowledge-and-relationship-based, requiring consistency and credibility on the part of those organizations seeking to promote it. This means that they must be prepared to observe the principles that they are espousing in the manner in which development programming is carried out. Unfortunately, development agencies have often fallen short in relation to continuity and coherence of programming and procedures, stakeholder participation, mutual cooperation and sharing of information, professionalism and courtesy, accountability and remediation of errors. Such deficiencies have undermined development partnerships and reduced their impact. Here too, a better understanding of rules and how they work may lead to useful practical tools.

The traditional institutional response to problems in the field has been for headquarters to introduce more detailed rules and controls, rather than to structure simpler rules and introduce practices that promote deeper knowledge, better decision-making skills and trust. Rules that set standards and promote accountability have an important role to play but a multiplication of cumbersome rules and procedures impedes motion in all directions. Rules are a counterproductive substitute for local knowledge, judgement and flexibility in environments that are already beset by many forms of transactional friction. As a further consequence of excess rule complexity, there has been a tendency in some development agencies

---

71 The conflict in the Niger Delta provides an example. See Kingsley Kuku, *Remaking the Niger Delta: Challenges and Opportunities* (Mandingo Publishing, 2012) and Judith Burdin Asuni, *Understanding the Armed Groups of the Niger Delta, Council on Foreign Relations* (CFR 2010).

to recruit staff for a knowledge of their internal procedures in preference to a technical knowledge of the subject, region or culture.

Rules can only produce simplified models of real life circumstances. Displacing discretion and accountability on the part of staff with the straightjacket of more fixed rules represents a failure to understand and engage with rules systems properly. Associated with every rule are penumbral meta-rules to guide their application, such as those governing interpretation, exceptions, mitigation and the legal consequences of non-compliance. Staff who are forced to navigate these meta-rules without adequate training or objective reference points tend to make it up as they go along, sometimes weakening or discrediting the rule regime or the organization itself. In cases where there is micromanagement by rules and resulting gridlock, a more productive approach would include simplified rules, training in the legal requirements governing the exercise of discretion, improved real-time feedback and monitoring and evaluation focused on how effective donor rules systems are when applied in practice.

It may be that, in fragile governance environments, more pressing and easily identified capacity limitations of host countries – combined with donor bargaining power – have obscured or diverted dialogue on donor deficiencies in the past. As lessons are learned and a new interconnected and politically astute generation of development partners emerges, such shortcomings will be increasingly apparent and challenged. This will hopefully provide the impetus needed to (a) reduce rule complexity and bureaucratic barriers, (b) avoid sudden, unilateral changes of direction and priorities that cause delays and frustrate expectations and planning, (c) develop a deeper understanding of local culture, priorities and circumstances to enhance and understand the impact of programming, (d) improve institutional memory and lessons learned, (e) enhance transparency and accountability for decisions taken, (f) provide corrective mechanisms when mistakes are made and (g) develop certification systems, training programmes and reference materials, networks and rational career structures that promote professionalism and knowledge base of the experts used by donors. Unfortunately, present procurement rules work against many of these objectives.

Some of these deficiencies are addressed by Paris Declaration principles but institutional inertia is strong and implementation remains a challenge.[72] The next frontier in the provision of foreign aid may be the development of rules of engagement, codes of conduct and systems that genuinely reflect the fundamental governance principles being espoused. Unless there is a greater appetite for constructive self-examination, effectiveness in promoting the rule of law will continue to be a receding target.

---

72   See the Paris Declaration on Aid Effectiveness (2005) and the Accra Agenda for Action (2008) http://www.oecd.org/dataoecd/11/41/34428351.pdf (accessed 16 December 2012). See also OECD, Assessing progress on implementing the Paris Declaration and the Accra Agenda for Action, http://www.oecd.org/document/21/0,3746, en_2649_3236398_43385196_1_1_1_1,00.html (accessed 16 December 2012).

Conclusion

Different meanings, technical and colloquial, can attach to widely used expressions such as the rule of law. Those that focus on enforcement, especially in relation to failing States, have their place. However, in the context of development and economic productivity, there are compelling reasons for understanding its wider meaning and the full implications of its fundamental precepts that reach well beyond formal qualities, technical enforcement and compliance. If the rule of law is to realize its potential as an organizing principle of productive and humane societies globally, the focus of development and economic management will have to shift to embrace crucial elements such as the political legitimacy of law formation, the refinement of substantive rights, economic justice, and a more extensive use of administrative justice to improve the manner in which decisions are made by public authorities. Justice sector strengthening efforts with an excessively narrow remit are missing important opportunities and leverage points to transform societies through more optimized decision-making outcomes, a more level playing field and more inclusive engagement by marginalized citizens. Such techniques have the potential to transform the political and economic landscape of emerging and developed countries alike. Moreover, there is no other discipline or field of endeavour positioned to create and fully employ these tools. Unfortunately, a stunted, lay understanding of the rule of law has obscured from view many tools in the rule of law toolkit and limited their deployment.

It is somewhat striking that if one looks at one's own society through the same lens employed to promote the rule of law and good governance in developing countries, one discovers that many of the structural problems identified in the field feature in our own societies. 'Development' is therefore a more interdependent, two-way pursuit than believed by those who assume that it is about replication. This transformation to interdependence greatly enhances the authenticity and effectiveness of the development relationship. If we were serious about applying to our own institutions the principles we espouse to others, we would not only become more credible, professional and effective, we would also be in a better position learn from our development partners valuable lessons about how to make our own societies more balanced, humane and productive. If we can envisage what the world would look if the rule of law truly prevailed, then we might take seriously the intriguing prospect that the rule of law already has within it the practical means of its own realization.

References

Asuni, Judith B. *Understanding the Armed Groups of the Niger Delta*. New York: Council on Foreign Relations, 2010.

Austin, John. *The Province of Jurisprudence Determined.* Edited by Wilfrid Rumble. Cambridge: Cambridge University Press, 1995. (First published, 1832.)

Austin, John. *Lectures on Jurisprudence, or The Philosophy of Positive Law.* Two vols, edited by Robert Campbell. 4th edn, rev. London: John Murray 1879. (Bristol: Thoemmes Press reprint, 2002).

Barnes, J. (ed.). 'Politics, Book 3'. *The Complete Works of Aristotle*, The Revised Oxford Translation. Princeton: Princeton University Press, 1984.

Barron, Gordon. 'The World Bank and Rule of Law Reforms'. *LSE Working Paper Series*, no. 05-70, 2005.

Bingham, Tom. *The Rule of Law.* London: Allen Lane, 2010.

Carothers, Thomas. 'Promoting the Rule of Law Abroad', *Rule of Law Series*, no. 34, Carnegie Endowment for International Peace, January 2003.

Chesterman, Simon. 'An International Rule of Law?' *American Journal of Comparative Law* 56 (2008).

Cissé, Hassane, Sam Muller, Chantal Thomas and Chenguang Wang (eds). *World Bank Legal Review vol. 4, Legal Innovation and Empowerment for Development.* Washington: World Bank, 2013. http://issuu.com/world.bank. publications/docs/9780821395066 (accessed 7 February 2013).

Davis, Kevin E. and Trebilcock, Michael J. 'The Relationship Between Law and Development: Optimists versus Skeptics'. *American Journal of Comparative Law* 56, no. 4 (2008).

Davidson, Cathy N. and Goldberg, David T. *The Future of Thinking: Learning Institutions in a Digital Age.* Cambridge, MA: MIT Press, 2010.

Diamond, Larry. *The Spirit of Democracy.* Times Books, 2008.

Dicey, Albert V. *An Introduction to the Study of the Law of the Constitution.* 5th edn. London: Macmillan, 1897. (First published in 1885.)

Dixon, Norman. *On The Psychology of Military Incompetence.* London: Jonathan Cape, 1976.

Farrall, Jeremy. 'Impossible Expectations? The UN Security Council's Promotion of the Rule of Law after Conflict'. *The Role of International Law in Rebuilding Societies after Conflict*, ed. Brett Bowden, Hilary Charlesworth and Jeremy Farrall. Cambridge: Cambridge University Press, 2009.

Forsyth, Christopher and Matenje, Steve D. 'Some Reflections on Administrative Justice in Malawi: Practical Steps'. *Acta Juridica: Comparing Administrative Justice across the Commonwealth.* Sabinet, 2006.

Franck, Thomas. M. *Democracy, Legitimacy and the Rule of Law: Linkages.* NYU Law School, Public Law and Legal Theory Working Paper, No. 2. 1999.

Franck, Thomas M. *Fairness in International Law and Institutions.* Oxford: Clarendon Press, 1995.

Fuller, Lon. *The Morality of Law.* New Haven: Yale University Press, 1969.

Gallant, Kenneth S. *The Principle of Legality in International and Comparative Criminal Law.* Cambridge: Cambridge University Press, 2009.

Gerangelos, Peter. 'The Separation of Powers and Legislative Interference with Judicial Functions in Pending Cases'. *Federal Law Review* 30, no.1 (2002).

Habermas, Jurgen. *Between Facts and Norms: Contributions to a Discourse Theory of Law and Democracy*. Translated by William Rehg. Cambridge: Polity Press, 1996.

Harsanyi, John. 'Cardinal Welfare, Individualistic Ethics, and Interpersonal Comparisons of Utility'. *The Journal of Political Economy* 63, no. 4 (August 1955): 309–21.

Humphreys, Stephen. *Theatre of the Rule of Law: Transnational Legal Intervention in Theory and Practice*. Cambridge: Cambridge University Press, 2011.

Kleinfeld, Rachel. *Advancing the Rule of Law Abroad: Next Generation Reform*. New York: Carnegie Endowment for International Peace, 2012.

Kuku, Kingsley. *Remaking the Niger Delta: Challenges and Opportunities*. London: Mandingo Publishing, 2012.

Meyer, Lukas. *Legitimacy, Justice and Public International Law*. Cambridge: Cambridge University Press, 2009.

Narayan, Deepa and others. *Can Anyone Hear Us? Voices from 47 Countries*. Poverty Group, PREM, World Bank, 1999.

Peerenboom, Randall. 'Varieties of the Rule of Law: An Introduction and Provision Conclusion'. Randall Peerenboom, *Asian Discourses on Rule of Law*. London: Routledge Curzon, 2004.

Rawls, John. *A Theory of Justice*. Cambridge, MA: Belknap Press, 1971.

Raz, Joseph. 'The Rule of Law and its Virtue'. *The Law Quarterly Review* 93 (1977): 195.

Reitz, John. 'Export of the Rule of Law'. *Transnational Law and Contemporary Problems* 13 (2003): 429.

Rosenfeld, Michel, 'The Rule of Law and the Legitimacy of Constitutional Democracy'. *Southern California Law Review* 74 (2001): 1307.

Russell-Einhorn, Malcom L. and Fenton, Howard N. *Using Administrative Law Tools and Concepts to Strengthen USAID Programming*. USAID, February, 2008.

Schneider, Mark. 'Placing Security and Rule of Law on the Development Agenda'. *Development Outreach* 11, no. 2. Washington: The World Bank Institute, October 2009.

Shrader-Frechette, Kristin S. *Risk and Rationality: Philosophical Foundations for Populist Reforms*. Berkeley: University of California Press, 1991.

Sedley, Sir Stephen. *London Review of Books*, 34, no. 4 (23 February 2012): 15–16.

Sullivan, T., Warren, E. and Westbrook, Jay N. *The Fragile Middle Class: Americans in Debt*. New Haven: Yale University Press, 2001.

Tamanaha, Brian Z. 'A Concise Guide to the Rule of Law'. *Florence Workshop on the Rule of Law*. Edited by Neil Walker and Gianluigi Palombella. St. John's Legal Studies Research Paper no. 07-0082. Oxford: Hart Publishing Company, 2007.

Tamanaha, Brian Z. *On the Rule of Law*. Cambridge: Cambridge University Press, 2004.

Trebilcock, Michael. 'The Rule of Law and Development: In Search of the Holy Grail'. *The World Bank Legal Review vol. 3, International Financial Institutions and Global Legal Governance*. Edited by Hassane Cissé, Daniel D. Bradlow and Benedict Kingsbury, 207–239. Washington: World Bank, 2012.

USAID, *Guide to Rule of Law Country Analysis*, Washington: USAID, 2010.

Wade, William and Forsyth, Christopher. *Administrative Law*. Oxford University Press, 2009.

Wilkinson, Richard and Pickett, Kate. *The Spirit Level: Why More Equal Societies Almost Always Do Better*. London: Allen Lane, 2009.

World Bank Institute and NDI. *Strengthening Parliamentary Accountability, Citizen Engagement and Access to Information: A Global Survey of Parliamentary Monitoring Organizations*. Washington: World Bank Institute and NDI, 2011.

United Nations Documents and Reports Cited

United Nations Rule of Law Indicators: Implementation Guide and Project Tools, 2011.

Secretary-General's Report 'Annual report on strengthening and coordinating United Nations Rule of Law Activities' (A/64/298) (2009).

Secretary-General's Report 'Strengthening and Coordinating United Nations Rule of Law Activities' (A/63/226) (2008).

Secretary-General's Report 'Uniting Our Strengths: Enhancing United Nations Support for the Rule of Law' (A/61/636) (2006).

2005 World Summit Outcome (A/RES/60/1) (2005).

Secretary-General's Report 'In Larger Freedom: Towards Development, Security and Human Rights for All' (A/59/2005) (2005).

Secretary-General's Report 'The Rule of Law and Transitional Justice in Conflict and Post-Conflict Societies' (S/2004/616) (2004).

United Nations Millennium Declaration (A/RES/55/2) (2000).

'The Brahimi Report': Comprehensive review of the whole question of peacekeeping operations in all their aspects (A/55/305) (2000).

U.N.G.A. Res. 217A (III), U.N. Doc. A/810 (III) (1948).

Chapter 5

What Is 'International Impartiality'?

Frédéric Mégret

Among ethical values that are seen as central to an international rule of law, the idea of 'impartiality' has long been a major feature of the idea of international organization. William Rappard for example described it as going at the heart of the 'original conception' of the League of Nations (Rappard 1927, p. 813). The emergence of international institutions – legal, political, even military – starting in the nineteenth century generated a huge need for even-handedness, objectivity and the perception thereof. This need that has if anything been amplified by the tendency of international organizations to delve ever deeper in the fabric of states, notably as part of strategies of international reconstruction (Bali 2005; Majstorović 2009). That impartiality is often put in question and is sometimes an object of scorn or scepticism does not change that the idea is inseparable from that of international progress. Impartiality is said to be a condition of the credibility and legitimacy of international organizations and tribunals.[1]

International organizations, international judges, international experts, international civil servants, and even peacekeepers are all supposed to be 'impartial'. The essence of the idea of impartiality is that a person can come to an issue with a fresh mind and that only certain 'relevant' factors will be taken into account in decision-making, whereas 'irrelevant' factors will be excluded. But what are these factors? Aside from the most flagrant forms of personal self-interest, how far should international decision-makers go in expunging from their mind from any preconceived opinion? What does impartiality mean in the international context, and might it mean something different from what it means domestically? Is international impartiality even desirable?

The study of international impartiality has the quality of a discreet leitmotiv in international studies. Each generation of student of international law and relations has expressed qualms and hope about the notions, and sought to draw its contours in a way that seemed neither too cynical nor too credulous. Hersch Lauterpacht made much of the notion of impartiality in his famous 'The Function of International Law in the International Community' (Lauterpacht 2000, p. chapter 10) in which he described impartiality of the international judge as 'the Cape Horn of international judicial settlement' and 'undoubtedly one of the most urgent problems of the political organization of the international community'

---

1   For a recent emphasis on the importance of impartiality internationally see Amann 2005.

(Lauterpacht 2000, p. 202). The book was published in 1933, at a time when optimists about international impartiality were engaged in a race with some of its diehard opponents. Not long after, that era would end with the total collapse of international impartiality illustrated perhaps most starkly by the allegiance sworn by Avenol, the then French Secretary-General, to Maréchal Pétain (Barros and Studies 1969). Thirty-five years later, Thomas Franck wrote one of the only books specifically on the issue. His was a different time, one marked by the Cold War and its repeated assaults on the very possibility of impartiality. In this context, as he put it, 'Can any man, or group of men, administer justice impartially in an ideologically and culturally divided world?' (Franck 1968). Franck went on to provide a remarkably optimistic defence of impartiality rooted in a remarkably interdisciplinary understanding of the law and governance.

Yet perhaps because it seems less under threat, the study of impartiality, down to an understanding of its definition, has not of late elicited substantial attention, at least beyond narrow contexts such as the institution of ad hoc judges before the ICJ or the theory of peacekeeping. This chapter seeks to reflect on how the post-Cold War world has contributed to reframe some of the central dilemmas of impartiality, based on changing political circumstances but also epistemological shifts in our understanding of its cognitive texture. After outlining the origin of 'international impartiality' as an idea integral to international governance and order, it will outline some of the limitations of the idea and suggest some ways to better problematize it in this day and age.

The Origins of 'International Impartiality'

Although the idea of international impartiality originated in late nineteenth-century ideas about international arbitration and third-party settlement of disputes, it witnessed one of its finest expressions in the rise of an international civil service in the interwar period, and has gone on to shape the role of international experts, dominant concepts of peacekeeping and down to the very idea of international organization.

International Adjudication

The first clear manifestations of the idea of 'international impartiality' lie in the early promise of international adjudication in the late nineteenth century. The group of international lawyers who met in Ghent to create the Institut de droit international formed, as Martti Koskenniemi has described, a loose transnational community bound by a common vision of progress and civilization through international law, which were prone to conceive of international law as above the fray of national politics (Koskenniemi 2002). Their ideas would go on to form the backbone of many international adjudication projects in the twentieth century, where the promise of third-party *bons offices* resided in the ability to locate a world class of arbitrators

(Sacriste and Vauchez 2005). The idea of impartiality fitted well with international lawyers' sense of a profession marked by heroic virtue, a sense of *avant garde* destiny, and an ethics of responsibility (Koskenniemi 2002, pp. 76-80), tropes that, as we shall see, may go some way in explaining its subsequent vulnerability.

One of the earliest projects of international adjudication, the Permanent Court of Arbitration, proposed to provide states with arbitrators to resolve their disputes. Yet it soon became evident to the project's authors that, as Secretary of State Elihu Root put it in his address to the National Arbitration and Peace Congress in 1907, 'the great obstacle to the universal adoption of arbitration is not the unwillingness of civilized nations to submit their disputes to the decision of an impartial tribunal; it is rather an apprehension that the tribunal selected will not be impartial' (Dalfen 1967, cited in p. 136). For Denis Myers, writing in 1916:

> arbitration too often acts diplomatically rather than judicially; they measure their responsibility and their duty by the traditions, the sentiments, and the sense of honorable obligation which has grown up in centuries of diplomatic intercourse, rather than by the traditions, the sentiments and the sense of honorable obligation which characterize the judicial department of civilized nations. Instead of the sense of responsibility for impartial judgment, which weighs upon the judicial officers of every civilized country, and which is enforced by the honor and self-respect of every upright judge, an international arbitration is often regarded as an occasion for diplomatic adjustment. (Root 1916, p. 141)

To remedy that desultory state of affairs, what was required was very clear, and consisted in the further judicialization of international arbitration, based on a high-minded notion of international impartiality:

> What we need for the further development of arbitration is the substitution of judicial action for diplomatic action, the substitution of judicial sense of responsibility for diplomatic sense of responsibility. We need for arbitrators not distinguished public men concerned in all the international questions of the day, but judges who will be interested only in the question appearing upon the record before them. (Anon 1907, p. 45)

The essence of the idea of impartiality as it then emerged was that certain individuals, by vocation or necessity, could be expected to rise above their national moorings and function in 'true international manner'. Pushed to its extreme, this logic called for the effective de-nationalization of international judges and technocrats. This was evident in a mild, social form in that international judges were expected to socialize with their peers and, in the best of scenarios, become imbued with a genuinely and positively international outlook. In other words, they would eventually become through practice what one could not quite presume them to be at the outset. It is worth noting that some of the more radical proposals historically even called for a juridical denationalization of international agents.[2] Such suggestions may seem as unreachable today as they were then, but they do capture a form of flight to internationalism, sometimes reasonable sometimes desperate, to create an world class of jurisconsults that would stand as humanity's best hope for international peace.

The International Civil Service

The idea of international impartiality was then recycled with even more ambition after the First World War in that great crucible of internationalism: Geneva. In that context, it no longer described a handful of elite jurisprudes but was destined to become one of the characteristics of the then nascent international civil service, an emerging class of international technocrats working for the League of Nations.

Drummond, the first Secretary-General of the League of Nations, held the view that the Secretariat should be 'as far as was practicable, an international civil service, in which men and women of various nationalities might unite in preparing and presenting to the members of the League an objective and common basis of discussion' (Ellis 2003, cited at pp. 172–3). Drummond's principles of international impartiality were subsequently codified and reaffirmed by three League committees and published as the Balfour,[3] Nobelmaire,[4] and Committee of Thirteen Reports.[5] The central idea was what became known early on as the 'exclusively international character of the international civil service'. For Balfour, the British delegate to the League, 'members of the secretariat once appointed are no longer the servants of the country of which they are citizens, but become for the time being the servants only of the League of Nations'.[6]

International civil servants were thus to be thoroughly 'denationalized' and distinguished from the various national representatives also present in Geneva.[7] According to article 1 of the Staff Regulations of the League: '[t]he officials of

---

2   For example Eberhard Deutsch, the Chairman of the 'Peace and Law Through United Nations' Committee of the American Bar Association, suggested in 1963 that 'The most important single way ... by which the independence and integrity of the International Court of Justice could be assured, is to provide for the "internationalization" of its judges, and so the revised Statute of the Court requires that each member of the Court upon his accession should renounce his allegiance to the country of which he was a national when elected and is to be deemed to have become, for his natural lifetime, a citizen of the United Nations' (Deutsch 1977, p. 30).

3   *League of Nations Official Journal*, First Year, 1920, pp. 136–9.

4   Records of the Second Assembly, 1921, Meetings of the Committees, I, 174–229.

5   Records of the Eleventh Ordinary Session of the Assembly, 1930, Minutes of the Fourth Committee, pp. 290–370.

6   *League of Nations Official Journal*, First Year, 1920, pp. 137–9.

7   Report of the Committee of Enquiry on the organization of the Secretariat, the International Labour Office and the Registry of the Permanent Court of International Justice (Committee of Thirteen), *League of Nations Official Journal*, Special Supplement

the Secretariat of the League of Nations are exclusive international officials and their duties are not national but international'.[8] This notion of the international legal character of the League and the UN would eventually be given international judicial recognition in the ICJ's advisory opinion on reparations. Although the Court cautioned that the allegiance owed by international civil servants to the UN was not of the same nature as a link of domestic allegiance (nationality), it did push the internationalist scruple as far as to say that ultimately international civil servants should be able to rely only on the UN for their protection and not on their own state, lest that protection come at too high a price.[9]

This ideal of the impartial international civil servant involved significant constraints for international civil servants. According to the Noblemaire report, '[b]y accepting appointment, they pledge themselves to discharge their functions and to regulate their conduct with the interests of the League alone in view'.[10] Being an international civil servant would thus be incompatible with holding national office, political or otherwise, being in any way an agent of the state, or even receiving any honour or distinction from a government (except for services rendered before appointment). International civil servants would be responsible only to the Secretary-General, and could not solicit let alone receive instructions from any government. The League Staff regulations of 1930 reemphasized these points formally. Included for the first time in 1932 was an oath of allegiance.[11] After the Second World War, this core was made part of the Charter at Dumbarton Oaks thus endowing it with an even more solemn statutory character.[12] The Secretary-General of the United Nations, notably in the person of Dag Hammarskjöld, would come to see himself as a guarantor of that impartiality.[13]

Experts, Peacekeepers, and International Organs

It may be said that the idea of international impartiality has since diffused itself amongst international circles to become more generally characteristic of what international organization is about. Three examples can help illustrate this proposition.

No. 88, Records of the Eleventh Ordinary Session of the Assembly, Minutes of the Fourth Committee, Geneva, 1930, p. 295.

8   *Staff Regulations*, 1933, art. 1, cited in S.M Schwebel, The International Character of the Secretariat of the United Nations, 30 Brit. *Y.B. Int'l L.* 71, 73 note 1 (1953).

9   Reparations for injuries suffered in the service of the United Nations, Advisory Opinion: ICJ Reports 1949, 174 at 183–4. See also Scwhebel, ibid., at 98–100.

10   *Organisation of the Secretariat and of the International Labour Office*, L.N. Doc. C. 424, M. 305, 1921, X. and A. 140 (a), 1921.

11   Article 1.9.

12   UN Charter, article 100 para.1.

13   Cordier and Foote 1975, pp. 197–8, 'I would rather see (the office of the Secretary-General) break on strict adherence to the principle of independence, impartiality, and objectivity than drift on the basis of compromise.'

First, the requirements of impartiality have been extended beyond international judges and international civil servants to any manner of expert or rapporteur working for international organizations. International experts have been used for fact-finding missions in various UN contexts, notably in the peace and the human rights fields, which are often very sensitive and prone to charges of partiality (Bassiouni 1994). The Regulations on Experts in Mission, for example, anticipate that they should 'discharge their functions and regulate their conduct with the interest of the Organization only in view'.[14] The Human Rights Commission/ Council terms for the mandates of special rapporteurs also insist heavily on impartiality, even though the latter are independent individuals with no organic link to the United Nations. If anything, experts endowed with a fact-finding mandate should be even more strictly impartial than judges since they cannot claim that they engage in complex and subjective exercises of judicial interpretation.

Second, the UN's emblematic tool to intervene in conflicts, peacekeeping, has itself been deeply shaped by notions of impartiality from the start (i.e., the Suez crisis and its aftermath). Peacekeeping consists in the deployment of troops, typically to monitor a peace agreement or an armistice and prevent the emergence or resumption of hostilities. Impartiality is presented as one of peacekeeping's three core principles alongside consent of the parties and non-use of force (Yamashita 2008). It has been described as 'the oxygen of peacekeeping: the only way peace keepers can work is by being trusted by both sides ... The moment they lose this trust, the moment they are seen by one side as the "enemy", they become part of the problem they were sent to solve' (Tharoor 1995, p. 417). Many of the ways in which impartiality and the perception of impartiality are sustained in peace operations are reminiscent of other already explored areas.

Third and perhaps more controversially, it has increasingly been said that in addition to being a quality of individuals, impartiality should be seen as a quality of international bodies themselves. For example Thomas Franck stressed the 'role of impartiality not only in adjudication but also in other forms of decision-making'. He emphasized the need for UN resolutions, in order to be persuasive, 'to be based on principles that are generally and reciprocally applicable', and insisted that 'when a world body dependent on moral prestige acts the political opportunist, whilst it is expected to be the principled sage, it is affronting both justice and history' (Franck 1968, pp. 318–19). This is especially true of international bodies with a normative mandate. After decades of being decried for its partiality, the UN Human Rights Commission was reinvented as the Human Rights Council, to be 'guided by the principles of universality, impartiality, objectivity, and non selectivity, constructive international dialogue and cooperation, with a view to enhancing the promotion and protection of all human rights'.[15] Even with as blatantly political a body as the Security Council, members are careful to always formulate their vote as forwarding the general international interest, and attempts

---

14   GA/RES/56/280, of 27 March 2002.
15   GA/RES/60/250, 23 December 2005.

to use the process to blatantly favour the national interest have been universally decried (El Zeidy 2002).

The Limits of International Impartiality

Many ideas about international impartiality have been transposed from the domestic sphere. Of course, even there the very notion of impartiality is not without its critics. Legal realists have long doubted the cardinal role of a virtue such as impartiality in a context where 'judges fail to be impartial not because they are vicious but because in the process of decision their sense of values is inevitably involved' (Garlan 1941). There is also an old strand of particularly sociological and psychological oriented literature that has emphasized the importance of certain biases in judicial or administrative law-making. This is not to mention a philosophical scepticism about what impartiality as a moral quality might entail (Friedman 1989). Yet if one sees impartiality as a goal to strive for rather than something that can ever be fully achieved, devices exist to protect the rule of law and the public interest from at least the most obvious perversions: competitive recruitment, rule that one cannot be judge in one's own cause, oaths of impartiality, etc.

Such protections are relatively easily transposable in the international context. Judges and international civil servants can be selected carefully so that only the most suited to the task of impartiality are retained (competitive recruitment is the rule); they can be required to take an oath;[16] they can be prevented from sitting in cases in which they have already been involved in some personal or professional capacity or have an interest; peacekeeping missions will almost by definition not include nationals of the country involved or, for that matter, individuals with too blatant ethnic, religious, cultural or political ties to the populations they must separate; international civil servants should neither receive nor solicit instructions from their governments. The basic intuition here is that a certain quality of externality and separation from the domestic is one of the hallmarks of impartiality.

Yet there is also evidently something irreducible about the international sphere, which makes the lock, stock and barrel import of tools conceived domestically problematic. The risk is less that judges, experts, civil servants or peacekeepers will have a specific and personal interest in a case than more subtle national and ideological biases. If anything, concerns about impartiality are magnified, not lessened by transposition to the international arena. Domestic decision-makers can rely on long traditions, integrated polities, programmatic horizons, separation of powers and a high degree of legitimacy. Conversely, international decision-makers

---

16   Although there are to this author's knowledge no studies of the legal value of such oaths these are probably better viewed as purely unilateral commitments rather than something that would truly bind oath takers and expose them to serious consequences if at fault. They are part of the mystique and decorum of impartiality rather than a strict guarantee of it.

must confront an intensely political arena made of a juxtaposition of sovereigns, where much power remains within states, the social milieu is thin, the project questionable and the socialization superficial. The critique of the indeterminacy of international law, in particular, and of the dominance of 'experts' on matters of global governance sheds an ambiguous light on the ability of the international rule of law to simply rely on an abstraction such as 'impartiality'.

Moreover, the changing nature of international organization also inevitably has an impact on the nature and very possibility of impartiality. In times when international organization was restricted to managing technical standards and minimum cooperation between nations, impartiality might be more readily conceivable as an ideal. But as international organization has increased in ambition, encompassing a range of extremely sensitive issues for states in a context of international polarization, impartiality has seemed less tenable, or at least less evident as a standard assumption of the dominant model. This is particularly true in a context where human rights, international humanitarian and international criminal law have dramatized the moral stakes of international interaction. The international milieu thus raises highly unusual dilemmas for the very notion of impartiality, leading it to experience a triple crisis: of plausibility, desirability and even morality.

The Implausibility of Impartiality

Essential to the idea of impartiality is the ability of individuals to hoist themselves above their national identity to reach a sort of noumenon of internationalism. Lauterpacht spoke of the impossibility of achieving impartiality through 'formal safeguards', where the problem was, instead, the 'creation in the minds of judges of a sense of international solidarity resulting in a clear individual consciousness of citizenship of the civitas maxima' (Lauterpacht 2000, pp. 232–3) Needless to say, there has always been a certain dose of scepticism about such a possibility. Minéitcirô Adatci, the Japanese member of the 1920 Advisory Committee of Jurists for the Establishment of a Permanent Court of Justice, pointed out that it would 'not be easy to find persons prepared to denationalise themselves or to "deify" themselves, in other words, to separate themselves completely from their country' (Justice 1920, pp. 187–8). In the UN era, it is the Soviets who were at the forefront of a new and more radical challenge to impartiality. Khrushchev articulated the classical Soviet view when he insisted that 'while there are neutral countries, there are no neutral men', and that in 'this deeply divided world an impartial official is a fiction' (Lippmann 1961). Indeed, even after the Cold War and in a world released of bloc discipline, one may wonder whether some issues are not so divisive that impartiality becomes, for all purposes, largely illusory.[17]

---

17 The situation of Israel and Palestine, forever a profound fracture line, comes to mind. It is almost as if every statement made by international experts or resolution adopted by an international body on the issue is immediately interpreted as the expression of siding

Apart from the issue of the psychological makeup of international officials and the plausibility of their attempts at internationalization, there is also the more deeply perplexing question of what should take 'national partiality's' place. The harder it is to put one's finger on what 'international impartiality' is (aside from an absence of 'national partiality'), the more dubious claims made in its name will be. Is impartiality even philosophically plausible? Impartiality certainly implies that there is some universal guiding thread beyond particular interests, something that one can reasonably expect to be impartial about, which might be either international law (in the cases of judges), or the international public interest (international civil servants), or some value such as peace (international peacekeepers).

Earlier commentators, particularly in the interwar period, may have been more optimistic about the ability for such values to acts as referents. For Lauterpacht, the main danger was that states would 'distrust the impartiality of international judges in the unavoidable exercise of their creative function of filling the gaps in an undeveloped legal system' (Lauterpacht 2000, p. 202). If all that was at stake was applying international law, implicitly, then partiality would be less of a problem since international law would exercise its discipline on adjudicators. Today, however, one may wonder if a renewed contemporary appreciation of the inherent indeterminacy of international law, has not warned us that the exercise of international law-making is not a fundamentally creative exercise – and thus one highly vulnerable to biases – even when it comes to well-trodden areas of the law beyond gap-filling.[18] Impartiality, perhaps even more now than at the height of the Cold War when Franck wrote his book and when all that seemed to threaten it was the vulgarity and bad faith of Khrushchev, is thus suspicious because it is seen as a rudderless vessel, adrift in an ocean of passions, politics and discretion.

In an attempt to shake off the suspicion of indeterminacy and thus reinstate the value of impartiality, one temptation is to suggest that impartiality is not defined simply by the absence of national biases, but by something more positive. For Thomas Franck, 'the only way learned national biases can be vitiated is by balancing them through substituting an acquired *international* "bias"' (Franck 1968, p. 261). The idea of international law or the international public interest as what one ought to be partial to has the advantage of giving impartiality more spine as against national biases. But it also presumes that we know what that international public interest is when, precisely, it was meant to be the function of international lawyers, experts and judges, *on the basis of their impartiality*, to formulate it. There is a

---

more with 'one side' over the other. Hence both the Goldstone report and its follow-up by Christian Tomuschat have been assailed as partial both on the basis of their content and previous declarations by some of their authors. Of course, there is a difference between a perception of partiality and its reality, yet this does underscore the fact that impartiality is a certain *belief*, which to be sustained requires conditions where animosity and bad faith have not reached such a degree that no one is ever trusted to be above the fray.

18   Koskenniemi 2005, p. 553, 'How to fulfil the ideal of integrity in the absence of an objective law?'

fundamental circularity to putting the 'cart of international public interest' before the 'wheels of impartiality'. An alternative is to invoke international community of professionals who have become so internationalized as to be impartial to national interests. But the appeal to an international community of professionals assumes a little too readily that internationalist sentiment is homogeneous. The history of the international civil service and of international adjudication suggest that whilst the progresses of international mindedness is very real in all kinds of cultural and social aspects, it often also barely hides deep rifts (Mégret 2013).

It is also worth pointing out that there may be cases where the exact converse is true and where, far from being vague, international priorities will have been defined in such a robust and unmistakable way as to make the conceit of 'impartial internationality' hard to sustain. Partiality for the international interest may well involve one in muscular projects of international order enforcement in the service of the UN 'a political organization with overtly political goals – the maintenance of international peace and security, for one – that suggest a need to take "partial" positions' (Boulden 2005, p. 148). For example, there have been many UN peace operations in the last decades that cannot be convincingly described as conceptually and operationally impartial. At the very least, the presence of any international peace operation will affect the position of parties on the ground differently, and lead to the perception that, willy nilly, a differential outcome was envisaged, especially when use of force is envisaged.[19] In some cases, that differential impact will have been very much in the minds of the operation's creators, even though this may only appear by reading a mandate between the lines, or studying the details of their operational practices (Hughes 2002). Not even the Secretary-General is above the suspicion of implementing certain mandates according to a partial reading of them.[20]

Moreover, impartiality about certain interests only seems to be achievable by being partial against certain others, so that impartiality is occasionally likely to be perceived as a form of collusion against the excluded middle. This inevitably raises questions about whose impartiality? Consider, for example, the following passage from the memoirs of William Rappard:

> We may note ... that the League succeeded in appearing as a true representative
> of the world community in all those cases in which the factor of nationality was

---

19   As Secretary General Dag Hammarskjöld put it, 'it is common experience that nothing, in the heat of emotion, is regarded as more partial by one who takes himself the position of a party than strict impartiality' (Cordier and Foote 1975, p. 197).

20   This was the Soviet criticism of Dag Hammarskjöld's performance in the Congo (Cordier and Foote 1975, p. 175): 'the Secretary-General ... has failed to display the minimum of impartiality require do f him in the situation which has arisen. In the over-all workings of the United Nations organism, its chief has proved to be the very component which is functioning most unashamedly on the side of the colonialists, thus compromising the United Nations in the eyes of the world'.

eliminated, or at least repressed, and in which true international impartiality was thus secured. The outstanding example is that of the supervision of the mandated territories. As the Mandates Commission was composed not of national representatives but of individuals who were responsible solely to their own conscience for the steps they recommended, their advice to the Council was, from the start, characterized by a spirit of impartiality which was recognized even in Germany. (Rappard 1931, p. 78)

Is it not ironic that this apex of interwar 'impartiality' was only attained as part of a neo-colonial scheme, in an organization dominated by a few great European powers,[21] and in reference to its backers rather than its beneficiaries? To describe the mandate system as impartial may be half-true in the way that Rappard describes it, but the system itself was steeped in a hugely partial view of the world in which a few nations presided over the destinies of the many. It is as if impartiality between the great powers could only be achieved at the cost of a broader and unquestioned partiality to European designs and the inability to question their policies ... A similar case could be made that the 'impartial' UN peace operation in the Congo in the 1960s was certainly a model of cooperation among the 30 states that contributed troops towards an international cause but, as seen through the opposition to the independence and Katanga, one very partial to US interests in particular (Gibbs 2000).

The Undesirability of Impartiality

Aside from its sheer implausibility, there have recurrently been questions about whether impartiality is that desirable. This is of course different from states trying to influence the impartiality of international decision-makers which they see as going against their national interest, as most big powers have over the twentieth century. What is at stake here is that even a certain form of *internationalist* point of view has occasionally been led to re-evaluate the radical dichotomy between the international and the domestic traditionally posited by the field.

Although international organizations by and large demand of their personnel that it be impartial, that may not always be rigidly true on pragmatic grounds, especially of the higher echelons of international administration such as Secretary Generals and Heads of programmes and agencies for which the temptation of enlisting the experience and influence of senior politicians with networks of connections has been strong. A purely internationalist staff, if such a thing were to exist, might remain relatively cut off from key domestic circles of power that any international organization must aspire to have access to if it is to remain relevant. Even the Noblemaire report, so often quoted for its classical approach to the idea of

---

21   The presence of non-European states (Latin American, Asian, African) was hardly felt at the League, where most had barely one member represented in the up to 600-strong staff. Wilson 1934, p. 149.

an international civil service, emphasized that the highest posts of the Secretariat should be 'filled by persons of any country whatsoever, who are of recognized importance and widespread influence among their own people and whose view and sentiments are representative of their national opinion' (Lemoine 1995, p. 83) The existence of Under-Secretaries-General has sometimes been defended not only as a compromise, but also as something that might more generally increase the influence of the Secretariat (Evans 1944, pp. 28–31).

It has been said, moreover, that 'top-level officials have often been seen as necessary channels of communication with their nation or region ... because attuned to the moods and institutions of their constituency, they are expected, in the service of the Organization, both to anticipate or explain the attitudes of that constituency and to expound to it the position of the organization in a more persuasive or at least more acceptable manner than a complete outsider, however skilful and well disposed' (Lemoine 1995, p. v). A good anecdotal illustration is given in Marrack Goulding's memoir. Goulding, who was the top British official at the UN in the 1980s, describes his position in the following terms:

> A senior UN official nominated by his or her government was ... assumed to be in the Secretariat to do that government's bidding ... I wanted to be an impartial international official ... and had already decided that I would decline invitations to stay at British embassies when on my travels ... What I did not foresee ... was that distancing myself from Whitehall could reduce my usefulness to the secretary-general himself ... It reduced my value to my boss ... Boutros Ghali, in particular, expected his British USG [under secretary-general] to give him private insights into Her Majesty's government's thinking and their likely reaction to initiatives which he might take. My insistence on my independence as an international civil servant this made me something of a misfit on the 38th floor. (Goulding 2003)

Thus international civil servants, especially at the top echelons, can be both sounding boards and influence demultipliers ('friends at court'). Again, there would not be much point in a flight to cosmopolitan internationality that translated in international organizations cutting themselves off from the very sources of power that sustain them.

When it comes to the international judiciary, a similar type of reasoning emerges. Having only purely impartial international judges (officially, very much the ideal) may be questioned as severing a necessary link with the states or societies involved. The long controversial practice of nominating ad hoc judges at the ICJ from the countries appearing before the Court in a dispute, for example, is often seen as a flagrant violation of the *nemo judex in causa sua* principle, and an unfortunate concession to states' interests. But it can also be seen as a subtle recognition that bench dynamics can benefit from the presence of individuals who are endowed with an outlook that is predetermined by a certain national rootedness. There has certainly never been much doubt about the partiality of such ad hoc judges, and the record bears out that they have almost always sided with their state. As a 1927 committee on the reform of the rules of the PCIJ put it, 'Of all influences to which men are subject, none is more powerful, more pervasive, or more subtle, than the tie of allegiance that binds them to the land of their homes and kindred and to the great sources of the honours and preferments for which they are so ready to spend their fortunes and to risk their lives. This fact, known to all the world, the [Court's] Statute frankly recognises and deals with.'[22]

Yet by the same token, Lord Phillimore, one of the authors of an influent draft for the Statute of Permanent Court of International Justice had stipulated that 'it would be preferable to give a national representative to both parties, not only to protect their interests, but to enable the Court to understand certain questions which require highly specialised knowledge and relate to the differences between the various legal system'.[23] Elihu Root similarly insisted that 'Nations should be able to go before the Court with the certainty that their case will be fully understood. For this purpose there must be … a judge of their nationality on the Court … it must be possible to tell the masses that there will be at least one person upon the Court who is able to understand them'.[24] Closer to us, Judge Elihu Lauterpacht, the son of Hersch Lauterpacht who had in his time vehemently opposed resort to ad hoc judges, found a similar, if more subtle, justification to the practice. Ad hoc judges, above and beyond their oath of impartiality, have 'a special obligation to endeavour to ensure that, so far as is reasonable, every relevant argument in favour of the party that has appointed him has been fully appreciated in the course of collegial consideration'.[25]

Similar issues have arisen in the history of international criminal justice. Hans Kelsen deplored the absence of judges from the defeated powers at Nuremberg as impugning the precedential value of the verdict (Kelsen 1947, p. 171). The creation of hybrid tribunals in Sierra Leone, Cambodia or Lebanon suggests the importance of having national judges sit alongside international ones. On such occasions, the argument seems to be that domestic judges will, in addition to providing a layer of legitimacy, be able to provide a much needed understanding of domestic realities.

Finally, although the impartiality of international experts is routinely presented as desirable, one may certainly wonder whether their strict impartiality is the

---

22   Fourth Annual Report of Permanent Court of International Justice, Series E, No.4, pp.75–6.

23   Procès-Verbaux of the Proceedings of the Advisory Committee of Jurists, 24th Meeting, 14 July 1920, pp. 528–9.

24   Ibid., pp. 532 and 538.

25   Application of the Convention on the Prevention and Punishment of the Crime of Genocide, ICJ Rep. 1993, pp.408–9. See also Scwhebel, 894: 'on occasion the national judge may have a uniquely useful ability to appraise facts the significance of which escape other members of the Court. The national judge may, because of his national knowledge and experience, appreciate what his colleagues do not.'

quality that states have most sought out. Although one would expect a pure fact-finder to be impartial, the needs of international organizations extend far beyond fact-finding to reflection and policy development where what constitutes impartiality aside from a minimal openness to dialogue is not evident. When the Human Rights Commission now Council designate special rapporteurs, whether country or theme specific, they have often shown a lack of interest for traditional impartiality, often choosing individuals known for their strong views on the subject. The ungenerous reading of this is that it is simply a perversion of the practice of resorting to international experts, essentially trying to get the rhetorical benefits of impartiality, whilst packaging a more fundamentally political message (Franck and Farley 1980). But a more generous reading might suggest that when it comes to fundamental issues of political assessment, states are getting what they are paying for when they nominate experts with a more explicit political background, and that this is a defensible use of resources for a domain that feeds on a diversity of views. Perfect impartiality is very hard to achieve and might lead to something bland that is of little use to political bodies.

The Immorality of Impartiality

In ordinary circumstances impartiality is very defensible as a moral category. Tom Franck has written on the 'morality of detachment' as opposed to 'commitment', where impartiality is contrasted with narrow interest maximization. Impartiality to the extent it describes a state prior to the decision rather than the flux of decision-making. Yet detachment also has its critics. To begin with, one may wonder whether an attitude of 'detachment' can by itself tie together the many loose threads that make adjudication or complex decision-making possible. Detachment suggests apathy, distance, even aloofness. It may be a recipe for juridical monstrosities, and has been at times in the twentieth century. One wonders whether to bring the law to life one does not need something more than impartiality, something more in the nature of a lived experience, an aesthetics and a sensitivity. A certain form of bland impartiality, therefore, may stand in tension with the sort of enlightened moral judgment that makes great justice and civil service.

In fact, impartiality has come under challenge as not only amoral, but also potentially dangerously immoral. Whilst the Soviet critique of impartiality emphasized the ideological polarization of the world, in times of seeming ideological homogenization that critique may lose some of its more immediate trenchancy. The post-Cold War world has discovered a new form of polarization, one rich with much deeper moral connotations, which opposes authors of 'international crimes' to their victims. The critique here is not so much that impartiality is made implausible by that polarity: there has in fact been a considerable effort to maintain impartiality in the face of atrocities. Rather, it is that to persist in the ways of impartiality when faced with international crimes creates a fundamental problem. That critique takes its root in a scathing assessment of the culture of impartiality during the Second World War, as incarnated notably by the International Committee of the Red Cross, accused of having failed to denounce the crimes of the Holocaust because of too rigid a doctrine of neutrality (Slim 2001).

More recently it is the UN's peacekeeping operations that have been assailed for being impartial where impartiality ended up objectively favouring criminals. As one author put it 'In the case of unintended human disasters, international impartiality is appropriate even essential. In the case of genocide ... international impartiality toward both the victims and the perpetrators is profoundly wrong' (Campbell 2001, p. 33). In Bosnia, it has been argued that 'the West's attempt at limited but impartial involvement abetted slow-motion savagery' (Betts 1994). Impartiality has been suspected of standing for a form of abandonment of responsibility, as a 'shield to cover inaction or to avoid greater action' (Boulden 2005, p. 158), in cases where the Security Council does not want to be involved in the dirty process of allocating blame for hostilities. The Secretary-General himself was forced to take a significant step back from what he described as an 'institutional ideology of impartiality even when confronted with genocide', following the Srebrenica massacre.[26] The UN report drawing the lessons of the Rwandan genocide similarly pointed out that General Romeo Dallaire had been issued instructions, following the downing of the presidential plane and in the midst of genocide, that '(he) should make every effort not to compromise (his) impartiality' and noted, in its final observations, that 'there can be no neutrality in the face of genocide, no impartiality in the face of a campaign to exterminate part of a population'.[27]

A much greater readiness to take sides, at least rhetorically, and thus engage in non-neutral behaviour is evident in some of the more recent international interventions. Impartiality, at least when it is understood as prioritizing right procedure over the good, takes second stand and is increasingly subsumed within an overarching attention to ethical principles that gives it its proper weight, and balances it against the risk, for example, of significant human rights violations (Lepard 2003, pp. 213–14). That the organization has moved on at least when it comes to peacekeeping is evident in the Brahimi report:

> impartiality is not the same as neutrality or equal treatment of all parties in all cases for all time, which can amount to a policy of appeasement. In some cases, local parties consist not of moral equals but of obvious aggressors and victims, and peacekeepers may not only be operationally justified in using force but morally compelled to do so.[28]

---

26 Report of the Secretary-General pursuant to General Assembly resolution 53/35, The fall of Srebrenica A/54/549, 15 November 1999.

27 Report of the Independent Inquiry into the Actions of the United Nations during the 1994 Genocide in Rwanda, 15 December 1999.

28 Report of the Panel on United Nations Peace Operations, A/55/305–S/2000/80, 2000, para. 50.

In this context and inversely, it should come as no surprise that 'impartiality' has at times become a code name for states to protect their sovereignty and oppose any form of strong moral judgment particularly about their human rights performance. This is evident in debates on the special procedures at the Human Rights Commission/ Council, where states have been known to argue strongly for the 'impartiality' of special rapporteurs.[29] It also manifests itself in the very ambiguous attempt to thrust on rapporteurs an ethics of impartiality that could effectively prevent them from taking a stand on country-specific human rights violations (Sunga 2007, p. 288; Subedi 2011, p. 219). Of course, special rapporteurs and the United Nations acknowledge the importance of impartiality, but disagree that impartiality should mean a stance of automatic deference to the state. Such a stance would defeat the purpose of international rights monitoring and amount to a moral abdication. As Paulo Sergio Pinheiro put it:

> There is an inescapable tension between impartial fact-finding and clear and sound public assessments. Objective fact-finding does not mean neutrality; special rapporteurs will sometimes be required to denounce abuses for which there is evidence. We may conclude that the principle of impartiality contradicts a personal assessment of the problem during a mission. If special rapporteurs witness a consistent pattern of allegations of gross human rights violations, summary executions, torture, of acts of genocide, we must denounce them and not be limited to discreet documenting. (Pinheiro 2003, p. 11)

The reproach against impartiality when faced with crimes or gross human rights violations is thus essentially that it abides by an ethics appropriate for a world of states and in which international organization can only survive if it is seen to be above the fray. Instead, what is necessary is increasingly an ethics for an integrated world, one in which the ethics of impartiality are tempered on occasion by the need to stand up against 'evil'.

---

29   For a typical manifestation of state discontent with Special Rapporteurs' lack of impartiality, see Report on the situation of human rights in Nigeria prepared by Mr. Bacre Waly Ndiaye, Special Rapporteur on extrajudicial, summary or arbitrary executions, and Mr. Param Cumaraswamy, Special Rapporteur on the independence of judges and lawyers, E/CN.4/1997/62, 4 February 1997. According to the Government of Nigeria, 'the Thematic Rapporteurs had at different international meetings conducted themselves in a manner that could undermine the spirit of the dialogue. The statements and utterances credited to the two Thematic Rapporteurs were not only unfortunate, they were also capable of undermining the impartiality and integrity of these independent and neutral experts appointed by sovereign independent states in the Commission of Human Rights in which Nigeria is an active member. We view the statements and utterances of the two Rapporteurs as capable of compromising their independence and neutrality'. In essence the rapporteurs had accused Nigeria of grave human rights violations.

Problematizing Impartiality

Whilst still presented as necessary, there is little doubt that impartiality is not what it used to be and that in particular the stereotypical image of the splendidly detached, exclusively international-minded individual is one that is increasingly hard to sustain in a complex and polarized world. If impartiality is to be saved, it needs to be better problematized.

National Bias v. Personal Worldview

As has been seen, one of the key fears in terms of impartiality historically, is that judges or civil servants will be biased in favour of their own country. This has of course occasionally turned out to be a well-founded fear. During the interwar period, Italian and German League of Nations civil servants notoriously emphasized their allegiance to their states, with disastrous consequences for the League.[30] It is true that statistically, judges have tended to vote in favour of their states on the occasions that their states have appeared before them. But national bias is less common than one might think if only because by chance or by design international judges or experts are unlikely to be involved directly in cases or affairs to which they have a direct national connection.

There is in fact significant evidence of national judges (judges already sitting on the bench when a case is brought to the Court) and even ad hoc judges (those specifically designated when a state does not have a national sitting on the court) voting 'against' their state of nationality, and the correlation between national origin and voting patterns is a very hard one to establish conclusively (Smith 2004; Hensley 1978, 1968). If anything, it is judges who are steeped in a legal culture that denies the value of impartiality and affirms the idea that judges are always involved in some form of politics who, unsurprisingly, tend to always vote for their state (Hensley 1978). International institutions/jurisdiction have, in fact, become quite good at dealing with the more blatant form of prejudice, the sort which their creation was so resolutely supposed to avoid. Yet it is not hard to see how bias might manifest itself beyond favouring the interest of a state in particular. 'National bias', as one commentator put it, 'is a much broader concept than partiality (and) is composed of the consideration of culturally inculcated values.'[31] Such 'national outlook' is inescapable. In such cases, as Thomas Franck put it, it may well be that

---

30   The Marquis Paulucci di Calboli Barone was Mussolini's chef de cabinet until he became the League's Under Secretary-General, and he made no secret of his passionate fascist beliefs. Some Italian League civil servants donated a gold bar to the Italian war effort in a show of defiance vis-à-vis their own organization after its condemnation of Italy's campaign in Abyssinia.

31   Hensley 1968.

'the devices of psychological bias are far too subtle to be fully counteracted even by an extensive network of categories and rules of recusation'.[32]

Beyond the subtler forms of national bias, moreover, lies an entire terrain of little explored *personal* biases that form what might be described as a world-outlook. International law has traditionally discounted these forms of non-national bias. But as international civil servants, judges and experts increasingly shift their gaze away from purely interstate matters to broadly societal ones, there is every reason to think that they have played an increasingly important role. For example, no one accused the judges of the Rwanda and Yugoslavia International Criminal Tribunal of being insufficiently sensitive to sexual violence as a result of coming from such or such country. Rather certain blind spots of international administration and justice will be increasingly blamed on the domination of certain groups and under-representation of others. Among the most obvious biases in this category are gender biases, but ethnic, cultural, religious, able-bodied or ageist biases may all have an impact on international decision-making. Past declarations or writings of judges, in this context, have at times come back to haunt them, although by no means all challenges to their impartiality have been successful (Mégret 2011).

This notion of the formulation of the international public interest and justice being easily influenced by general as opposed to national biases was at the heart of the Marxist critique of international decision-making, which saw in the idea of impartiality a typical manifestation of the chimera of bourgeois ethics. If international law was and should be nothing but an 'instrument of politics' (Soloveitchik 1952) (something that the Soviets, in their pursuit of socialism recognized, but which they argued Western nations sought to obfuscate for their gain), then what room could there be for impartiality? Beyond the association between certain political regimes and certain states (Western states = bourgeois capitalists), the critique targeted class as a factor shaping decision-making. Soviets jurisprudes may have had a hard time pinpointing what in ICJ decisions was specifically a manifestation of class consciousness,[33] but it was certainly plausible that the Court's bench had not exactly been working class in extraction,[34] and that some decisions betrayed at least an aloofness to the plight of third world peoples. Judge Krylov insisted, for example, that in the South West Africa decision the 'International Court showed clear partiality and indulgence towards the South African imperialists and colonizers' (Zile 1964, p. 383). Of

---

32   Franck 1968, p. 260.

33   One possibility is that the ICJ did not decide that many cases with evident economic implications. It is harder to see class-consciousness affect a decision on border or maritime delimitation.

34   There is, to my knowledge, no serious study of the sociological composition of the ICJ or even of the UN's staff. It is therefore very difficult to speculate, although it stands to reason that at the very least senior international judges have tended to belong to (often established) elites and, anecdotally, there is much evidence, particularly among European judges, of upper-class extraction.

course, Soviet international lawyers could hardly exempt themselves – nor would have – from the heavy taint of partiality themselves: all Soviet judges at the ICJ were Communist Party members *de rigueur* (Zile 1964, pp. 387–8).

Gender bias is a form of bias that has increasingly come to the fore in the contemporary era, for example in the form of requirements of parity or quotas. Whilst there was a time when it was hardly ever remarked that the ICJ and the PCIJ benches had forever consisted of men, or that women formed only a very small fraction of the League of Nations and UN staff, such glaring lack of balance is now hard to miss. Partiality to one's gender may manifest itself individually, but more realistically in aggregate, as a result of a sort of gender group-think. In practice of course it is male prejudice, reinforced by a masculine domination of international courts and organizations that has been problematic. Its manifestations are subtle, especially given the range of issues that do not immediately seem to rely on gender. It includes the failure by international criminal tribunals to take certain forms of violence done to women in a way commensurate with their gravity or, more potently, a vision of international law and order shaped by gender and emphasizing 'public' harms at the expense of violence committed in the 'private' sphere. The fact that women in international organizations are traditionally assigned to social issues, whilst men dominate the security sector reinforces the sense of the UN as an organization polarized by gender.

Although gender representation claims internationally are oftentimes based on notions of justice and equal access, and on an appeal to the legitimacy needs of international organizations (Grossman 2011), they also operate against the background of feminist theories that have suggested that at the very least judgment may be influenced by gender (Wilson 1990; Schafran 1989; Peresie 2005). Recently, the claim that there is a specific link between the gender composition of an international bench and its normative production has been made more insistently, particularly in the case of international criminal tribunals (Grossman 2011). Although it is perhaps too much to say that a mono-gender bench is necessarily biased, a mixed bench, particularly but not only in cases involving a gender element is very likely to better capture some of the underlying complexity of cases and to cancel at least the more obvious forms of gender bias.[35] Interestingly, the case for the presence of women on the bench of international courts is sometimes made by invoking the fact that all international benches are already to an extent engineered to reach a certain composition, if only by ensuring an equitable geographic representation. The issue then becomes why nationality or geographic origin are considered worth representing but not something like gender (Kenney 2002).

---

35 For this sort of minimalist defence of having women on the bench of the ICC see Peterson 2008, pp. 221–2, 'this female presence on the ICC's staff will not only make some female victims more comfortable discussing their attack, it will also ensure the presence of a much-needed female perspective to help male judges understand the victim's viewpoints and reactions to their attacks'.

Negative v. Positive Impartiality

Much of the confusion that surrounds impartiality is linked to definitional issues, and a certain tendency to portray impartiality as an attitude of distance or even aloofness. This calls for a measure of clarification about what impartiality is not necessarily, and what it could be, especially if one understands impartiality to be constituted by much more than not favouring one's state.

First, impartiality is often described as an 'absence' (absence of prior commitments, prior ideas, or prior opinions on a given case). This 'blank slate' approach to impartiality stretches credulity, which may only increase suspicions about it. In practice, international judges and decision-makers will often have developed preliminary views on the issues they have to decide, not to mention a whole range of background views on the nature of international law or administration. In fact, they may well have been specifically chosen to serve because of such of the depth and sophistication of their outlook. As Theodor Meron put it, 'judges are not empty vessels that the litigants fill with content', (Meron 2005, p. 365) and in a sense their general knowledge of the world may also be what protects them from undue influence and manipulations. In this context, impartiality should rather be seen as an awareness, an alertness to inevitable existence of one's biases. Impartiality, thus conceived, is a form of self-critique. It implies that one is not entirely a dupe of one's own beliefs, and that one is willing to question them. The cardinal sin, in this perspective, is not with having a worldview, but with not knowing one has one or worse, taking one's worldview for a universal truth.

Second, a contemporary take on impartiality would emphasize the degree to which it is a process rather than a state, and something that must be reached rather than assumed. For example, one might emphasize the importance of transparency, deliberation, and accountability as factors that go towards fostering impartiality. An openness to discuss one's views, to expose them in order, through dialogue, to uncover biases that one may not have suspected, are all hallmarks of the modern practice of impartiality. The practice of including individual opinions in international adjudication is one that encourages jurisprudes to take responsibility for their views before a community of peers.

Third, impartiality should not be confused with the neutrality of 'doling out blame to both sides' (Friedman 1989). It can and should be viewed as compatible with an ability to take sides and as the opposite of wishy-washiness. One way of looking at it, is as involving a temporal element involved. Impartiality refers to a state of mind prior to decision-making. In that respect it is crucial that decision be informed only by factors that are relevant. For example, judicial decisions should not be made or policies decided on the basis of maximizing the national interest of certain states. As a principle, this is recognized even in the Security Council. Yet a priori impartiality does not mean that the decision process, once it has occurred, then inevitably leads to the same, i.e., a continuation of 'impartial' policies that would prolong the starting point impartiality. Impartiality only exists for a brief and important theoretical moment, but it cannot be a stultifying and paralyzing policy of not discontenting anyone. As one author suggested, what is needed in peace operations for example, is not 'a gentle, restrained impartiality but … an active, harsh impartiality that overpowers both sides: an imperial impartiality' (Betts 1994).

Individual v. Collective Impartiality

The focus has traditionally been on impartiality of the *individual*, the idea being that a collective of impartial individuals will produce impartial institutions. However, a closer look at the practice of international tribunals and organizations suggests that built into the system is a certain understanding of the frailty of individual impartiality, and an attempt to engineer institutional impartiality through a system of collective cancellation of excessive biases. It is worth noting in this respect the collegial nature of much international decision-making. Whether one is dealing with courts or international organizations or peacekeeping missions, opportunities for deliberation exist within each where transparency guarantees a certain level of discipline and discourages manifest partiality.

This explains in part the insistence on representativeness in international courts and organizations. The original, interwar concept of impartiality aspired to have individuals entirely dissociated from their national moorings to become a new species of 'homo internationalis'. Their recruitment was to be based on purely technical criteria for excellence in the case of international organizations, and prestige as jurisprudes in the case of international tribunals. Yet in practice, for historical reasons that cannot be explored here, this often meant that international civil servants and judges were selected from a remarkably narrow section of the world's population. The League of Nations had been dominated by the British and the French, and more than half of the staff of United Nations after the War was West European or American. The benches of international tribunals, notably the International Court of Justice, have been extraordinarily masculine.

This monochromatic nature of much of international technocracy is what eventually prompted calls that all major legal cultures should be represented before tribunals; international organizations even introduced a regional quota system to instil a sense of representativeness. Part of this is of course simply an attempt to get one's 'share of the pie', for example as recently independent countries vied to have their nationals represented in international organizations. In some cases, as in Krutschev's 1960s proposal that there be three Secretary Generals (one US, one Soviet and one non-aligned), one is dealing with little more than an attempt to reintroduce Great Power intergovernmentalism over the relative impartiality of a Secretary-General. There is also a mere concern with the 'optics' of impartiality, and the idea that international organizations will be all the more able to lead that they resemble the people of the world.

But it is notable that representativeness is also frequently justified in more principled terms as one of the ways of securing a truly unbiased international governance and rule of law. If the relative homogeneity of international decision-makers reinforces the partiality of their world-outlook, then diversity will help reconstruct international decision-making in its image. This is what might be called the 'pot-pourri' vision of impartiality; the idea that even if individual impartiality is unachievable, or at any rate unverifiable, at least various forms of discreet partiality will cancel each other in each other's presence. Such reasoning has been applied in the context of both benches and international organizations. For example as Bert Rölling put it, 'the more nations ... an international court of justice represents the smaller the risk [of reality being strained]; for distortion or camouflage of history is then more limited because certain distortions or disguises are mutually begrudged' (Rölling 1960, p. xiii).

Diversity is also one of the ways in which an 'international outlook' can be encouraged. As one author already pointed out in the context of the League of Nations, '[n]on-European demands for new posts are actuated frequently by *the desire to secure a fuller appreciation of the overseas point of view* and conditions rather than simply for additional posts' (Wilson 1934, p. 149). Better, more *international* policy, it was argued, would result from a fairer representation and more diverse Secretariat.[36] As the General Assembly put it, 'the policies and administrative methods of the Secretariat should reflect, and profit to the highest degree from, assets of various cultures and the technical competence of all member nations'.[37] The Secretary-General himself has been at pains to emphasize that geographic representation 'is no contradiction at all (with) a demand for a truly international Secretariat' and that it 'was indeed necessary precisely in order to maintain the exclusively international character of the Secretariat'.[38]

In addition, there if a sense that with the passage of time this process will engender the very conditions of its realization, as the practice of institutional decision-making helps nurture the sort of impartiality that it might not be able to presume:

> association in the analysis and development of international law and co-operation in judicial decision would develop inevitably and esprit de corps which would necessarily influence each judge in the performance of his duties. Acting

---

36   'Only staffs which represent the cultural, racial, ideological, and linguistic diversity in the world can hope to function effectively in today's international environment' (Renninger 1977, p. 394).

37   GA/Res 1852 (1962). To this day, about 75% of staff come from 24 countries. Regularly, certain geographic groups have been irked by what they see as the bias of the UN towards certain constituencies. Over the years, the fiscal contribution aspect has remained somewhat dominant (55% as opposed to 40% for membership and only 5% for population), and the UN has encountered some difficulties in tilting the balance towards underrepresented states.

38   *Introduction to the Annual Report of the Secretary General on the Work of the Organization, 16 June 1960 – 15 June 1961*, UN GAOR Supp. No. 1A (A/4800/Add.1), UN Doc. A/4800/Add.1 (1961) at 6.

under judicial responsibility, individual opinion, indeed prejudice, would lose something of its rigidity, and the decision of the Court would offer the highest guarantees for international impartiality (Carnegie Endowment for International Peace. 1920).

This is a very different concept of impartiality. Impartiality ceases to be a quality of the individual, and instead becomes a quality of the system, to be constructed by a careful effort to combine individuals from very different horizons in the hope that, over time, they will produce outcomes that are in the image of their diversity.

Conclusion: Impartiality's Evolving Status

International impartiality as an idea is not what it was in the late nineteenth century or the interwar period, or even the Cold War. At each period, it has been tied to a certain configuration of international order, its limitations and aspirations, as well as certain conceptions about the nature of governance. The nineteenth-century view of impartiality as detachment was appropriate for a world where the international community stood for little else than peaceful coexistence, and where the most it could offer was *bons offices* between equal sovereigns. The interwar ideal of a purely international class of technocrats was severely put in question by the failures of the League and the outbreak of the Second World War. Today and in retrospect, we would not judge kindly its impartial Eurocentrism. Dag Hammarskjöld's vigorous, substantive view of impartiality may have helped the organization sail through the Cold War, but it also provoked a lasting suspicion from some quarters that impartiality was at times the mask of certain political agendas.

All along, the thicker the international project has become and the more the international community has stood for something – peaceful settlement of disputes rather than war, order rather than territorial dismemberment, sovereignty rather than occupation, human rights rather than a range of other domestic regimes – the more quibbles it has tended to pick with states, and the less evidently impartial it has appeared. Moreover, the less traditionally 'international' and the more 'global' its core mission becomes, the more its societal impact will be felt, and the more it will have to confront challenges to impartiality more familiar from the domestic context.

Accordingly, the very concept of impartiality has come under challenge, and will continue to do so. The view of impartiality as a psychological quality that one has or does not has, for example, begs more questions than it answers. One temptation has been to escape the indeterminacy of law, for example, to embrace the supposed determinacy of science, particularly in the environmental realm, but it is difficult to imagine that scientific expertise can entirely escape the political economy of knowledge production (Andresen 89). Yet even as it is threatened from all sides, impartiality continues to encapsulate a core intuition about the necessity for international law and governance to be based on something else than the national interest, bias or solitary 'deification'. Impartiality is increasingly seen as a quality of governance that must emerge from fundamentally representative institutions, avoid serving as an excuse for neutrality, and draw its strength not on the denial of bias but its critical deconstruction.

However, as the definition of impartiality has changed, its role in defining legitimate international governance has evolved. Internationalists today may think twice before investing considerable hope, as Lauterpacht could in the interwar period, in a concept that presupposes something that is likely to be regularly belied in practice or, perhaps more relevantly, to be implausible in principle. Impartiality remains important as a goal to be attained but, since it can no longer be simply presumed, it does not serve the overarching legitimizing goal that it did in earlier times, when the hope of international order was sustained on the basis of the rise of a species of 'international men'. Part of the chronic crisis of international law and governance is surely traceable to our continuing doubts about true impartiality. Yet even if an international community of impartial international lawyers (e.g., Schachter's (1977) 'invisible college of international lawyers') and international civil servants were to exist as the very global incarnation of technocratic legitimacy, one may wonder whether it would provide – with its elitism, aristocratic, cosmopolitanism and lack of accountability – an appropriate foundation for international governance.

What takes international impartiality's place as a legitimizing principle is not clear at this stage, but it is certainly not, at least not yet, some form of global democracy. As issues of representation come to the fore, impartiality as such is increasingly secondary. Representation becomes a goal in itself and not merely a means to impartiality. This probably reflects a more psychologically and politically realistic view of the nature of international governance and law-making, one in which nothing is served by idealizing impartiality, even as something is lost by abandoning it totally. It also blurs the line between executive, legislative, judicial and administrative functions as all entail a demand for impartiality, yet none can be satisfied with a purely abstract definition of what it entails.

References

Amann, D., 2005. Impartiality deficit and international criminal judging. Manuscript for publication in forthcoming volume on transitional justice. Tokyo: United Nations University.

Andresen, S. et al., 1989. *International Resource Management: The Role of Science and Politics*. Fridtjof Nansen Institute, Oslo; British Crop Protection Council.

Anon., *Proceedings of the National Arbitration and Peace Congress*, New York, April 14th to 17th, 1907. Reprint. Hong Kong: Forgotten Books, 2013.

Bali, A.U., 2005. Justice under Occupation: Rule of Law and the Ethics of Nation-Building in Iraq. *Yale J. Int'l L.*, 30, p. 431.

Barros, J. and Studies, P.U.C. of I., 1969. *Betrayal from Within: Joseph Avenol, Secretary General of the League of Nations, 1933–1940*, Yale University Press.

Bassiouni, M.C., 1994. The United Nations Commission of Experts Established Pursuant to Security Council Resolution 780 (1992). *The American Journal of International Law*, 88(4), pp. 784–805.

Betts, R.K., 1994. The Delusion of Impartial Intervention. *Foreign Affairs*, pp. 20–33.

Boulden, J., 2005. Mandates Matter: An Exploration of Impartiality in United Nations Operations. *Global Governance*, 11, p. 147.

Campbell, K.J., 2001. *Genocide and the Global Village*, Palgrave Macmillan.

Carnegie Endowment for International Peace. 1920. Division of International Law, *The project relative to a Court of Arbitral Justice: draft convention and report adopted by the Second Hague Peace Conference of 1907*, The Endowment.

Cordier, A.W. and Foote, W., 1975. *Public Papers of the Secretaries-General of the United Nations*, Columbia University Press.

Dalfen, C.M., 1967. The World Court in Idle Splendour: The Basis of States' Attitudes. *International Journal*, 23(1), pp. 124–39.

Deutsch, E., 1977. *An International Rule of Law*, University Press of Virginia (Charlottesville).

El Zeidy, M., 2002. United States Dropped the Atomic Bomb of Article 16 of the ICC Statute: Security Council Power of Deferrals and Resolution 1422. *The Vand. J. Transnat'l L.*, 35, p. 1503.

Ellis, C.H., 2003. *The Origin, Structure & Working of the League of Nations*, Lawbook Exchange.

Evans, A.A., 1944. The International Secretariat of the Future. *Public Administration*, 22(2), pp. 64–74.

Franck, T.M., 1968. *The Structure of Impartiality*, Macmillan.

Franck, T.M. and Farley, H.S., 1980. Procedural Due Process in Human Rights Fact-Finding by International Agencies. *Am. J. Int'l L.*, 74, p. 308.

Friedman, M., 1989. The Impracticality of Impartiality. *Journal of Philosophy*, 86.

Garlan, E.N., 1941. *Legal Realism and Justice*, Columbia University Press.

Gibbs, D.N., 2000. The United Nations, International Peacekeeping and the Question of 'Impartiality': Revisiting the Congo Operation of 1960. *The Journal of Modern African Studies*, 38(03), pp. 359–82.

Goulding, M., 2003. *Peacemonger*, Johns Hopkins University Press.

Grossman, N., 2011. Sex on the Bench: Do Women Judges Matter to the Legitimacy of International Courts? *SSRN eLibrary*. Available at: http://papers.ssrn.com/sol3/papers.cfm?abstract_id=1773015 [Accessed 18 October 2011].

Hensley, T.R., 1978. Bloc Voting on the International Court of Justice. *Journal of Conflict Resolution*, 22(1), p. 39.

Hensley, T.R., 1968. National Bias and the International Court of Justice. *Midwest Journal of Political Science*, pp. 568–86.

Hughes, A., 2002. Impartiality and the UN Observation Group in Lebanon, 1958. *International Peacekeeping*, 9(4), pp. 1–20.

Justice, L. of N.A.C. of J. for the E. of a P.C. of I., 1920. *Procès-verbaux of the proceedings of the Committee, June 16th – July 24th 1920, with annexes*, The Lawbook Exchange, Ltd.

Kelsen, H., 1947. Will the Judgment in the Nuremberg Trial Constitute a Precedent in International Law? *Int'l LQ*, 1, p. 153.

Kenney, S.J., 2002. Breaking the Silence: Gender Mainstreaming and the Composition of the European Court of Justice. *Feminist Legal Studies*, 10(3), pp. 257–70.

Koskenniemi, M., 2002. *The Gentle Civilizer of Nations: The Rise and Fall of International Law*, Cambridge University Press.

Koskenniemi, M., 2005. *From Apology to Utopia: The Structure of International Legal Argument*, Cambridge University Press.

Lauterpacht, H., 2000. *The Function of Law in the International Community*, Lawbook Exchange Ltd.

Lemoine, J., 1995. *The International Civil Servant: An Endangered Species*, Martinus Nijhoff Publishers.

Lepard, B.D., 2003. *Rethinking Humanitarian Intervention: A Fresh Legal Approach Based on Fundamental Ethical Principles in International Law and World Religions*, Penn State Press.

Lippmann, W., 1961. Interview with Khrushchev. *Survival*, 3(4), pp. 154–8.

Majstorović, D., 2009. Generic Characteristics of the Office of the High Representative's Press Releases. *Critical Discourse Studies*, 6(3), pp. 199–214.

Mégret, F., 2011. International Judges and Experts Impartiality and the Problem of Past Declarations. *The Law and Practice of International Courts and Tribunals*, 10(1), pp. 31–66.

Mégret, F., 2013. The Rise and Fall of 'International Man'. In P. Singh (ed.), *Critical International Law: Post-realism, Post-colonialism and Transnationalism*. New Delhi: Oxford University Press.

Meron, T., 2005. Judicial Independence and Impartiality in International Criminal Tribunals. *American Journal of International Law*, 99(2), pp. 359–69.

Peterson, L., 2008. Shared Dilemmas: Justice for Rape Victims under International Law and Protection for Rape Victims Seeking Asylum. *Hastings International and Comparative Law Review*, 31, p. 521.

Pinheiro, P.S., 2003. Musings of a UN Special Rapporteur on Human Rights. *Global Governance*, 9, p. 7.

Rappard, W.E., 1927. The Evolution of the League of Nations. *Am. Pol. Sci. Rev.*, 21, p. 792.

Rappard, W.E., 1931. *The Geneva Experiment*, Oxford University Press.

Renninger, J.P., 1977. Staffing International Organizations: The Role of the International Civil Service Commission. *Public Administration Review*, pp. 391–6.

Rölling, B., 1960. The Law of War and the National Jurisdiction Since 1945. *RCADI*, 100.

Root, E., 1916. *Addresses on International Subjects*, Ayer Publishing.

Sacriste, G. and Vauchez, A., 2005. Les 'bons offices' du droit international: la constitution d'une autorité non politique dans le concert diplomatique des années 1920. *Critique internationale* (1), pp. 101–17.

Schachter, O., 1977. Invisible College of International Lawyers. *Nw. UL Rev.*, 72, p. 217.

Schwebel, S.M, 1953. The International Character of the Secretariat of the United Nations, 30 Brit. *Y.B. Int'l L.*, 71, p. 73 note 1.

Slim, H., 2001. Review Article – Humanitarianism and the Holocaust: Lessons from ICRC's Policy towards the Jews. *The International Journal of Human Rights*, 5(1), pp. 130–44.

Smith, A.M., 2004. 'Judicial Nationalism' in International Law: National Identity and Judicial Autonomy at the ICJ. *bepress Legal Series*, p. 428.

Soloveitchik, S., 1952. International Law as Instrument of Politics. *U. Kan. City L. Rev.*, 21, p. 169.

Subedi, S.P., 2011. Protection of Human Rights through the Mechanism of UN Special Rapporteurs. *Human Rights Quarterly*, 33(1), pp. 201–28.

Sunga, L.S., 2007. Introduction to the 'Lund Statement to the United Nations Human Rights Council on the Human Rights Special Procedures'. *Nordic Journal of International Law*, 76(2/3), p. 281.

Tharoor, S., 1995. The Changing Face of Peace-Keeping and Peace-Enforcement. *Fordham Int'l LJ*, 19, p. 408.

Wilson, B., 1990. Will Women Judges Really Make a Difference? *Osgoode Hall Law Journal*, 507, p. 28.

Wilson, F.G., 1934. *Labor in the League System: A Study of the International Labor Organization in Relation to International Administration*, Stanford University Press.

Yamashita, H., 2008. 'Impartial'Use of Force in United Nations Peacekeeping. *International Peacekeeping*, 15(5), pp. 615–30.

Zile, Z.L., 1964. Soviet Contribution to International Adjudication: Professor Krylov's Jurisprudential Legacy, A. *Am. J. Int'l L.*, 58, p. 359.

Chapter 6

Professions without Borders: Global Ethics and the International Rule of Law

Charles Sampford

Introduction

> The time has come for mankind to make the rule of law in international affairs as normal as it is now in domestic affairs. Of course the structure of such law must be patiently built, stone by stone. The cost will be a great deal of hard work, both in and out of government particularly in the universities of the world. Plainly one foundation stone of this structure is the International Court of Justice … [and] the obligatory jurisdiction of that Court … One final thought on rule of law between nations: we will all have to remind ourselves that under this system of law one will sometimes lose as well as win. But … if an international controversy leads to armed conflict, everyone loses. President Dwight D. Eisenhower[1]

Those who believe that good governance should start at home and extend abroad will easily agree, but may be surprised at the source of the quote and be more optimistic about its achievement. In this chapter, I will argue that the emergence of strong sovereign states after the Treaty of Westphalia turned two of the most cosmopolitan professions, the law and the military, into the least cosmopolitan. Sovereign states determined the content of the law within their borders – including what elements of ecclesiastical law, law merchant and international law applied. Similarly, states sought to ensure that all military force was at their disposal in national armies. The erosion of sovereignty in a post-Westphalian world may significantly reverse this process.

The erosion of sovereignty is likely to have profound consequences for the legal profession and the ethics of how, and for what ends, it is practised. As we shall see, lawyers have played a major role in the civilization of sovereign

---

1   D. Eisenhower (1959) *Remarks Upon Receiving an Honorary Degree of Doctor of Laws at Delhi University* 11 December 1959 <http://www.eisenhowermemorial.org/speeches/1959>. Those who are surprised by the source of the quote should recall that this soldier-turned-politician used federal troops to protect a black student in Little Rock and warned of the military industrial complex. In Delhi, the old warrior who had masterminded the 6 June Normandy landings of the 'United Nations' (a phrase used in newspapers on that day) made his plea for law not war.

states through the articulation and institutionalization of key governance values – starting with the rule of law. An increasingly global profession must take on similar tasks – and may find unexpected allies within the profession of arms. This lecture apply these ideas to the rule of law, reviewing the concept of an international rule of law and its relationship to domestic conceptions and outline the task of building the international rule of law and the role that lawyers and soldiers can and should play in it.[2]

Westphalian States and Two Cosmopolitan Professions

Pepo, Bologna and Pre-Westphalian Professions

The gradual evolution of the institutions that gave rise to universities means that there is no precise date for when particular institutions became 'universities' and which can claim the mantle of the 'first'.[3] Some ancient bodies might claim as much right to call themselves 'universities' as the eleventh and twelfth century European centres of learning in Bologna, Paris and Oxford. China's Nanjing (*c.*200), Morocco's Al-karouine (859) and Egypt's Al Azar (975) could claim to be the oldest continuing universities while India's Odantapuri (*c.*550 BC to *c.*AD 1040) and Jalanda (*c.*450 BC to AD 1193) have respectable claims to being the earliest institutions that could be called universities. Although predated by a medical school at Salerno, the institution with the claim to be the first university in Europe is the University of Bologna, and there is evidence of law lectures being given by the monk Pepo as early as 1076.[4] Universities and university law teaching thus predated the modern state by nearly six centuries (and predate the joint stock company, which they have latterly been encouraged to emulate, by nearly eight centuries). They were originally among the most cosmopolitan of institutions.

---

2   In so doing, it will expand on views expressed in C. Sampford, 'Challenges to the Concepts of "Sovereignty" and "Intervention"', closing keynote World Congress on Legal and Social Philosophy, 1999, published in T. Campbell and B.M. Leiser (eds), *Human Rights in Philosophy and Practice*, Aldershot: Ashgate, 2001, pp. 335–91; C. Sampford, 'What's a Lawyer Doing in a Nice Place like This? Lawyers and Applied Ethics', *Legal Ethics* 1, 1998; C. Sampford, 'Get New Lawyers', *Legal Ethics* 6, 2003, 185–205; C. Sampford, 'More and More Lawyers But Still No Judges', *Legal Ethics* 8, 2005, 16–22; and C. Sampford, *Retrospectivity and the Rule of Law*, Oxford: Oxford University Press, 2006.

3   See http://en.wikipedia.org/wiki/List_of_oldest_universities_in_continuous_operation for Wikipedia's discussion of the issue with the claims of Nanjing and Academy of Gundishapur in Iran as well as University of Al-Karaouine in Morocco and Al Azar in Cairo.

4   C. Phillipson, 'Andrea Alciati and His Predecessors', *Journal of the Society of Comparative Legislation* New Series 13(2), 1913, 245–64.

The students of the time learnt Roman Law, Canon Law and, as it developed, the Law Merchant.[5] Such law was not made by territorial sovereigns but was developed by jurists, priests and traders and covered most of mediaeval Europe. Indeed, the re-emergence of international trade involved issues which the existing local laws were not equipped to address, but which the preserved Roman Law could. Accordingly, the legal education gained by students at Bologna and, later, Paris, Oxford and other mediaeval universities allowed them to work for any of the princes of Western Europe and to argue in many courts – making the profession of law highly cosmopolitan. There was no 'dingo fence' in mediaeval Europe.[6] Indeed, most professions were cosmopolitan – not just the oldest profession but also the most venerated profession – medicine. This applied not only to medicine and law but also the profession of arms, where there was a claimed transnational affinity between knights and a code of chivalry setting out how one could and could not fight. Most soldiers did not fight directly for kings but for local lords or as mercenaries following 'captains' of 'military bands' or 'military companies'. They might be part of armies organized by kings. But they might also fight against kings or in civil wars – or for foreign princes as individuals or groups who would fight in return for land or money.

However, the rise of strong sovereign states in the seventeenth century turned these two, most cosmopolitan, professions into two of the least cosmopolitan. Those who like a convenient date look to the Treaty of Westphalia in 1648, which provided the basis for state sovereignty. These transitions arguably commenced long before Westphalia and were not fully completed 300 years later when the United Nations (UN) Charter enshrined key aspects of the Westphalian system.[7]

---

5   For a discussion generally see: W Mitchell, *An Essay on the Early History of the Law Merchant*, Cambridge: University Press, 1904.

6   The 'dingo fence' was erected in Australia to keep dingoes (wild dogs brought that were present in Australia before European settlement) out of south east Australia. The restrictive practices for keeping southern lawyers from appearing before Queensland courts were colloquially referred to as a 'dingo fence').

7   For example Chapter 1, Article 2, principles 1 and 7: 'The Organization is based on the principle of the sovereign equality of all its Members' and 'Nothing contained in the present Charter shall authorize the United Nations to intervene in matters which are essentially within the domestic jurisdiction of any state or shall require the Members to submit such matters to settlement under the present Charter; but this principle shall not prejudice the application of enforcement measures under Chapter VII'. The concept of universal standards provided increased support for the human rights instruments which accompanied the Charter. The preamble of the *Universal Declaration of Human Rights* (UDHR), G.A. res. 217A (III), U.N. Doc A/810 71 (1948), explains that human rights are a 'common standard of achievement for all peoples and all nations'. Article II of the UDHR explains the universal application of human rights by stating: 'Everyone is entitled to all the rights and freedoms set forth in this Declaration, without distinction of any kind, such as race, colour, sex, language, religion, political or other opinion, national or social origin, property, birth or other status. Furthermore, no distinction shall be made on the basis of

The Westphalian Legal Profession

The claim of sovereign states to determine the content of the law within their borders – including which, if any, ecclesiastical law, what form of economic regulation and what, if any, international law was to apply – meant that those who sought to study law would study the law of a particular sovereign state. Admission to practice was determined by domestic institutions – Courts, Inns of Court and various forms of apprenticeship and professional examination[8] In common law countries, universities were not initially engaged in educating lawyers for such practice. English law was not even taught at Oxford until 1758 when William Blackstone commenced his series of lectures on English Law.[9] However, after six centuries, even Oxford came around to teaching primarily English laws.

Two other developments profoundly affected the law and lawyering:

1. The rise of printing, which allowed legislation and case law to be disseminated more widely and in far greater detail than had ever been possible.
2. The decline of feudal land tenure, the gradual decline in the importance of land in European economies and the extension of the market led to the idea that landholding typically involved an 'owner' with sole dominion over it.[10]

Over some 300 years, these developments came to be seen as so entrenched that they were perceived to be natural, and the legal pluralism of pre-Westphalian Europe seemed contrary to the very nature of law.[11] However, the last 10–15 years have seen the emergence of trends that involve profound challenges to the nature of law in Westphalian sovereign states. The challenges to sovereignty include the rise of transnational law – including international law, free trade treaties, the extra territorial reach of United States (US) law and the development of universal jurisdiction.[12]

---

the political, jurisdictional or international status of the State or territory to which a person belongs, whether it is independent, trust, non-self-governing or under any other limitation of sovereignty.' The *International Covenant on Civil and Political Rights* (ICCPR) and the *International Covenant on Economic, Social and Cultural Rights* (ICESCR) both support the notion of universality in their preambles when they state that nations are obliged to give 'universal respect for, and observance of, human rights and freedoms'.

8   See, e.g., P. Lemmings, Introduction, *Gentlemen and Barristers: The Inns of Court and the English Bar 1680–1733*, Oxford: Oxford University Press, 1990.

9   See W. Twining, *Blackstone's Tower*, London: Stevens, 1994.

10   This development is in sharp contrast to feudal law when land was at the centre of life and likely to be subject to a range of rights. In a sense, it was 'too important' to be simply owned by one person.

11   Which was, since Austin, seen as norms emerging from a sovereign.

12   See, e.g., R. O'Keefe, 'Universal Jurisdiction: Clarifying the Basic Concept', *J Int Criminal Justice* (2004) 2 (3), 735–60.

The rise of international and transnational organizations in the public, corporate and voluntary sectors has also increased the move towards pluralism. The growth of the UN and the other pillars of the UN system (the International Monetary Fund (IMF) and World Bank) have led to a profusion of international organizations for global public purposes. The International Court of Justice (ICJ), the International Criminal Court (ICC) and now the World Trade Organization (WTO) are international judicial institutions capable of enforcing an increasing volume of international law, and universal jurisdiction allows domestic courts to apply international law in certain circumstances. While the WTO has real 'teeth', the growth of transnational supply chains and global corporations led to calls to establish internationally acceptable norms to bind corporations to international human rights norms. In response to the growth of corporations and their increased recognition as actors under public international law, the UN established the Global Compact.[13] The Global Compact is a corporate social responsibility scheme where corporations agree to be bound by 10 principles in return for the perception of being a good corporate citizen. This scheme is the largest corporate citizenship group in the world with approximately 40,000 stakeholders across 100 nations.[14] Despite the current limitations on the enforcement of international law, states have created regulatory vehicles to hold non-state actors accountable for unethical business practices. The Organization for Economic Cooperation and Development (OECD) Guidelines for example, provide voluntary guidance for corporations in their international affairs and are enforced by member states.[15] While these guidelines have limited impact upon many corporations to which those guidelines are directed, they do represent moves by states to impose universal standards across jurisdictions.[16] There is no barrier to OECD member states agreeing to

---

13   The UN General Assembly on 5 December 2007 unanimously adopted a Resolution which supported the work of the UNGC Office: United Nations General Assembly, 62nd sess, 3 December 2007, Agenda item 61, Res Towards Global Partnerships; United Nations Global Compact; 'UN General Assembly Renews and Strengthens Global Compact Mandate', *Compact Quarterly* 12, 2007; see for a comprehensive discussion: A. Rasche, 'A Necessary Supplement' – What the United Nations Global Compact Is and Is Not, *Business & Society* 48, 2009.

14   United Nations Global Compact, *Annual Review 2006* 2, 2007. The UN General Assembly on 5 December 2007 unanimously adopted a Resolution which supported the work of the UNGC Office: United Nations General Assembly, 62nd sess, 3 December 2007, Agenda item 61, Res *Towards Global Partnerships: United Nations Global Compact*; 'UN General Assembly Renews and Strengthens Global Compact Mandate', *Compact Quarterly* 12, 2007.

15   S. Cooney, 'Improving Regulatory Strategies for Dealing with Endemic Labour Abuses', SJD thesis, Columbia University, 2005, pp. 155–8; S. Cooney, 'A Broader Role for the Commonwealth in Eradicating Foreign Sweatshops?', *Melbourne University Law Review* 28, 291, 2004, 315–16.

16   For a criticism of the OECD Guidelines for Multinational Enterprises (2000), see J. Ruggie, 'Protect, Respect and Remedy: A Framework for Business and Human Rights' Report of the Special Representative of the Secretary-General 2008.

implement similar ethical guidelines for the way lawyers conduct themselves in international affairs and they should be encouraged to do so.

In the not-for-profit sector, the growth of international and transnational NGOs from the Red Cross to Greenpeace and Transparency International has given such NGOs a larger place in the global community than in most sovereign states. On the other hand, institutionalized religion has a more limited place than in pre-Westphalian Europe, despite attempts by fundamentalists in the 'middle east' and 'mid west' whose aspirations for states dominated by particular religions are distinctly pre-Westphalian.[17]

More generally, the challenges of globalization, involving the movement of people, goods, services and ideas across boundaries, have increased the growth of a global community. One important aspect of this is the emergence of the Internet, which has created substantial difficulties for states that desire to regulate their citizens' access to information.[18]

The issue of sovereignty has been substantially challenged by the environmental problems facing the global community. Arguably, the greater ease of movement of organisms that damage flora, fauna and people and the unintended effects on the environment of human activity, are leading to an awareness that the land is, once again, too important to be the subject of the private dominion of individual citizens. The perception that the environment should be regarded as a global issue arguably gained traction with the Convention on Climate Change and has obtained increased recognition with the Kyoto Protocol.[19] The Kyoto Protocol 'creates significant responsibilities for the participating countries, and brings together many of the most industrialized countries of the world to limit gas emissions in an unprecedented way'.[20]

Sovereignty is also challenged by the flow of debt (toxic or otherwise), political ideology (toxic and otherwise), capital (mostly legitimate but including the proceeds of corruption) and viruses of varying degrees of virulence. None of

---

17   The caliphate predated Westphalia by 800 years and the establishment of religiously defined colonies predated it by 30 years.

18   See for a discussion on attempts to regulate the Internet: S. Deva, 'Corporate Complicity in Internet Censorship in China: Who Cares for the Global Compact or the Global Online Freedom Act?' *George Washington International Law Review* 39, 2007, 255.

19   United Nations Framework Convention on Climate Change, opened for signature on 4 June 1992, 31 ILM 849 (entered into force on 21 March 1994); Kyoto Protocol to the United Nations Framework Convention on Climate Change, opened for signature 16 March 1998 (entered into force on 16 February 2005); See for discussion of the impact: D.G. Victor, *The Collapse of the Kyoto Protocol and the Struggle to Slow Global Warming*, New York: Princeton University Press, 2001.

20   H.D. Shumaker, 'The Economic Effects of the European Union Carbon Dioxide Emission Quota on the New Member States of the European Union: Can They Become Equal Economic Partners of the European Union While Complying with the 2008–2012 Quota?', *Pennsylvania State Environmental Law Review* 17, 2008, 99.

these problems can be addressed by sovereign states attempting to act alone within their borders – though they can contribute to global solutions.

Most of these trends will intensify over the next few decades and could lead to fundamental changes to the nature, practice, structure and content of law over the professional lifetimes of those students we are currently teaching. By the time that students entering laws schools this year (2011) retire in the mid twenty-first century, the law and the legal profession may be as different from its Westphalian sovereign paradigm as that paradigm was to the world of Pepo's students.

The Westphalian Profession of Arms

The profession of arms was also transformed by the rise of the nation state. The European feudal system involved direct loyalty to local lords rather than to princes, kings or, in the Holy Roman Empire, the Emperor. Outside the feudal system, mercenaries had been a common feature[21] – particularly in pre-Westphalian Europe where soldiers' loyalties were often to their immediate captain rather than to a sovereign.

The growth of sovereign states resulted in standing armies that claimed the loyalties of their soldiers directly, rather than through their lords or captains. States claimed a monopoly of legitimate violence. If the soldiers' loyalty and duty were to the nation state, it was inappropriate for them to give their loyalty to, and fight for, one part of the state against another, risking the newly established order which it was the prime responsibility of the state to engender for the protection of its citizenry. Professional soldiers saw themselves as maintaining order rather than contributing to disorder. Similarly, it was also totally inappropriate for a soldier to fight for another state as 'mercenaries' became dirty word. These principles were not always followed. Occasionally, the military would break up and join opposing sides in a civil war – something that was seen as the ultimate tragedy for a professional military force. More often, the military would remain unified in suppressing insurgency – or unified in overthrowing governments in *coups d'état* – one of the curses of the modern state. On the external front, some states continued to recruit mercenaries, but they were generally looked down upon as not real soldiers.[22] The use of mercenaries became less popular and in the twentieth

---

21   D. Stinnett, 'Regulating the Privatization of War: How to Stop Private Military Firms From Committing Human Rights Abuses', *Boston College International and Comparative Law Review* 28, 211, 2005, 213–16; The main instruments banning mercenary activities are the Additional Protocols to the Geneva Conventions of 12 August 1949 (Protocol I) 42 and the International Convention against the Recruitment, Use, Financing and Training of Mercenaries (UN Mercenary Convention) U.N. GAOR, 44th Sess., Supp. No. 43, U.N. Doc. A/RES/44/34 (1989) (entered into force Oct. 20, 2001).

22   While some would argue that the Ghurkhas are a potentially contradictory example, there were attempts to avoid considering them as mercenaries and their rights were never as extensive as Britain's citizen soldiers.

century there were national and international steps taken to outlaw the use of private military forces.[23]

The forces of globalization are changing the profession of arms as surely as the profession of law. The last 20 years has seen the rise of private military forces associated with the US military, corporations and criminal gangs.[24] The largest remaining forms of private military forces exist in private military companies (PMCs). These PMCs can provide training, security or direct military support. The 'Sandline affair' involved an attempt to bypass the Papua New Guinea military in suppressing a secessionist movement.[25] Where PMCs perpetrate human rights abuses within a sovereign state on behalf of that state or an invading state, these forces have largely been immune from prosecution. More recently, the international community has been examining vehicles to hold PMCs responsible under international law.[26]

While the monopoly of legitimate force was a matter of definition, in most states, most of the time, the military forces of the state could prevail over any and all other coercive forces ranged against them. For mainstream military forces, the development of the laws of war has entrenched codes of behaviour that can now be enforced by the International Criminal Court. The increasing range and intensity of cooperation between military forces through participation in each other's training programmes, joint exercises and UN deployments are reinforcing the sense that soldiers are part of a common global profession of arms. Indeed, their common code of conduct is in some senses far more advanced than that of lawyers, being distilled into a number of international agreements – with the four Geneva Conventions and the three amendment protocols the most significant.[27]

---

23 W. Singer, 'Corporate Warriors: The Rise of the Privatized Military Industry and Its Ramifications for International Security', *INT'L SEC.* 26 186, 188–9, 2001/02, 191.

24 See P.W. Singer, *Corporate Warriors: The Rise of the Privatized Military Industry*, New York: Cornell University Press, 2003.

25 S. Dinnen, R. May and A. Regan (eds), *Challenging the State: The Sandline Affair in Papua New Guinea*, ANU Canberra: NCDS and Department of Political and Social Change, RSPAS, 1997; S. Dorney, *The Sandline Affair: Politics and Mercenaries and the Bougainville Crisis*, Sydney: ABC Books for the Australian Broadcasting Corporation, 1998.

26 D. Morgan, 'Professional Military Firms under International Law', *Chicago Journal of International Law* 9, 2008, 213; D. Ridlon, 'Contractors or Illegal Combatants? The Status of Armed Contractors in Iraq', *The Air Force Law Review* 62, 2008, 199.

27 First Geneva Convention 'For the Amelioration of the Condition of the Wounded and Sick in Armed Forces in the Field' (first adopted in 1864, last revision in 1949); Second Geneva Convention 'for the Amelioration of the Condition of Wounded, Sick and Shipwrecked Members of Armed Forces at Sea' (first adopted in 1906); Third Geneva Convention 'relative to the Treatment of Prisoners of War' (first adopted in 1929, last revision in 1949); Fourth Geneva Convention 'relative to the Protection of Civilian Persons in Time of War' (first adopted in 1949, based on parts of the 1907 Hague Convention IV); Protocol I (1977): Protocol Additional to the Geneva Conventions of 12 August 1949, relating to the Protection of Victims of International Armed Conflicts; Protocol II

Building Global Professions as Important Institutions in a Globalizing World

Global Values and Global Institutions

The trends towards globalizing the legal and military professions and others are important. Indeed, given the absence of any equivalent to national governments within the international order, such professions may need to play a disproportionate role in building and sustaining that international order. The basis for this argument is a narrative that has much influenced my thinking over the last 10 years, outlined in my earlier chapter in this book and summarized here. Good governance requires the articulation of governance values (for example, liberty, equality, citizenship, community, democracy, human rights, the rule of law and environmental sustainability)[28] and the institutions that can realize those values. Since the seventeenth century, governance debates have centred on sovereign states rather than relations between them. Late seventeenth-century states were generally highly authoritarian and justified as such. Hobbes argued that rational people would mutually agree to subject themselves to an all-powerful sovereign to avoid a 'state of nature' in which the life of man would be 'solitary, poor, nasty, brutish and short'.[29]

Once internal order had been restored, this social contract did not seem such a good bargain. The eighteenth-century Enlightenment sought to civilize these authoritarian states by holding them to a set of more refined and ambitious values – notably liberty, equality, citizenship, human rights, democracy and the rule of law. Some of these values were adaptations of classical city-state ideals to the much larger polities of the time. Nineteenth-century thinkers extended the range of rights championed and added concern for environment and for practical and social equality.

Most importantly, the key to the Enlightenment governance project was a 'Feuerbachian' reversal of the way rulers and ruled related to each other. Before the Enlightenment, 'subjects' had to demonstrate their allegiance and loyalty to their 'sovereign'. The Enlightenment proclaimed that 'governments' had to justify their existence to 'citizens' who chose them. Once the reversal of the relationship was suggested, it was very hard to go back.

Values are rarely self-implementing: they require institutions to realize them. Institutional innovations included an independent judiciary exercising judicial review of the executive, representative institutions, bicameral parliaments, federal division of functions, government and civil society watchdogs, universal

---

(1977): Protocol Additional to the Geneva Conventions of 12 August 1949, relating to the Protection of Victims of Non-International Armed Conflicts; Protocol III (2005): Protocol Additional to the Geneva Conventions of 12 August 1949, relating to the Adoption of an Additional Distinctive Emblem.

28   Though, not as recently as might be imagined, nineteenth-century environmentalists sought to clean up the Thames and protect the countryside via the National Trust.

29   T. Hobbes, *Leviathan*, Cambridge: Cambridge University Press, 1991, p. 89.

education, questioning media and 'responsible' (or 'parliamentary') government.[30] This development of governance values and the institutions to realize them can be seen as an 'enlightenment project'.

Debates have rightly continued over the precise meaning and relative importance of these governance values and the best institutional means of achieving them. However, the centre of gravity in governance debates has remained the sovereign state, with the 'enlightenment project' becoming a 'UN project' in which all the peoples of the world might become members of strong sovereign states securing their citizen's universal human rights.

This 'UN project' has been shaken by the 'globalizing' flow of ideas, people, goods and services flooding over international borders and weakening many sovereign states. Liberal democratic values were formed *in and for* strong states. Citizenship, democracy, welfare, and community have clear meaning *within* sovereign states but lack apparent application in a broader, more diffuse, globalized world. The institutions that sustain, promote and realize those values are very much state-based. The rights, duties and 'sense of belonging' that citizenship carries are attached to state institutions. Democracy is realized through citizen participation in national and sub-national legislatures – and loses mileage if the real power and range of choice open to those legislatures is restricted. Welfare rights like education and healthcare are only implemented through the institutions of strong, sovereign (and wealthy) states – and even their capacity to do so is increasingly questioned.

Two common responses are to abandon inconvenient governance values such as democracy and welfare or to resist globalization and strengthen the state. I have long argued for a third approach, because globalization exposes a flaw in the 'enlightenment project' and later 'UN project'.[31] How can universal rights be secured by geographically limited entities? Why should the welfare rights of the citizens of some states be a tiny fraction of the welfare rights of others? This approach suggests a fundamental rethinking of our governance values and the mix of institutions that can achieve them – a 'global enlightenment' in which, as in the eighteenth century, the ideals will come first and the practical institutional solutions will come later.[32] As in the eighteenth century, when city-state values and institutions were reworked and re-combined for nation states, sovereign state values and institutions may need reworking and recombining.

I have argued that the institutional arrangements that are most likely to emerge and which are most likely to secure such values will not resemble 'sovereign states writ large'. It is more likely to look like pre-Westphalian Europe. States

---

30   A feature shared by all long-standing democracies other than the United States.

31   Sampford, 'Challenges to the Concepts of "Sovereignty" and "Intervention"', pp. 335–91.

32   While deferring the institutional issues, I would emphasize that this does not amount to an argument for global government – the sovereign state writ large. A more likely result is a mix of institutions reflecting both pre-Westphalian Europe and the modern ideal of an integrity system made up of public, corporate and NGO bodies.

and multilateral institutions will be important but other institutions – corporations, superannuation funds,[33] professions and NGOs – may play a larger role.[34] In this light, I will be considering the roles of the legal and soldierly professions in a future order and I will suggest that lawyers and the military should see themselves as part of an international profession, respecting international values.

Towards Global Professions

I suggest that the legal profession is, and should be, breaking free of its Westphalian shackles. Professions are not bound by their employers, let alone their states. This principle is the whole point of an independent profession.[35] The concept of a profession involves a group who develops and deploys a body of knowledge and skills for a public purpose. Such knowledge and skills can be used for good or ill – for the ostensible purpose which justifies the powers and privileges of the relevant profession, or abused for other purposes. As argued elsewhere,[36] the justification of a profession (indeed, institutions generally) should be in terms of the values it furthers on behalf of the community in which it operates. Those values provide the core for ethical standard setting (both aspirational and disciplinary), legal regulation and institutional reform.

The importance of ethical guidelines is axiomatic in the case of the military – whose knowledge and skills may involve the deployment of organized deadly force against other states in defiance of international law or deployed against the state itself (and generally the human rights of its citizens) in a *coup d'état*. The oft-asked question about the difference between a government and a band of robbers is repeated in asking the difference between the army and an organized group of violent gangsters. The answer cannot simply lie in following orders of the civilian 'commander-in-chief' as to which groups of people are to

---

33 Especially if driven to engage in sustainable investment that meets the values and interests of their unit holders who have longer-term interests than the investment managers.

34 There is also likely to be a place for unions or faith based organisations – though I am not sure that their role will be larger or smaller. It is relevant to observe that faith-based NGOs have been involved in pressuring corporations to date on good corporate citizenship: L. Allen, 'Religion and Corporate Social Responsibility: The Interfaith Centre on Corporate Responsibility and the Corporate Withdrawal Movement from Burma', PhD thesis, Boston University, 2003.

35 In describing the profession as 'independent', this does not mean that it is entirely self-regulating. However, the main impetus for enunciating and developing legal ethics and the structure and role of the profession comes from lawyers, with many of the regulatory and most of the disciplinary decisions in the hands of the judicial branch of the profession.

36 See C. Sampford, 'Law, Institutions and the Public Private Divide', invited keynote address Australasian Law Teachers Association Conference, Canberra, September 1990; C. Sampford and C. Parker, 'Legal Ethics: Legal Regulation, Ethical Standard Setting and Institutional Design', in S. Parker and C. Sampford (eds), *Legal Ethics and Legal Practice: Contemporary Issues*, Oxford: Oxford University Press, 1995, p. 11.

be killed en masse, as that does not guarantee that the military is more than a reliable accomplice. The answer must lie in the values the military forces claim to espouse, the codes of honour and ethics they develop to realize those values, the commitment to that code and the institutional means that they provide in order to make that realization probable – including mechanisms for reviewing the actions of soldiers and applying appropriate sanctions.

While lawyers cannot directly deploy lethal force, if they are not bound by ethical restraints they can provide advice, which can result in spectacular individual and social harm. Where lawyers give advice on the legality of wars or torture, the consequences can be catastrophic for those who suffer invasion and/ or torture. The fact that those who sought selective legal advice may leave office with their reputations shattered is small consolation and an insufficient deterrent.

While the abuse of the knowledge and skills of lawyers is not as spectacular as the deployment of military force, it is potentially insidious if the knowledge and skills of lawyers are used to deny justice. Sometimes globalization makes this task easier – when lawyers forum-shop for jurisdictions wherein their clients can engage in lawful practices, which would be regarded as criminal in their home state.[37] A similar question arises with regard to the difference between a lawyer and a 'spin-doctor' – saying whatever suits the client's interest and, in effect, making lawyers figuratively rather than literally 'guns for hire'. I have previously argued that, where the client refuses to have disputes heard in a court of competent jurisdiction, there is a temptation for clients to seek, and lawyers to give, advice they want to hear. Under such conditions, they are not acting as lawyers but as spin-doctors, no better than the much despised Jamie Shea who was lent by Prime Minister Blair to NATO during the Kosovo conflict. Egregious examples include some of those who provided opinions to governments on the legality of the Kosovo and Iraq wars[38] and the treatment of prisoners.[39] As with the military, the answer for lawyers must lie in values, ethics, commitment and the institutional means for keeping lawyers to their task.

In both cases, the professionals act, with very few exceptions, on instructions by the commander-in-chief or client. However, they do so in an institutional context designed to further the core values of that profession and reduce the likelihood that the professionals' knowledge and skills will be abused. In the case of the

---

37   For a discussion of where this has occurred in relation to bribery and medical trials see: P. Ala'i, 'The Legacy of Geographical Morality and Colonialism: A Historical Assessment of the Current Crusade against Corruption', *Vanderbilt Journal of Transnational Law* 33, 2000, 877; D. Fidler, '"Geographical Morality" Revisited: International Relations, International Law, and the Controversy over Placebo-Controlled HIV Clinical Trials in Developing Countries', *Harvard International Law Journal* 42, 2001, 299.

38   See Sampford, 'Get New Lawyers', 185–205; Sampford, 'More and More Lawyers but Still No Judges', 16–22.

39   The subject of numerous papers in the 2006 and 2008 International Legal Ethics Conferences.

military in Western states, the core values are the protection of the civil population and constitutional authority from external attack and, rarely, internal insurrection. For lawyers, the core values are the rule of law, due process, and human rights – sometimes packaged under an overall value of doing justice according to law. For the military, it is civilian control by constitutional authority (only using force when legally permitted) and that force should be used against citizens under very strict rules and specific safeguards. However, there is considerable overlap. The core values of the military reflect core values for lawyers. Likewise, the rule of law and human rights can be central to some conceptions of the role of the military. The Hon. Mike Kelly, Parliamentary Secretary for Defence, had argued that the military would be more likely to be successful if it subjected itself to the rule of law in interventions, because others knew when force would be used and when it would not.[40] In a workshop on 'Reconceiving the Rule of Law in a Globalizing World' in 2001, he argued that the Australian army was the largest human rights organization in Australia because it did more to further human rights through its peacekeeping operations than any other organization.

I emphasize *furthering* core values of the relevant profession. It is not sufficient for a profession to avoid actions that compromise their core values. Professions take a lead role in promoting certain values. Lawyers were critical in developing and proselytizing the rule of law and the institutional mechanisms to make it effective within strong sovereign states. The military have taken a lead role in the strongest democracies in emphasizing their subordination to the Constitution, to law and to constitutional authority. Lawyers and soldiers should now do the same in international affairs, recognizing that the profession of arms may be an ally. My earlier chapter set out an approach to the rule of law – as a contested concept with largely reinforcing and supportive meanings. It stands for a fundamental value or ideal, an ethic for lawyers and officials, the basic principles of constitutionalism and a set of institutions that supports its attainment. These meanings are appropriate for both the 'domestic' and 'international rule of law'. The rest of the essay discusses how the globalizing professions of arms assisted the former and may be play a critical role in developing the latter.

Role of the Legal Profession in Developing the International Rule of Law

If one looks at the various difficulties in developing and institutionalizing the international rule of law, one could conclude that, in many areas where the rule of law seems most needed, it is as distant as it would have seemed to those living under the largely absolutist regimes that emerged in Western Europe after the Treaty of Westphalia. The fact that the heroic efforts by lawyers and revolutionaries over several centuries led to a remarkable transformation in those

---

40   Discussions with the then Lt Col Kelly in 1999 during our work on an ARC linkage grant on 'Preserving and Restoring the Rule of Law in the Asia Pacific'.

states may offer little comfort. The international community cannot wait that long and cannot sustain the violent struggles that were often necessary for the rule of law to emerge domestically. However, the rule of law is a very strong domestic ideal on which we can build support. It is an ideal that is not only endorsed, but in many cases sincerely so, by various leaders' summits.[41] To make the attainment of an international rule of law realistic, there needs to be coordinated action to address some of the institutional limitations of international law. Lawyers can and should take a lead in such action – just as they did in the development of the domestic rule of law and the institutions that underpin it. This is not the time or place to set out a comprehensive strategy for building the rule of law in international affairs to match the rule of law in domestic affairs (something we hope to be closer to at the end of the above-mentioned projects). However, I will suggest some things lawyers may do and the reasons they may find unexpected allies in the military.

Developing and Promoting the Rule of Law as a Fundamental Governance Value in International Affairs

Just as lawyers were major contributors to the development and promotion of the rule of law in domestic affairs, so they should be in international affairs. However, they should not be so as narrow lawyers, but as lawyers who understand the philosophical, political and economic issues it raises. Indeed, they should recognize that the rule of law was developed at a time when those disciplines had not yet become distinct. While mastering these disciplines in their entirety is not a realistic goal for individuals, it is for groups of lawyers who respect those disciplines and bring their insights to bear.

If the rule of law becomes a fundamental value of the profession and a value that it uses to justify the profession, lawyers need to reflect carefully and debate publicly its meaning, value and relationship to the nature of the profession and its work to a global community.

Ethical Standard Setting through Codes

Lawyers can contribute to the articulation of more specific codes for lawyers and others – not least the military who are, as we have seen, potential allies in building the international rule of law. Lawyers should begin by developing a code of ethics for international lawyers and lawyers operating across borders. However, this should not be done in isolation. One of the most important underpinnings of the rule of law in modern states is the importance it plays in the ethics of key participants. Lawyers have 'duties to the court' or, more generally, to 'the law' or 'justice'. Civil servants are concerned with ensuring that all action taken in the name of the state has legal authority. More generally, the rule of law is an ethic

---

41   Such as the UN World Summit in 2005 (UNGA 15 September 2005, clause 134).

for the wielders of power – to exercise powers they have for the purposes that are entrusted to them. Codes need to be developed for:

- International lawyers; International judges and tribunal members; and international civil servants. Such codes cover a variety of issues but centrally concern how entrusted power is handled and a commitment to international law and the rule of law in international as well as national affairs. Lawyers have made a good start on developing voluntary codes. The International Bar Association consulted with the American Bar Association and the Council of Bars and Law Societies of Europe in October 2008 to create an anti-money laundering code that provides a risk-based approach to avoid participation in money laundering, including monitoring processes and training for lawyers. The International Bar Association has a two page 'International Code of Ethics'[42] and the Union Internationale des Avocats has developed the "Turin Principles for the Legal Profession in the 21st Century" (2002). The only area with developed codes that are authorized and (in theory at least) enforced by courts are in the International Court of Justice and the various ad hoc criminal tribunals for the Rwanda, Sierra Leone and the Former Yugoslavia. The NYU/UCL Project on International Courts and Tribunals (PICT)[43] developed a code of ethics for lawyers appearing before international tribunals. The committee (which included the author) met in London, Geneva Utrecht between June 2009 and April 2010, finally reporting to the International Law Association in August 2010.
- Member states and their delegates to General Assembly (GA), United Nations Security Council (UNSC) and international bodies (analogous to codes of ethics for parliamentarians in domestic systems).
- Military forces which are acting under UN authority and military forces engaging in international action – reflecting the same kind of respect for international law and particularly the UN Charter that they are expected to show for domestic laws and domestic constitutions.

The nature of the code development would vary depending on the work already undertaken and completed by others. In all cases, the code development should consider the dilemmas, apparent and real conflicts of duties, as well as the pressures and temptations of practice that may lead participants to 'read down' their ethical duties. However, the focus of the work will vary depending on the codes and principles already in place and the degree to which those codes and principles are controversial. For example, where there are rival codes or principles, it is very important to tease out the reasons for disagreement and make suggestions. Also, where most of the relevant ethics codes are domestic (for example, practicing lawyers and, to a lesser extent judges), it is important to deal with issues involving

---

42   First adopted in 1956, last amended in 1988.
43   See www.pict.org.

the extension of existing codes, potential conflict between codes, the relationship between the duties to domestic courts and clients and relevant duties to international courts and clients.

In all cases, the relationships between the codes must be considered carefully by examining the ways in which they may unintentionally conflict and ways in which they may be mutually supportive (for example, in the complementarity of the ethics of judges and advocates).

Once relevant international codes for lawyers acting and advising in international matters are developed, their principles should be incorporated into domestic legal ethics codes so that respect for international law and the rule of law in international affairs is built into the codes by which most lawyers practice. Similar domestic implementation should be followed in professional civil service codes and military ethics.

Other Forms of Ethical Standard Setting

The creation of codes is a high priority for a number of reasons. For example, there is a current opportunity to do so with the Project on International Courts and Tribunals (PICT) project and there is a great deal of disquiet about the 'torture memos' discussed elsewhere in this volume. Further, the creation of an international code will emphasize the responsibilities of international lawyers to the international legal system separately from their responsibilities as lawyers within their domestic jurisdictions; and such codes can provide inputs for those who want to reform the domestic legal ethics codes following the torture memos.

While the creation of codes is a high priority and is a natural activity for lawyers, it should be recognized that this does not exhaust the ethics of this or any other profession. If legal ethics were co-extensive with codes of ethics, two counter intuitive consequences would follow. First, it would mean that there would be no sense in complimenting or criticizing the ethics codes. Second, it would make no sense to criticize the ethics of some and praise others. It would be pointless to compliment Lord Goldsmith for the first advice and to criticize him for the second advice.[44] It would also be pointless for to refer to the temptation for clients to seek, and lawyers to give, the advice the client wants to hear rather than the advice the client should hear if they are facing court. If the client has no intention of accepting the jurisdiction of a court of competent jurisdiction, lawyers should make it clear that they will not give such advice or, if they do, they will not be acting as lawyers and there should be no privilege.

Before there are codes, people can debate what kind of conduct they admire as ethical and which they criticize as unethical. They can advocate new rules to bolster these normative claims. Even where there are codes in place, they generally set minimum standards of behaviour. There is room to articulate and

---

44 See Sampford, 'More and More Lawyers but Still No Judges', 16–22, for discussion and sources.

practise according to what the proponents believe to be higher standards. These will help set standards even while they are supererogatory. While they may affect code development, there will always be room for such higher standards, and they are part of a dynamic profession.

In all cases, the pressures for and against compliance should be considered. While the initial focus of code development would involve the clarification of ethical standards for those subject to the pressure, and those who may be applying the pressure, suggestions would also be made for institutional changes that remove or reduce dilemmas, temptations and pressures for unethical behaviour.

Simultaneously, the legal profession should be actively involved in strengthening institutions that will support the international rule of law and the participation of all states in it. Lawyers made tremendous contributions to the institutionalization of the rule of law domestically – not always succeeding, and risking occasional death or imprisonment.

Role of the Military in Developing the International Rule of Law

I will not spend as much time on the role of the military, as my research and expertise lies primarily in the profession of which I am a part. However, the following thoughts may be helpful.

As I have emphasized throughout this chapter, lawyers should seek suitable allies within the military. During the lead up to the Iraq war, two of those most implicated in what seems to most international lawyers to be a serious breach of international law were lawyers-turned-prime ministers. Prime Minister Blair appears to have been instrumental in persuading Lord Goldsmith to produce a short and misleading opinion claiming the proposed war would be legal, omitting the caveats in his original advice.[45] On 6 March 2003, Prime Minister Howard told the Australian Parliament that there was ample legal authority for the war, although virtually no legal authorities supported it.[46] Some members of the military behaved much more creditably. Admiral Sir Michael Boyce, the Chief of the UK armed forces, refused to cross the Kuwait border without written legal advice that the war was legal.[47] If the lawyers providing written advice for public consumption had been prepared to acknowledge the limited support their arguments had and the unlikelihood of being able to succeed in a court of competent jurisdiction, the British military may have stopped the war.

---

45 R. Whitaker, 'The Crawford Deal: Did Blair sign up for war at Bush's Texas ranch in April 2002?' *The Independent*, 27 February 2005.

46 Sampford, 'More and More Lawyers But Still No Judges', 16–22.

47 A. Barnett and M. Bright, 'British military chief reveals new legal fears over Iraq war', *Observer*, 1 May 2005.

Later in the Iraq war, it was serving soldiers who first reported and then leaked what had happened at Abu Ghraib.[48]

While soldiers who are also lawyers may play an important role, it is the respect for international law by other soldiers that is determinative. In the Kosovo and Iraq wars, JAG officers in the armed forces advised against some targeting.[49] The differential response of different militaries indicates the importance of their role and the extent to which the adherence to international law is built into their ethics and the way they see themselves serving their countries. In the Iraq war, this respect for JAG advice could have been motivated by an awareness of the ICC and the possibility of criminal conviction. However, the differential response in the Kosovo war indicates a difference in ethics of different militaries.

The idea of professional obligation is deeply entrenched in the military – so deep that they are prepared to die for it – something other professions are rarely called upon to do. But this is cross-fertilized by the fact that a number of military officers are members of two professions – with engineers and doctors being more numerous than lawyers. While being a member of two professions may be potentially confusing, it is more likely to help in developing codes in underdeveloped areas. Some cross fertilization between professions in the military may assist.

Conclusion

This chapter endorses the idea that the rule of law should become as fundamental a governance value within the international community as it is within sovereign states. The legal profession should take a lead in developing our understanding of that value and the ethical and institutional means of realizing that value. The military profession is a potential ally and Americans have traditionally been, and hopefully will again become, natural allies in this process. Our good work in the twentieth century has been tarnished by a poor end to the twentieth century and a poor start to the twenty-first. However, those who are either unduly optimistic or pessimistic about major institutional change might do well to recognize that history is, what I call, a 'long game'. But the way that long game will play out is not a matter of prediction but of action. What lawyers and soldiers do during the next 50 years will be crucial to how it plays out. Lawyers were critical to the crystallization of the rule of law in seventeenth-century England – soldiers all but undid it, and a bloody civil war almost destroyed the country. This century – or more likely quarter-century – we are playing for much bigger stakes. The international rule of law has been sufficiently conceptualized. This is the time when the international rule of law may be articulated, advocated and institutionalized. But we cannot afford a global civil war along the way. This is

---

48   Suzanne Goldenberg, 'Abu Ghraib leaked report reveals full extent of abuse', *The Guardian*, 17 February 2006.

49   Confidential but reliable source.

why the international rule of law must be a key goal of the newly cosmopolitan and globalizing legal profession – and the increasingly cosmopolitan profession of arms must go along with them – not just to avoid conviction in the ICC, but because of their conviction that internationally, as well as domestically, their use of force must be lawful.

Ten years ago, I was asked to deliver the final keynote the World Congress on Legal and Social Philosophy held in the World Trade Centre. I was asked to talk about sovereignty and intervention and I spent a good deal of time talking about the international rule of law. I drew a link between domestic and international rule of law and suggested that it was a great tragedy that the US, so long a leader in articulating and practising the domestic rule of law, was setting such a bad example in the international rule of law. When I described illegal bombing from 15,000 feet as a new 'high crime and misdemeanour' I was told I must be a Republican. Had my interlocutor known of Eisenhower's quote, he might have pressed me. But the answer is that the rule of law is neither Republican nor Democratic, Liberal or Labour, Left or Right. It is a fundamental governance value, a basic rule of the game – indeed it is the commitment to the idea that the game HAS rules.

One truly disturbing trend that has emerged is the abandonment of the rule of law by some who consider themselves conservative – or the oxymoronic category of 'neo-conservative'. The corollary of this trend is that the argument for the rule of law has so often to be run by the left, and those genuine conservatives who fight for it are often ranged against those who call themselves conservatives – and those conservatives who fight for it are treated as if they are left-wing radicals.

Let us hope that the implosion of the oxymoronic 'neo-conservatism' allows conservative, liberal and social democratic lawyers can make common cause on the rule of law – and take a lead in its realization internationally as well as democratically – bringing with them the profession of arms and the vocation of politics.

Chapter 7

International Civil Service Ethics, Professionalism and the Rule of Law

Lorne Sossin and Vasuda Sinha[1]

The idea of public service independence and its relationship to the rule of law is a topic that has been well-canvassed with respect to the operation of democratic principles within national contexts.[2] Less consideration, however, has been given to the question of whether an analogous set of ethical norms operates with respect to bureaucrats who work at the international level, in settings such as the United Nations and its agencies, the European Commission and other fora of multilateral governance. Given the established role of public service independence ensuring the rule of law within a state, at least two corollary questions arise when we consider international or global governance issues:

a. Is an independent, global or multilateral civil service a necessary precondition for an international rule of law?
b. By what mechanisms does the operation of bureaucracy in multilateral governance strengthen (or erode) the international rule of law?

In this brief chapter, we examine the ethics and professionalism of the international civil service – the individuals who collectively comprise the international organizations ('IO's) that exercise authority through the auspices of entities recognized by international law[3] – and reflect on the potential of the operation of such ethics and professionalism to define and enhance the concept of the international rule of law.

The rule of law is not self-executing. It depends on decision-makers understanding and respecting the limits of their authority and oversight mechanisms with the capacity and commitment to enforce the rule of law when necessary.

---

1   Valerie Crystal provided superb editing and research support for this chapter.

2   Lorne Sossin, 'Speaking Truth to Power? The Search for Bureaucratic Independence' (2005) 55 UTLJ 1; and a subsequent version of this research commissioned by the Inquiry into the Sponsorship Affair (the 'Gomery Inquiry') was published by the Gomery Inquiry as Lorne Sossin, 'Defining Boundaries: The Constitutional Argument for Bureaucratic Independence and Its Implication for the Accountability of the Public Service' (February 2006).

3   While there are many IOs which might fit these criteria, for the purposes of this study, we focus on the United Nations and its agencies.

While enforcement takes on a different character in international settings, the role of civil servants both in reflecting and instilling a rule of law culture is no less, and perhaps even more, important.

As in any public organization, the most significant bulwark against infringements of the rule of law is the rank and file members of the organization itself. Jose Alvarez describes the emergent role of international civil servants in these terms:

> Of course, the move to IOs has created a new category of actor on the world scene: international civil servants. These new non-state actors owe their power to their titles and function, whether we call them 'secretary general,' 'UN expert,' or 'special rapporteur,' or 'international judge.' Their capacity to act and their legitimacy as actors stem from the fact that they are agents of neutrality or of centralization. They are treated as legitimate insofar as they are not the mere agents of particular states but the representative of all of them, and perhaps of the global public interest. These actors are supposed to be autonomous from the nations they come from.[4]

The notion of an international civil servant's autonomy from her country of origin is important, as it suggests that her loyalty is owed not to that country, but to a different master. At a high level these questions about loyalty raise issues that are analogous to domestic tensions that have been examined in the context of liberal democracies, between a civil servant's political neutrality and the danger of civil servants advancing the partisan aims of a particular political party. In global and multilateral settings, the tension lies not between public servants and the partisanship of elected politicians but rather between public servants and the politics of national governments. Just as public servants also rely on elected politicians in liberal democracies for their legitimacy, so international public servants rely on national governments for their legitimacy.

In this study, taking the United Nations as the example, we explore how, as a matter of employment, international civil servants at the UN must follow direction from their supervisors, in a chain of command, with the Secretary-General as the Chief Administrative Officer. But UN officials, we suggest, must also be seen to owe a broader (and, when necessary, overriding) duty of loyalty to a set of foundational principles rooted in the global public interest, and the foremost such principle, we argue, is the international rule of law. While it is beyond the scope of this chapter to articulate fully the concept of an international rule of law, we suggest some of its constitutive elements below. We also highlight the evolutionary nature of these obligations. For example, while impartiality is a key element of the international rule of law, the nature of impartiality evolves in accordance with other global dynamics.

---

4   Jose E. Alvarez, 'Distinguished Speaker Series: Governing the World: International Organizations as Lawmakers' (2008) 31 Suffolk Transnat'l L Rev 591 at 597–8.

Our analysis of this claim proceeds in three parts. First, we attempt to situate the international rule of law within the foundational principles of the UN, and to ascribe to it some tangible features that impose obligations on those engaged in decision-making at the organization. Second, we explore the implications of the independence of the international civil service, and what mechanisms exist to resolve disputes which might arise around their potentially competing duties. Third, by way of conclusion, we suggest several areas of uncertainty which will need to be resolved if the international civil service is to function as guardian of the international rule of law.

Part One: The International Rule of Law

While ideas on the scope and nature of the rule of law will (and should) differ, the concept may be seen, at a minimum, to capture four central ideas. The first idea is that no one is above the law.[5] Those who hold power and influence, in other words, must abide by the same rules as those who do not. The second and related idea is that all power has limits.[6] Discretion is never unbounded and authority always comes with enforceable constraints. That is, no one can be empowered to act arbitrarily in relation to the rights and interests of others. Third, the rule of law includes a commitment to fairness and equality in the exercise of authority.[7] Fourth, the rule of law demands accountability and remedy where demonstrable infringements to fairness and equality have occurred.[8]

The Report of the Secretary-General on 'The Rule of Law and Transitional Justice in Conflict and Post-Conflict Society' elaborates a similar understanding of the rule of law within the UN:

> For the United Nations, the rule of law refers to a principle of governance in which
> all persons, institutions and entities, public and private, including the State itself,
> are accountable to laws that are publicly promulgated, equally enforced and
> independently adjudicated, and which are consistent with international human

---

5   See, for instance, A.C. Dicey, *Introduction to the Study of the Law of the Constitution* (London: Macmillan, 1915) at 189, where the author states: 'We mean in the second place, when we speak of the "rule of law" as a characteristic of our country, not only that with us no man is above the law, but (what is a different thing) that here every man, whatever be his rank or condition, is subject to the ordinary law of the realm and amenable to the jurisdiction of the ordinary tribunals.'

6   *Roncarelli v. Duplessis*, [1959] SCR 121 at 140 ['*Roncarelli*']. For a discussion of the significance of this case in the context of the rule of law, see L Sossin, 'The Unfinished Project of *Roncarelli*: Justiciability, Discretion and the Limits of the Rule of Law' (2010) 55 McGill LJ 661.

7   T.R.S. Allan, 'Deference, Defiance and Doctrine: Defining the Limits of judicial Review' (Winter 2010) 60:1 UTLJ 41 at 44.

8   *Roncarelli* at 142.

rights norms and standards. It requires, as well, measures to ensure adherence to the principles of supremacy of law, equality before the law, accountability to the law, fairness in the application of the law, separation of powers, participation in decision-making, legal certainty, avoidance of arbitrariness and procedural and legal transparency.[9]

Protecting and advancing the rule of law in domestic and international settings is at the heart of the UN's mission. As the Secretary-General's Report suggests, instilling respect for the rule of law is fundamental to resolving conflicts and to the transition from war to peace. It is also central to the promotion of human rights, social cohesion and economic development.

The General Assembly considered the rule of law as an agenda item several times in the 1990s; interest in this area has been renewed since 2006.[10] The Security Council has held a number of debates on the rule of law,[11] resulting in resolutions that speak to its importance in framing rights in the context of women, peace and security, children in armed conflict, and the protection of civilians in armed conflict.[12] According to the UN's 'Rule of Law' unit, over 40 UN entities are engaged in rule of law issues and the rule of law operations and programming takes place in over 150 countries in all regions of the globe, with the largest presence in Africa. At least five different entities are currently working simultaneously on the rule of law in at least 35 countries, with a focus on conflict and post-conflict situations.[13]

Principles underlying the rule of law are embedded in the Charter of the UN and pertain to the conduct of state-to-state relations. The UN's major components, including the General Assembly and the Security Council, which must accord with

---

9   S/2004/616. See also Secretary-General's report 'Uniting Our Strengths: Enhancing United Nations Support for the Rule of Law', A/61/636; and 'Strengthening and Coordinating United Nations Rule of Law Activities', A/63/226.

10   A/RES/61/39, A/RES/62/70, A/RES/63/128.

11   See S/PRST/2003/15, S/PRST/2004/2, S/PRST/2004/32, S/PRST/2005/30, S/PRST/2006/28.

12   http://www.un.org/en/ruleoflaw/index.shtml.

13   United Nations Secretary-General, Strengthening and coordinating United Nations rule of law activities, UNGA, 66th Sess, UN Doc A/66/133 (2011) at 3, online: UN <http://www.unrol.org/files/Third%20Annual%20Report%20of%20the%20Secretary-General.pdf>. The Rule of Law activities of the UN itself requires a substantial civil service commitment. Responsibility for the overall coordination of rule of law work rests with the Rule of Law Coordination and Resource Group, chaired by the Deputy Secretary-General and supported by the Rule of Law Unit. The membership of the Group consists of the Department of Political Affairs (DPA), the Department of Peacekeeping Operations (DPKO), Office of the High Commissioner for Human Rights (OHCHR), the Office of Legal Affairs (OLA), United Nations Development Programme (UNDP), The United Nations Children's Fund (UNICEF), UNHCR, the United Nations Development Fund for Women (UNIFEM) and the United Nations Office on Drugs and Crime (UNODC).

the Charter from which they derive, play a critical role in this regard.[14] However, it falls to the international civil service (and international judicial bodies such as the International Court of Justice and ad hoc criminal tribunals) to transform commitment to the rule of law into tangible action.[15] It is to a discussion of the ethics of the international civil service, including its commitment to the rule of law, which we now turn.

Part Two: Rules and Regulations Governing the International Civil Service

The Charter of the United Nations contemplates that a civil service is needed to bring the other commitments enshrined in its provisions to life. Article 97 of the Charter, for example, provides that the UN Secretariat 'shall comprise a Secretary-General and such staff as the Organization may require. The Secretary-General shall be appointed by the General Assembly upon the recommendation of the Security Council. He shall be the chief administrative officer of the Organization.'

Articles in the Charter that speak to the independence of the Secretary-General and her or his staff provide:

Article 100
1. In the performance of their duties, the Secretary-General and the staff shall not seek or receive instructions from any Government or from any other authority external to the Organization. They shall refrain from any action which might reflect on their position as international officials responsible only to the Organization.
2. Each Member of the United Nations undertakes to respect the exclusively international character of the responsibilities of the Secretary-General and the staff and not to seek to influence them in the discharge of their responsibilities.
Article 101
1. The staff shall be appointed by the Secretary-General under regulations established by the General Assembly.
2. Appropriate staffs shall be permanently assigned to the Economic and Social Council, the Trusteeship Council, and, as required, to other organs of the United Nations. These staffs shall form a part of the Secretariat.
3. The paramount consideration in the employment of the staff and in the determination of the conditions of service shall be the necessity of securing the highest standards of efficiency, competence and integrity. Due regard shall be

---

14   http://www.un.org/en/ruleoflaw/index.shtml.

15   For discussion of the commitment of these bodies to developing an international rule of law, see Chandra Lekha Sriram, 'International Rule of Law? A Comparative Analysis of Domestic and International Courts and Tribunals' prepared for the 'Ethical Supports for Strengthening the International Rule of Law' Conference of the Institute for Ethics, Governance and Law, 19 October 2009.

paid to the importance of recruiting the staff on as wide a geographical basis as possible.

Article 105

1. The Organization shall enjoy in the territory of each of its Members such privileges and immunities as are necessary for the fulfilment of its purposes.

2. Representatives of the Members of the United Nations and officials of the Organization shall similarly enjoy such privileges and immunities as are necessary for the independent exercise of their functions in connection with the Organization.

These provisions lay the groundwork for, and provide legitimacy to, an independent civil service within the UN, which is composed of public servants to the international community, who have an obligation to respect and promote the values of international law.[16]

The seemingly clear, traditional mandate of the international civil service notwithstanding, the boundaries of international civil service ethics are not easily defined. Civil servants at the UN owe a duty of loyalty to the UN and to follow the direction of those delegated authority within the organization. The Charter also speaks to the duty of UN civil servants to adhere to ideals of efficiency, competence and integrity and not to openly disparage their employer. Beyond these regular duties of an employee to his employer, the special context of the UN is taken also to impose broader duties on international civil servants to uphold fundamental UN principles (which include, of course, respect for the rule of law, as indicated above).

The primary source for civil servant ethics at the UN is the 'Staff Regulations',[17] the provisions of which include:

General rights and obligations
Regulation 1.2

---

16   See Aamir Ali, 'The International Civil Service: The Idea and the Reality, in International Administration' in *Law and Management Practices in International Organisations* (Chris de Cooker ed., Martinus Nijhoff Publ. and UNITAR, 1990). See also Jacque Lemoine, *The International Civil Servant: An Endangered Species*, Dordrecht: Kluwer Academic, 15–27 (1995).

17   According to the Staff Regulations, they are intended to 'embody the fundamental conditions of service and the basic rights, duties and obligations of the United Nations Secretariat. They represent the broad principles of human resources policy for the staffing and administration of the Secretariat. For the purposes of these Regulations, the expressions "United Nations Secretariat", "staff members" or "staff" shall refer to all the staff members of the Secretariat, within the meaning of Article 97 of the Charter of the United Nations, whose employment and contractual relationship are defined by a letter of appointment subject to regulations promulgated by the General Assembly pursuant to Article 101, paragraph 1, of the Charter. The Secretary-General, as the chief administrative officer, shall provide and enforce such staff rules consistent with these principles as he or she considers necessary'.

Core values

(a) *Staff members shall uphold and respect the principles set out in the Charter, including faith in fundamental human rights, in the dignity and worth of the human person and in the equal rights of men and women.* Consequently, staff members shall exhibit respect for all cultures; they shall not discriminate against any individual or group of individuals or otherwise abuse the power and authority vested in them ...

(c) Staff members are subject to the authority of the Secretary-General and to assignment by him or her to any of the activities or offices of the United Nations. In exercising this authority the Secretary-General shall seek to ensure, having regard to the circumstances, that all necessary safety and security arrangements are made for staff carrying out the responsibilities entrusted to them;

(d) In the performance of their duties staff members shall neither seek nor accept instructions from any Government or from any other source external to the organization;

(e) By accepting appointment, staff members pledge themselves to discharge their functions and regulate their conduct with the interests of the Organization only in view. *Loyalty to the aims, principles and purposes of the United Nations, as set forth in its Charter, is a fundamental obligation of all staff members by virtue of their status as international civil servants*;

(f) While staff members' personal views and convictions, including their political and religious convictions, remain inviolable, staff members shall ensure that those views and convictions do not adversely affect their official duties or the interests of the United Nations. They shall conduct themselves at all times in a manner befitting their status as international civil servants and shall not engage in any activity that is incompatible with the proper discharge of their duties with the United Nations. They shall avoid any action and, in particular, any kind of public pronouncement that may adversely reflect on their status, or on the integrity, independence and impartiality that are required by that status;

(g) Staff members shall not use their office or knowledge gained from their official functions for private gain, financial or otherwise, or for the private gain of any third party, including family, friends and those they favour. Nor shall staff members use their office for personal reasons to prejudice the positions of those they do not favour;

(h) Staff members may exercise the right to vote but shall ensure that their participation in any political activity is consistent with, and does not reflect adversely upon, *the independence and impartiality required by their status as international civil servants*;

(i) Staff members shall exercise the utmost discretion with regard to all matters of official business. They shall not communicate to any Government, entity, person or any other source any information known to them by reason of their official position that they know or ought to have known has not been made public, except as appropriate in the normal course of their duties or by authorization of the Secretary-General. These obligations do not cease upon separation from service ... [18] [Emphasis added].

While these provisions speak to a variety of ethical priorities, the highlighted passages above point to the importance of the twin ethical pillars of 'internationalism' and 'independence.' The principle of internationalism is somewhat self-explanatory: it requires international civil servants to conduct themselves not in the interests of particular states but in accordance with the multilateral interests of the UN. The meaning and implication of the principle of independence requires more careful elaboration. Most importantly, it raises the questions of from whom and what must international civil servants be independent: national governments? The UN General Assembly? Other international actors, such as multinational corporations and NGOs? To some extent, the independence of the international civil service must address each of these concerns. Independence requires objective guarantees and protections. In other words, if civil servants are vulnerable to being terminated or sanctioned for decisions which certain states dislike, independence may be compromised by the mere possibility of such a form of reprimand, without the need for any realization on the threat thereof. Independence is as much a matter of perception as one of reality.

A full discussion of civil service independence as a legal guarantee is beyond the scope of this study.[19] Generally, independence has been developed with the rule of law and fairness in the adjudicative process in mind. It is well established that international human rights law entitles each individual to a fair and public hearing by an independent and impartial tribunal in the determination of his or her rights and obligations. This right is expressly guaranteed in several international declarations and conventions, including the Universal Declaration of Human Rights,[20] the International Covenant on Civil and Political Rights, the European Convention for the Protection of Human Rights and Fundamental Freedoms and the American Convention on Human Rights.[21]

With respect to adjudicative independence, it has been observed, based on a wide-ranging review of state constitutions, legislation and supporting state practice, that 'the general practice of providing independent and impartial justice is accepted by

---

18   ST/SGB/2011/1. In addition to the Staff Regulations, a series of Staff Rules are also set out for UN civil servants, which cover a range of topics from the duty of loyalty to the Secretary-General, to conflict of interest and improper influence provisions, to discrimination and harassment, and rules prohibiting acceptance of gifts.

19   For discussion of independence as a legal guarantee both in national and international contexts, see Gerald Heckman and Lorne Sossin, 'How Canadian Administrative Law Protections Measure up to International Human Rights Standards' (2005) 50 McGill LJ 193.

20   GA Res. 217(III) UN GAOR, 3d Sess., Supp. No. 13, UN Doc. A/810 (1948) 71, Art. 10.

21   22 November 1969, 65 A.J.I.L. 679, Art. 8.

states as a matter of law' and is thus a customary norm of international law.[22] This is because adjudicative mechanisms that are both formally and operationally separate from the political cosmos within which they exists are needed to guard against political interference, or any appearance thereof, in the administration of justice. This principle is easier to invoke, however, than to implement, when we consider that the legitimacy of an adjudicative body derives not only from its independence but also its accountability to the same principles that it is meant to operationalize.

If the justice to be found at the United Nations is independent of the General Assembly and its member states, it raises the question of to whom and to what decision-makers and adjudicators are to be accountable. Clearly, the legitimacy of the international civil service derives, at least in part, from the UN's legislative arm, as the source of delegated authority. As such, bureaucrats within the UN must discharge duties that are set out in the resolutions and other legislative instruments of the UN, and must answer to the Secretary-General as set out above in the Staff Rules. While these bureaucrats must act to further the mandates created for them by the General Assembly as a whole, care must also be taken to ensure that those same bureaucrats not beholden to the whims of any particular member or interest within that legislative body. In this sense, the entrenchment and advancement of the rule of law in that international realm is requires independence and accountability being regarded as mutually reinforcing.

The international civil service does not exist in a vacuum. Rather, civil servants work for public bodies with particular mandates and powers. IOs are initiated by states attempting to serve public purposes. Starting in 1865, with the establishment of the International Telegraph Union, more than 80 IOs are now recognized. A number of these early IOs depended on impartial and independent administration (for example, the Bretton Woods agencies such as the International Monetary Fund). Such IOs typically enjoy immunity from the jurisdiction of member states' courts so as to preserve their independence and international character.

This commitment to independence in IOs evidences the normative importance of fairness and equity in the application of public authority that has been delegated outwards into the international realm. The effects of decisions made by IOs have the capacity of permeating into the lives of individuals worldwide, in areas ranging from the allocation of economic resources, humanitarian assistance, regulatory oversight, and military intervention. In light of the breadth of the nature of the decisions made and the wide constituencies that may be affected by them, fairness in the decision-making process is an important norm for achieving and maintaining the legitimacy of an international civil service.

---

22 Commission on Human Rights, Sub-Commission on Prevention of Discrimination and Protection of Minorities, *Independence and Impartiality of the Judiciary, Jurors and Assessors and the Independence of Lawyers – report by the Special Rapporteur Param Cumaraswamy*, UN Doc. E/CN.4/1995/39 (1995) at para. 35.

The ILO Administrative Tribunal

While the immunity of IOs vis-à-vis national courts is critical to their independent operation, a significant ancillary effect thereof was to preclude their employees from having recourse to any national employment laws. While organizational independence is one critical component to achieving the rule of law on an international level, the symbolic and actual value of such independence is undermined when the organizations that benefit from rule law of law principles do not act in accordance with them. In particular, the failure of an IO to treat its employees – i.e. the individual members of the international civil service responsible for making and implementing global policies and programmes – with the same kind of fairness and equity considerations under which the organization itself is able to operate, may well detract from the legitimacy of that organization as a manifestation and an agent of the international rule of law.

With these concerns in mind, historically, it fell on administrative tribunals generally, and the International Labor Organization (ILO) Administrative Tribunal (the 'ILO Tribunal') specifically, to elaborate and enforce the independence of members of the international civil service. The Tribunal was established in 1946 as the successor to the League of Nations Tribunal (1927 to 1946). The seven judges of the ILO Tribunal are appointed for three-year renewable terms by the ILO Conference, the highest organ of the ILO. The judges are of different nationalities and typically have been well-regarded judges in their countries. Usually, they sit in panels of three, but larger panels are permitted for exceptional cases. Another tribunal with a similar jurisdiction is the United Nations Administrative Tribunal (UNAT), established in New York in 1949 to receive complaints from the UN and the UN specialized agencies. The World Bank and the IMF also have their own administrative tribunals which deal with, among other disputes, complaints from staff at those organizations.

The ILO Tribunal (and, to a lesser extent, the other employment tribunals of multilateral entities) have performed a critical rule of law function in ensuring oversight in relation to the professionalism of the international civil service.

For example, in *Bustani v. Organization for the Prohibition of Chemical Weapons*,[23] the ILO Tribunal found that Jose Bustani was unlawfully dismissed from the post of Director-General of the Organization for the Prohibition of Chemical Weapons (OPCW)[24] in April 2002 as a result of political interference. In reaching this conclusion, the Tribunal affirmed the importance of the independence

---

23   Judgment No. 2232, Administrative Tribunal of the International Labour Organization, 16 July 2003 ('*Bustani*') available online at <http://www.ilo.org/public/english/tribunal/>.

24   The OPCW was established in 1997 under the 1993 Convention on the Prohibition of the Development, Production, Stockpiling and Use of Chemical Weapons and on Their Destruction (CWC).

of IOs and their secretariats, and condemned political interference by member states in their workings.

Bustani was appointed as the first Director-General of the OPCW in May 1997, with a four-year term. During his time at the OPCW, he and his inspectors oversaw the destruction of 2 million chemical weapons and two-thirds of the world's chemical weapons facilities. A year before the expiry of his term, the Conference unanimously extended it for another four years.

In March 2002, in the lead up to the American invasion of Iraq,[25] the United States submitted a no-confidence motion at the twenty-eighth session of the Council. Alleging mismanagement, demoralization of the Technical Secretariat, and ill-considered initiatives, the motion called for Bustani to resign. The motion failed, and the United States called a special, April 2002 session of the Conference, where the motion to dismiss narrowly carried.

In July 2002, Bustani commenced proceedings before the ILO Tribunal, claiming unlawful termination of his employment contract. For the first time in its history, the Tribunal reviewed the decision of an international organization to remove its head.[26] The Tribunal held, however, that a decision terminating the appointment of an international civil servant prior to the expiry of his/her term of office is an administrative decision, even if it is based on political considerations. The fact that the decision is a political one made by the UN's highest decision-making body cannot exempt it from the necessary review applying to all individual decisions which are alleged to be in breach of the terms of an appointment or contract, or of statutory provisions. Politics, in other words, does not come before law.

The Tribunal condemned the political interference exerted by states, and particularly the United States, in the operation of the OPCW. The Tribunal stated that 'the independence of international civil servants is an essential guarantee, not only for the civil servants themselves, but also for the proper functioning of international organisations'.[27] It argued that appointments for fixed terms are the means of ensuring that the heads of international organizations remain independent. If the Conference, for example, were given unfettered discretion to terminate Bustani's appointment, he and others would become 'vulnerable to pressures and to political change'.[28]

The Tribunal held that only in exceptional cases involving grave misconduct and the like should heads of international organizations be removed, but even then the decision to terminate such an appointment must be 'taken in full compliance

---

25   Bustani and Hans Blix both advocated a non-violent approach to claims about Iraq's possession of weapons of mass destruction.

26   The OPCW challenged the jurisdiction of the Tribunal to hear the case, alleging that the director-general position was a political appointee and not a civil servant able to challenge termination. The Tribunal ruled that Bustani was an 'official' and therefore able to seek a remedy before the Tribunal.

27   *Bustani* at para. 16.

28   Ibid.

with the principle of due process, following a procedure enabling the individual concerned to defend his or her case effectively before an independent and impartial body'.[29] Bustani received 50,000 euros in moral damages and 'the amount he would have received in salaries and emoluments' between the date of his dismissal and the end of his second four-year term.[30]

In a comment on this case,[31] David Caron and Ana Stanic observe that the ramifications of the case extend beyond questions regarding the independence of the OPCW, and go to the very foundation of the international legal and political framework. They note that the fundamental premises of our present international framework are the equality of states, the multilateral nature of international organizations, and the functional autonomy of such organizations. The *Bustani* case, in their view, highlights the urgent need to develop new procedures and mechanisms to ensure that international organizations and their staffs remain immune from such interference. Otherwise, the multilateral nature of the present international order will be reduced to being 'unilateralism in a multilateral disguise'.[32] Thus, cases such as *Bustani* are cautionary tales that cut both ways. On the one hand, the case demonstrates that there is a mechanism for accountability once the independence of the civil service has been compromised. On the other hand, this form of accountability did nothing to undo the decision, and is unlikely on its own to deter such occurrences in the future.

Other cases have led to more significant institutional changes. For example, the ILO Tribunal had earlier confronted the issue of citizens of Eastern European states in the international civil service during the Cold War. The general practice followed by the United Nations in recruiting national civil servants during the early 1980s was to request that the government concerned release them for UN service, whether on secondment or otherwise. Sometimes a candidate would resign from the national civil service, while other times, a secondment was arranged. A seconded civil servant, whose government was opposed to his or her reappointment by the Organization, could resign from the national civil service and be appointed as an international civil servant. This option was not available for staff members from Communist states.

The 1980 decision by the ILO Tribunal in *re Rosescu*[33] explored the issue of the independence of the international civil service from the perspective of proper and improper loyalties of civil servants. Rosescu, the complainant in the case and a Romanian citizen, joined the staff of the International Atomic Energy Agency (IAEA) in 1975 as a safeguards inspector, following a referral by the Romanian authorities, on a two-year contract. In 1977 the Romanian authorities asked the IAEA to extend Rosescu's contract for five years, but the Agency renewed the

---

29   Ibid.
30   Ibid. at para. 17.
31   (2004) 98 AJIL 810.
32   Ibid. at 814.
33   *In re Rosescu* (1980) ILOAT 431.

appointment for only two years. In June 1978, however, it was the IAEA that asked the Romanian authorities in writing whether they would agree to a five-year extension. This request was refused and the IAEA extended the appointment for only eight months. Rosescu appealed directly to the Tribunal with the agreement of the Agency.

The Tribunal ruled that the decision by the Director-General of the IAEA not to extend a fixed-term appointment of a safeguards inspector of Romanian nationality was reached through 'misuse of authority' because he let 'the interests of a member State [Romania, which opposed the extension of the appointment] prevail over the Agency's'. The Tribunal found that the letter seeking instructions from the Romanian authorities and the Director-General's compliance with the direction of the Romanian authorities represented an abuse of his authority. Although it was understandable for the Director-General to consult a state member before appointing one of its senior civil servants, Rosescu claimed, it was improper for the organization to consult after the appointment, since by then he had become an international official with independent status. Once again, rather than reinstatement, the Tribunal awarded the affected staff person with damages.

In commenting on the case, Theodor Meron identified the mischief at work in this case as the absence of any security of tenure among UN civil servants from Eastern Bloc countries. He observed:

> It is not necessary to discuss here the pros and cons of permanent appointments vis-a-vis fixed-term appointments. Suffice it to suggest that persons dependent on their governments' consent for reappointment and who have no prospects of permanent appointment often lack the moral courage to be truly independent international civil servants able to resist pressures from their governments.[34]

Cases such as Rosescu establish that independence within the international civil service depends on cutting the ties between those civil servants and their national state governments.

The UN Office of Administration of Justice

The UN's recognition of the need to entrench the application of a rule of law approach in the treatment of its own civil servants was recently evidenced by the General Assembly's resolution to establish the Office of Administration of Justice (OAJ).[35]

---

34 Theodor Meron, 'Note and Comment: In Re Rosescu and the Independence of the International Civil Service' (1981) 75 AJIL 910 at 923.

35 Administration of Justice at the United Nations, GA Res 61/261, UNGAOR, 61st Sess, Supp No 261, UN Doc A/61/261 (2007).

At the World Summit of 2005, the member states of the UN committed to a broad strengthening of the UN's oversight capacity, including the Office of Internal Oversight Services, expanding oversight services to additional agencies, calling for developing an independent oversight advisory committee, and further developing a new ethics office.[36] This initiative set in motion both the opening of various ethics offices to address disputes involving international civil servants and a restructuring of the UN's dispute resolution and justice system, that latter leading to the creation of the OAJ in 2009.[37] The OAJ's mandate includes providing a forum for addressing disciplinary measures that are taken against UN employees.

When an administrative decision is made that concerns the imposition of a disciplinary measure, or if it is a decision taken by the administration based on the advice of an expert or advisory board, the decision can be appealed directly to the newly established UN Dispute Tribunal. Article 2 of its governing statute outlines the purpose and scope of competence and jurisdiction of the Dispute Tribunal. Its substantive jurisdiction includes:

> 1. The Dispute Tribunal shall be competent to hear and pass judgement on an application filed by an individual, as provided for in article 3, paragraph 1, of the present statute, against the Secretary-General as the Chief Administrative Officer of the United Nations:
>
> (a) To appeal an administrative decision that is alleged to be in non-compliance with the terms of appointment or the contract of employment. The terms 'contract' and 'terms of appointment' include all pertinent regulations and rules and all relevant administrative issuances in force at the time of alleged non-compliance;
>
> (b) To appeal an administrative decision imposing a disciplinary measure;
>
> (c) To enforce the implementation of an agreement reached through mediation pursuant to article 8, paragraph 2, of the present statute.

In these matters the Dispute Tribunal has the power to make binding judgments once it has examined the facts of a case and conducted an oral hearing as necessary.

Decisions of the Dispute Tribunal can be appealed to the aptly named UN Appeals Tribunal. Article 2 of the Appeals Tribunal's governing statute sets out the general scope of its jurisdiction:

> 1. The Appeals Tribunal shall be competent to hear and pass judgement on an appeal filed against a judgement rendered by the United Nations Dispute Tribunal in which it is asserted that the Dispute Tribunal has:
>
> (a) Exceeded its jurisdiction or competence;
>
> (b) Failed to exercise jurisdiction vested in it;
>
> (c) Erred on a question of law;

---

36   See 'Implementation of Decisions from 2005 World Summit Outcome for Action by the Secretary General' A/60/430 (the '2005 World Summit Outcome') at p. 2.

37   A/RES/62/228; A/RES/63/253.

(d) Committed an error in procedure, such as to affect the decision of the case; or

(e) Erred on a question of fact, resulting in a manifestly unreasonable decision.

The very fact of the review mechanisms set out by the Dispute and Appeals Tribunals speaks to the entrenchment of the rule of law within the UN as it confirms the Organization's recognition of the necessity of permanent forum with clear procedures for examining administrative decisions that may compromise the independence and integrity of its civil service. This is further evidenced by the Secretary-General's Bulletin about the OAJ, which states:

> The Office of Administration of Justice is an independent office responsible for the overall coordination of the formal system of administration of justice, and for contributing to its functioning in a fair, transparent and efficient manner.[38]

The manner in which the OAJ, through the Dispute and Appeals Tribunals, helps to achieve fairness, transparency and efficiency in attaining the independence of the relationship between an international civil servant and the UN as her employer can be observed though some of the Tribunals' jurisprudence.

In *Hepworth v. Secretary-General of the United Nations*,[39] the Applicant, Hepworth, contested the decision of the Executive Director of the United Nations Environment programme to not renew his fixed-term employment as Executive Secretary of the Secretariat of the Convention of Migratory Species of Wild Animals ('CMS'). Included in the Applicant's grounds for complaint was an allegation that the decision not to renew his employment as Executive Secretary for the CMS was motivated by political considerations, and, more specifically, pressure and influence from the German Government to remove the Applicant from this post. The primary basis for the Applicant's allegation derived from two letters from the German Ministry for the Environment, Nature Conservations and Nuclear Safety to the CMS. The first letter was to the Applicant himself, asking that he turn his attention immediately to rectifying certain concerns that the German Ministry had with operations at the CMS. The second letter was addressed to the Executive Director of the CMS. In this letter the German Ministry expressed concern about the Applicant's failure to address the previously outlined concerns; the letter noted that rather than addressing the concerns, the Applicant instead hardened his position.

The Dispute Tribunal's consideration of the allegation occurred within an analysis of whether or not the non-renewal decision was 'based on improper motives or otherwise constituted an abuse of discretion.' The Dispute Tribunal ultimately found against the Applicant on this point. In its decision it noted that the Applicant's allegation was primarily based on letters from the German Ministry that expressed concern about the operations and management of the CMS Secretariat but did not

---

38   ST/SGB/2010/3.

39   Judgment No. UNDT/2010/193.

do so in manner that would 'allow the Tribunal to conclude that the decision not to renew the Applicant's appointment was due to political pressure'.

While this decision did not fall in the Applicant's favour, it does confirm that one function of the Dispute Tribunal is to ensure the political neutrality of administrative decisions affecting the employment of UN employees. That is, while in this case the Dispute Tribunal did not find that the decision not to renew the Applicant's appointment was influenced by undue political considerations, it is the fact that it considered the argument to be a legitimate one worthy of consideration that suggests the Dispute Tribunal is a mechanism for preserving the rule of law within the UN[40]

Gabaldon v. Secretary-General of the United Nations,[41] while not a case about politically motivated administrative decisions, is relevant insofar as the decision in the case confirms the existence of a unique relationship between the UN and its civil servants. In this case, Gabaldon, the Applicant, was offered a six-month appointment as a Humanitarian Affairs Officer. The offer was conditional on Gabaldon being cleared by a UN Medical Doctor, and it was to elapse automatically if he did not receive the required medical clearance. After he received the medical clearance, the Applicant fell ill. Prior to being able to commence his new appointment, he was required to re-sit for a medical exam; he was declared not fit, and his offer of appointment was subsequently withdrawn. When Gabaldon requested administrative review of the decision he was advised by the Administrative Law Unit of the Office of Human Resources Management at the UN Secretariat that he was not actually a staff member and the internal justice system was therefore not available to him.

Gabaldon appealed against this decision.[42] This appeal required the Dispute Tribunal to address the preliminary question of whether or not the Applicant held a contract of employment with the UN. The Dispute Tribunal ultimately held that the record did not indicate the Applicant received a letter of employment or that such a letter was ever signed by an authorized official. Accordingly, the Dispute Tribunal held that Gabaldon was never actually a staff member of the UN and therefore could not avail himself of its internal justice system. This decision was subsequently reversed by the Appeals Tribunal, which held that 'the UNDT Judge committed an error of law in denying Mr. Gabaldon access to the Tribunal solely

---

40   It should be noted that subsequent to this case being heard Hepworth received an unfavourable management review, which he unsuccessfully appealed again to the Dispute Tribunal in 2010. Hepworth went on to appeal that decision to the Appeals Tribunal in 2011 on the grounds that he was unlawfully denied the opportunity to call certain witnesses at trial, and was not permitted to able to consider the reasons for his transfer, among other grounds. The Appeals Tribunal agreed that a procedural error had been made, and sent the case back to Dispute Tribunal for 'a determination of the facts and the merits of the application'.

41   Judgment No. UNDT/2011/132.

42   Judgment No. 2011-UNAT-120.

on the grounds that the Appellant had never received a letter of appointment signed by an authorized official, without seeking to ascertain whether, following a thorough examination of the facts of the case, Mr. Gabaldon had satisfied all the conditions of the offer of employment and was entitled to contract-based rights with a view to his employment as a staff member within the Organization'.[43]

It is important to note that the Appeals Tribunal did not itself make a substantive determination on the obligations owed to Gabaldon, only that the Dispute Tribunal had erred in concluding that the absence of a signed letter of employment was itself sufficient to deny the existence of any such obligations. In this vein the Appeals Tribunal stated that it was for the Dispute Tribunal to determine if 'following a thorough examination of the facts of the case, Mr. Gabaldon had satisfied all the conditions of the offer of employment and was entitled to contract-based rights with a view to his employment as a staff member within the Organization'.[44]

While, at a high level, this case appears merely to be matter of employment and administrative law and practice within the UN, what is notable within the context of this study is the line of jurisprudence that was relied on by the Dispute Tribunal in its consideration of the merits. The Dispute Tribunal referred to the cases of *El-Khatib v. Secretary-General of the United Nations*[45] and *James v. Secretary-General of the United Nations*,[46] which both characterized the employment relationship between a UN employee and the UN as more than a contract between private parties. Accordingly, the reason for the Dispute Tribunal's rejection of Gabaldon's appeal was rooted in the 'special relationship between the United Nations and its civil servants'. The characterization of this relationship as special implies that particular rights and responsibilities arise from the relationship between the UN and its civil servants, and that those rights and responsibilities delineate the boundaries of the rules that the internal justice system has been mandated by the General Assembly to interpret and apply. Although the Appeals Tribunal rejected the Dispute Tribunal's narrow interpretation of the *El-Khatib* and *James* cases, notably, it did not reject the cases themselves. Instead, it appears that the Appeals Tribunal expanded the scope of their application by holding that if good faith offer and acceptance of a job within the Organization has occurred, the lack of a letter of appointment does not obviate an otherwise binding contract and the obligations that it entails. Accordingly, the Appeals Tribunal stated:

> a contract concluded following the issuance of an offer of employment whose conditions have been fulfilled and which has been accepted unconditionally, while not constituting a valid employment contract before the issuance of a letter of appointment under the internal laws of the United Nations, does create obligations for the Organization and rights for the other party, if acting in good

---

43   Ibid. at para. 31.
44   Ibid.
45   Judgment No. 2010-UNAT-029bis.
46   Judgment No. 2010-UNAT-009.

faith. Having undertaken, even still imperfectly, to conclude a contract for the recruitment of a person as a staff member, the Organization should be regarded as intending for this person to benefit from the protection of the laws of the United Nations and, thus, from its system of administration of justice and, for this purpose only, the person in question should be regarded as a staff member.

Although the Dispute Tribunal and the Appeals Tribunal differed as regards to what is required for an individual to constitute 'staff', most important within the context of this chapter is the fact that there was no dispute that an individual who does fall within that definition (whatever it is determined to mean) must be able to avail himself of the Organization's internal justice system.[47]

As jurisprudence of the OAJ develops, it appears to be further enshrining the role of basic principles underlying the rule of law in determining the obligations of the UN and its constituent bodies towards the individuals they employ.

In *Diop v. Secretary-General of the United Nations*,[48] the Applicant was a staff member of the United Nations Office on Drugs and Crime (UNODC) based in Mali, whose position was contingent on the project achieving sufficient funding. While such funding had been secured, in January, 2011, he received notice from his supervisor that his contract would not be renewed. Diop was later told by his supervisor that he had received a 'very embarrassing', yet confidential, email from the Minister of Justice in Mali. Subsequent to being so told, the Applicant requested reasons for the non-renewal of his contract, which were not given. When the Applicant asked the Minister of Justice in Mali about the email, the Minister denied it, and went on to provide a letter stating that he was completely satisfied with the Applicant's work.

At the Dispute Tribunal the Applicant argued that the decision not to renew his contract was based on the alleged email from the Malian Minister, and that this email should not be taken into account, as '[t]he staff of the United Nations enjoys independence in the exercise of their duties and this would be seriously compromised if the views of a Member State were taken into account when considering whether or not to renew a contract'. The Dispute Tribunal agreed, ruled in favour of Diop and ordered a suspension of the decision not to renew his contract pending review by management of the decision.

---

47   Two recent cases do suggest that while the Appeals Tribunal had employed an expanded definition 'staff' in the Gabaldon case, the Dispute Tribunal will impose limits on its own jurisdiction. Thus, for instance, in *Fagundes v. Secretary-General of the United Nations*, Judgment No. UNDT/2012/056, the Dispute Tribunal found it lacked jurisdiction where the applicant had been identified as a preferred candidate for a position, but had not actually been appointed to it. In *Basenko v. Secretary-General of the United Nations*, Judgment No. 2011-UNAT-139, the Dispute Tribunal held, which the Appeal Tribunal later upheld, that it lacked jurisdiction over a withdrawn offer for an unpaid UN internship.

48   Judgment No. UNDT/2012/029.

Included in the Dispute Tribunal's decision was a passage highlighting the importance of ensuring that employment decisions within the organization remain free of political interference from state pressures (in this case, pressure not from the Applicant's home state, but from the state in which the relevant project was operating):

> If any reliance was placed on an email purporting to come from the Minister of Justice of Mali in the decision-making process, it is morally offensive and unquestionably unlawful. Furthermore, reliance on a letter purportedly coming from the Ministry of Justice of a sovereign State which is a member of the Organization is not only embarrassing to the Organization itself, but could have far-reaching political and diplomatic consequences.[49]

In *Zedan v. Secretary-General of the United Nations*,[50] the Applicant had expected his position as Executive Secretary, Convention on Biological Diversity ('CBD') to be extended for two years, when it was actually renewed for only six months. While the Bureau of the Conference of Parties to the Convention ('COP'), the governing body of the CBD, had unanimously recommended that Zedan be given a new two-year contract, the United Nations Environment Program ('UNEP') had recommended a different candidate for the position of Executive Secretary. Zedan claimed that decision was essentially retaliation for complaints he had made regarding insufficient support from the UNEP. While the Dispute Tribunal refrained from comme nting on motivations that may have been underlying the decision, it ruled in Zedan's favour, awarding him US$70,000 in compensation.

Notably, the Dispute Tribunal's decision was premised on an understanding of the importance of transparency and the appearance of fairness in employment matters. Focusing on the fact that the Secretary-General had not been able to produce an audit trail of the decision to replace Zedan with the UNEP-recommended candidate, the Dispute Tribunal stated:

> As a general principle of good governance and administration, it should be obligatory on those involved in decisions on selection for recruitment or promotion to create and maintain proper records in order to give full effect to the commitment of the General Assembly to integrity and transparency at every stage in the decisionmaking process. Whilst this principle should be regarded as being of general application, it is of particular importance where the Secretary-General has personal responsibility for making the appointment. He must be

---

49 Ibid. at para. 35. In 2012, Diop once again applied to the Dispute Tribunal when his employer tried to find other means not to renew his contract. However, the UNDT stated that it had 'ample reason to suspect that this is a case of retaliation and/or pure prejudice in the decision-making process, given the history of the case'. The tribunal, once again, ordered the decision suspended pending management review.

50 Judgment No. UNDT/2012/006.

entitled to accept in good faith that when a recommendation is made to him, all
the necessary procedural requirements and safeguards have been complied with.
The integrity of the office requires no less.[51]

Transparency, openness and independence, the importance of which have been
underscored in the recent decisions of Zedan and Diop, are critical to maintaining
the rule of law in any context. The fact that these principles are highlighted by the
OAJ in its jurisprudence suggests an ongoing effort by the organization to play a
defining role with respect to identifying the obligations between UN entities and
their respective employees. Indeed, the combination of the developing case law
out of the Dispute and Appeals Tribunals, the body of jurisprudence emanating
from the ILO Tribunal, and the foundations in other legislative and executive
instruments at the UN, suggests that there is a non-partisan international civil
service that both owes and is owed loyalty vis-à-vis the UN.

The mutual obligation of loyalty evidences the embodiment of the UN as
guardian to a set of constitutive principles including the rule of law. If such a
broader obligation exists, it must mean that contexts exist where an international
civil servant's obligation to the rule of law (or other principles) will take
precedence over competing obligations. Working out the scope of such an
obligation, and the circumstances under which it may justify an international
civil servant's conduct which otherwise would be in contravention of a specific
order or direction, likely will fall to the Dispute Tribunal. In our view, as we
discuss below, it is possible to achieve both independence and accountability in
the oversight of the international civil service.

Part Three: Issues for Future Consideration Surrounding the Relationship between the International Rule of Law and the International Civil Service

The relationship between the independence and professionalism of the international
civil service has never been more closely observed. As in many domestic settings,
the reputation of international civil servants has become closely scrutinized and
criticized. As Alvarez has observed, 'Trust in international civil servants has
been … undermined by contemporary revelations (e.g., from the UN oil-for-food
scandal to widely publicized rapes attributed to UN peacekeepers).'[52]

Corruption, venality and abuse of power remain important threats to the
professionalism of international civil servants. The potential for external, national

---

51   Ibid. at para. 27.

52   Jose E. Alvarez, 'Centennial Essay: In Honor of the 100th Anniversary of the AJIL
and the ASIL: International Organizations Then and Now' (2006) 100 AJIL 324 at 344. For
details on these and other scandals involving international civil servants, see See Michael
N. Barnett and Martha Finnemore, The Politics, Power and Pathologies of International
Organizations, 53 INT'L ORG. 699 (1999).

political considerations to affect the composition of – and, therefore, the operations and policies pursued by – bodies within the UN is no less concerning, as the legitimacy and effectiveness of the decisions made by such organizations relies on their ability to make them independently. Given the political accord that animates the UN and other IOs, the first question we have considered is how to ensure accountability at the same time as guarding the independence of the international civil service.

Domestically, national constitutions provide for mechanisms of accountability. For example, in parliamentary democracies such as Canada, ministerial responsibility ensures political oversight over public administration. The General Assembly has no equivalent of Cabinet in this sense. Thus, alternative mechanisms of accountability for the actions of international civil servants remain an issue both for the UN and for its member states to address. In our view, transparency itself may be seen as a meaningful form of accountability. Therefore, requiring justification of employment-related decisions by UN officials, subject to review by independent oversight bodies such as the Dispute Tribunal, may provide a framework of accountability.

The second question we have considered relates to the need to safeguard the independence of the UN civil service from political interference. This non-partisan sphere cannot be guaranteed by legal and ethical precepts alone. If it is to be sustained, all participants and stakeholders in the UN must understand and appreciate the critical importance of its bodies (and those responsible for their operations) being able to make decisions free from the improper imposition of external political pressure. Again, in many domestic systems, this task of promoting and overseeing the professional ethics of the public service falls to non-partisan public bodies, such as Canada's Public Service Commission.[53] Certainly, the ILO Tribunal and now the OAJ play an important role in safeguarding the international civil service's independence by way of dispute resolution, and in articulating the administrative boundaries that must contain decision-making within the UN. However, the meaning, and perhaps even effect, of these formal activities risk being undermined if the Ethics Office that is charged with, *inter alia*, ongoing monitoring, training and oversight is not active and engaged in fulfilling these duties.[54]

The third and final question we have addressed relates to uncertainty about the duty of international civil servants to the international rule of law. Uncertainty about the nature and scope of the rule of law inexorably leads to the problem of whose definition of this concept ought to guide the international civil service. Does the rule of law require that international civil servants follow duly enacted directives from the General Assembly or should they refuse to follow and implement General Assembly directives that contradict core rule of law values such as fairness and equality? Are the individual laws that collectively rule to

53   See http://www.psc-cfp.gc.ca/index-eng.htm.

54   The Ethics Office was established by resolution, as a result of the above-mentioned, 2005 World Summit Outcome, A/Res/ 60/248. See also the Secretary-General's bulletin with respect to the Ethics Office, ST/SGB/2005/22 at para. 30.

be determined by international judicial tribunals, or is this determination open to subjective interpretation by the individual civil servants who are charged with implementing them? Must a civil servant be guided by how her supervisor approaches the rule of law? Is it up to international tribunals or national courts to delineate the scope of the rule of law?

These questions go to the heart of the independence of the international civil service and will define the possibility of any notion of the international rule of law becoming a reality. The ethical implications of the international rule of law for the UN civil service (or any global and/or multilateral public service) remain a work in progress. The advent of the OAJ and the Dispute and Appeals Tribunals suggests an improved infrastructure at the UN to explore the questions set out above. In so doing, the Tribunal will need to determine the cultural reference points for civil service obligations. While liberal democracies such as Canada provide only one example, we believe the experience of countries such as Canada demonstrates that an independent and accountable public service is vital to the development and application of the international rule of law. Or, put more starkly, without well understood and well accepted civil service values, the international rule of law will be little more than a hollow slogan.

Chapter 8

International Rule of Law? Ethics and Impartiality of Legal Professionals in International Criminal Tribunals

Chandra Lekha Sriram[1]

Introduction: International Rule of Law and International Courts

This chapter argues that despite being created to promote what might be called the international rule of law, international courts and tribunals have generally not been subjected to the degree of professional ethics regulation that domestic courts are, in ways that might affect the consistency of their operation with basic principles of the rule of law and could also affect their legitimacy. I suggest that more fully elaborated professional rules of conduct for judges, staff, and counsel should be developed, whether along the lines of regulations in most domestic jurisdictions, or model codes which have been proposed for international courts.

International rule of law might, in common with domestic rule of law, be defined in a wide variety of ways. Many, particularly positivist, definitions of rule of law at the domestic level have both procedural and substantive elements. The procedural requirements emphasize rules for the creation, application and enforcement of the law and the adjudication of the rights and duties created by the law.[2] Substantive requirements involve concepts of justice, often understood in terms of equal respect and protection of fundamental human rights. Any core concept of rule of law might include many of the principles laid out by the United Nations (UN) Secretary-General in his 2004 report on the subject in the context of states emerging from conflict, which includes principles of supremacy of the law, equality before the law, legal certainty, fairness in application of the law, avoidance of arbitrariness, and procedural and legal transparency. It entails a range of protections for the accused as well as addressing past wrongs and protection of the interests of victims.[3]

---

1 cs79@soas.ac.uk. I would like to thank Olga Martin-Ortega and Vesselin Popovski, and participants in the October 2009 conference on Ethical Supports for an International Rule of Law at CIGI for extremely helpful comments on earlier drafts. Any errors are mine alone.

2 H.L.A. Hart, *The Concept of Law* (Oxford: Clarendon, 1961).

3 *The Rule of Law and Transitional Justice in Conflict and Post-Conflict Societies. Report of the Secretary-General*, UN Doc. S/2004/616 (August 23, 2004), paras 6–7. Of course, rule of law promotion in post-conflict settings confronts particular challenges not present in ordinary domestic settings. Chandra Lekha Sriram, Olga Martin-Ortega, and

Such principles should, ideally, be transposable to the international level, where we might expect that international courts and tribunals would follow similar principles.[4] In *Uniting Our Strengths. Enhancing United Nations Support for the Rule of Law*, the UN Secretary-General treats rule of law at the international level as related to documents, processes, and institutions such as the Charter of United Nations, multilateral treaties, international dispute resolution mechanisms, the International Criminal Court (ICC) and advocacy, training and education regarding international law.[5] While UN-led initiatives such as the *Bangalore Principles of Judicial Conduct*, and the office of the UN Special Rapporteur on the Independence of Judges and Lawyers demonstrate a commitment to professionalism in the legal sector at the national and international levels, specific rules of professional ethics for international tribunals remain scarce, even though these tribunals are considered pillars of international rule of law.[6] The relative dearth of such professional regulations and the potential for deviation from the rule of law that may follow may undermine the legitimacy of international courts and tribunals.

In this chapter, I focus specifically on international and internationalized criminal tribunals rather than the wider array of international courts and tribunals for reasons of space and comparability, but do observe that other international courts have relatively limited ethical regulations. However, as I discuss in more detail, the relative absence should be of particular concern in international *criminal* proceedings both because the due process rights of individuals who are at risk of losing their liberty are at stake, and because the institutions themselves purport to uphold human rights norms.

International Rule of Law and the Problem of Legitimacy

Why should we care about whether international courts and tribunals are perceived as legitimate? As Thomas Franck so cogently argued, states are more likely to comply with international legal regimes which are perceived as legitimate. He argues that legal regimes have a greater compliance pull if they have four features. The first, determinacy, is the clarity of a rule. The second, symbolic validation,

---

Johanna Herman (eds), *Peacebuilding and Rule of Law in Africa: Just Peace?* (London: Routledge, 2010).

4   See Simon Chesterman, "An International Rule of Law?" *The American Journal of Comparative Law* vol. 56 (2008), pp. 331–61, on the challenges of defining rule of law at the international level, and elaborating on a range of understandings of what it might mean.

5   *Uniting Our Strengths. Enhancing United Nations Support for the Rule of Law*, UN Doc A/61/636-S/2006/980 (December 14, 2006).

6   The Bangalore Principles of Judicial Conduct (2002), at http://www.unodc.org/pdf/crime/corruption/judicial_group/Bangalore_principles.pdf; the webpage of the Special Rapporteur on the Independence of Judges and Lawyers can be found at: http://www2.ohchr.org/english/issues/judiciary/index.htm.

involves the ritual and pedigree of particular rules. The third, coherence, involves the coherent and consistent application of a rule. Finally, adherence to a normative hierarchy involves the way in which rules are interpreted are consistent with a primary rule of obligation. While Franck was examining legitimacy of legal regimes, rather than specific courts or institutions which might apply the law, the same logic and criteria might apply.[7] While international courts and tribunals might apply relatively determinate rules, they may be subject to challenge on the other three criteria. States, and state officials, often challenge the pedigree of rules which challenge their power, suggesting for example that certain aspects of international criminal law or international human rights law are shaped by Western states and values and are an illegitimate imposition from outside. Similarly, states and state officials under scrutiny by international courts often challenge the courts' legitimacy by claiming the institutions themselves are improperly selective.[8] Institutions such as the ad hoc tribunals for the former Yugoslavia and Rwanda faced early challenges that their very creation by the United Nations Security Council (UNSC) was an improper exercise of power by that body, and that their creation by a political body undermined their legal integrity and credibility.[9] The fact that the UNSC can refer situations to the International Criminal Court and also has the authority to defer proceedings at the court for 12 months has also been criticized as a politicization of a judicial body.[10] Finally, some states and officials sometimes claim that the institutions themselves deviate from their own

7   Thomas Franck, *The Power of Legitimacy among Nations: Fairness in International Law and Institutions* (Oxford: Oxford University Press, 1990); Thomas M. Franck, "Legitimacy in the International System," *American Journal of International Law* vol. 82 (1988), pp. 705–59.

8   This has been the cornerstone of complaints by the Sudanese regime in response to the arrest warrant issued by the International Criminal Court for President Omar al-Bashir. For a scholarly analysis of the issue of selectivity, see Robert Cryer, *Prosecuting International Crimes: Selectivity and the International Criminal Law Regime* (Cambridge: Cambridge University Press, 2005).

9   Vesselin Popovski, "Legality and Legitimacy of International Criminal Tribunals," in Richard Falk and Vesselin Popovski (eds), *Legality and the Legitimacy of International Order* (Oxford: Oxford University Press, 2011). International Criminal Tribunal for the former Yugoslavia, *Prosecutor v. Dusko Tadic, Decision on the Defence motion for interlocutory appeal on jurisdiction* (October 2, 1995) at http://www.icty.org/x/cases/tadic/acdec/en/51002.htm; International Criminal Tribunal for Rwanda, *Prosecutor v. Kanyabashi, Decision on Jurisdiction*, Case No. ICTR-96-15-T (June 18, 1997).

10   Rome Statute for an International Criminal Court, Articles 13(b) and 16; see generally Mahnoush H. Arsanjani, "The Rome Statute of the International Criminal Court," *The American Journal of International Law* vol. 93, no. 1 (Jan., 1999), pp. 22–43. However, it is worth noting that the ICC is considerably more independent of the UNSC than some earlier drafts of the statute by the International Law Commission envisioned and more than the United States would have preferred. See William A. Schabas, "United States Hostility to the International Criminal Court: It's All about the Security Council," *European Journal of International Law* vol. 15, no. 4 (2004), pp. 701–20.

principles.[11] Recent challenges to the legitimacy of the International Criminal Court by indicted Sudanese President Omar al-Bashir, member states of the African Union, and others are illustrative in this regard.[12]

The 2004 report of the UN Secretary-General on rule of law similarly emphasizes that clear adherence to principles of rule of law is important to state legitimacy in the domestic context. Some socio-legal scholars have also suggested, in the domestic context, that adherence to the law occurs less out of fear of punishment than out of a belief that laws have been properly constituted and implemented, even if individuals disagree with their content.[13] So too would such a belief be critical in principle to the legitimacy of a range of international bodies, including international courts. This may be particularly so, given that such courts are often accused of having a democratic deficit. Proponents of the democratic deficit argument claim that because such courts are not democratically accountable to the populations of individual states, they are not legitimate. Such courts are also subject to attacks which question their legitimacy for purely political reasons.[14] In the context of assertions that there is no functional rule of law at the international level in the wake of the US-led invasion of Iraq, international bodies, such as courts, purporting to promote rule of law may be subject to stricter scrutiny.[15]

International courts and tribunals are designed to adjudicate disputes regarding state adherence to international legal obligations and in some instances to impose individualized criminal accountability for violation of the most serious crimes in international law. As such, they might be assumed to be critical elements in the promotion of international rule of law, and that they are as such well-regulated procedurally and ethically. They generally do adhere to key principles of the rule

---

11   Brandeis Institute for International Judges, "Toward the development of ethics guidelines for international courts," (July 24, 2003), p. 6, at http://www.brandeis.edu/ethics/pdfs/internationaljustice/ethics/EthicsGuidelines.pdf.

12   Robert Cryer, "Prosecuting the Leaders: Promises, Politics and Practicalities," *Göttingen Journal of International Law*, vol. 1, no. 1 (2009). pp. 45–75.

13   Tom Tyler, *Why People Obey the Law* (Princeton: Princeton University Press, 2006).

14   On the "democratic deficit," see Madeline Morris, "The Disturbing Democratic Deficit of the International Criminal Court," *Finnish Yearbook of International Law* vol. 12 (2001), pp. 109–18; but compare Leila Nadya Sadat, "The International Criminal Court and Universal International Jurisdiction: A Return to First Principles," in Thomas J Biersteker, Peter J. Spiro, Chandra Lekha Sriram, and Veronica Raffo (eds), *International Law and International Relations: Bridging Theory and Practice* (London: Routledge, 2006). The tirades of Slobodan Milosevic before the International Criminal Tribunal for the Former Yugoslavia are an example of an individual with a vested interest challenging the legitimacy of an international court.

15   Balakrishnan Rajagopal, "Invoking the Rule of Law: International Discourses," in Agnes Hurwitz and Reyko Huang (eds), *Civil War and the Rule of Law: Security, Development, Human Rights* (Boulder, CO: Lynne Rienner, 2008), pp. 58–61, makes this point cogently.

of law, including due process and the promotion of substantive justice; they may nonetheless face serious legitimacy challenges.

Legitimacy may depend not merely on the procedural and substantive elements of court proceedings themselves outlined above, but clear protections that underpin due process, such as ethics and professional regulations. Yet many international courts lack ethics regulations for attorneys, staff, or judges, despite the risks of corruption and abuse that might arise. Even at the ad hoc international criminal tribunals for the former Yugoslavia and Rwanda, regulations were developed rather late, and partly in the wake of serious allegations of corruption. The International Criminal Court does have more robust professional ethics rules, yet it is worth noting that even at the ICC, such rules are less developed than in a range of domestic jurisdictions. Further, controversy over the treatment of evidence and witnesses in the court's first completed prosecution against Thomas Lubanga Dyilo suggests further refinement of ethics rules might be in order. The absence of such protections may weaken the real and perceived protections of both due process and substantive rights in practice.

International Courts and Tribunals: Limited Professional Ethics Regulations

As would be expected, major international courts and tribunals have significant rules of procedure and evidence to guide their daily operation. Yet many such courts have limited rules or in some cases no rules of professional or ethical conduct. The International Court of Justice (ICJ), for example, has detailed rules of court with over 100 articles, but there are no specific codes of conduct for judges or counsel. The absence of specific codes of conduct for judges at the ICJ might be of particular concern, given that each is nominated by his/her country and might be expected, or at least perceived, to be biased in cases involving that country's interest.[16] Tribunals such as the International Tribunal for the Law of the Sea, the Inter-American Court of Human Rights, and the European Court of Justice similarly lack such codes. The European Court of Human Rights has no official codes, although the plenary of the court adopted a resolution on judicial ethics in mid-2008, comprising just two substantive pages.[17]

This lack of formal ethics regulations may seem surprising in comparison to the extensive regulations present in many domestic jurisdictions, as I discuss below. It might seem particularly surprising if we consider that such tribunals are expected to not only uphold the substantive rules of law embedded in the treaties

---

16   International Court of Justice, *Rules of Court* (1978). See Leigh Swigart, "Symposium: Judicial Ethics and Accountability: At Home and Abroad: The "National Judge": Some Reflections on Diversity in International Courts and Tribunals," *McGeorge Law Review* vol. 42 (2010), p. 223; Frederic Mégret, "The Judge Who Talked Too Much," in this volume for a discussion of these risks.

17   European Court of Human Rights, *Resolution on Judicial Ethics* (June 23, 2008).

and conventions which they apply and present in customary international law, but are also meant to enforce rule of law at the international level. As in domestic jurisdictions, the preservation of rule of law might be expected to depend upon judges and counsel behaving in an ethical, professional fashion. One explanation for the absence of such regulations in many international courts might be that, save for the courts considering human rights claims against states, the proceedings heard in the bodies noted here involve claims of one state against another, and thus that individual punishment and due process are not at stake. If this is the case, we might therefore expect that international courts which involve criminal trials of individuals would have significantly higher ethical and professional standards, but as we shall see these regulations are still relatively limited and were generally created only some time after the creation of the original institutions. There have been several efforts to create model codes of conduct for counsel in international tribunals for just this reason, without great success.[18]

Are International Criminal Tribunals any Different?

We might expect that the International Criminal Court, and two ad hoc international criminal tribunals, the International Criminal Tribunal for the former Yugoslavia (ICTY) and the International Criminal Tribunal for Rwanda (ICTR) would have greater protections and regulations in place than are present in other international courts and tribunals. After all, they were designed to punish violations of the most severe crimes in international law, crimes that violate *jus cogens* norms, which are peremptory norms in the international system because they are understood to be fundamental. And indeed, international criminal tribunals and trials are often expected not merely to prosecute crimes, but to contribute to a range of other social goods, including domestic reconciliation, the establishment of an historical record, promotion of the interests of victims, and promotion of democratization and rule of law in the societies affected. They are clearly different than ordinary courts, whether at the international level where state obligations rather than individual rights and harms are at stake, or at the domestic level where narrower expectations are placed on courts, even those trying serious criminal offenses.[19]

---

18   United Nations Guidelines on the Role of Prosecutors (adopted at the Eighth United Nations Congress on the Prevention of Crime and the Treatment of Offenders, Havana, Cuba, August 27 to September 7, 1990) at http://www2.ohchr.org/english/law/prosecutors. htm; International Prosecutors Association, Standards of Professional Responsibility and Statement of the Essential Duties and Rights of Prosecutors (April 23, 1999) at http://www. iap-association.org/ressources/Standards_English.pdf and adopted by the United Nations Economic and Social Council, UN Doc. E/CN.15/2008/L.10/Rev.2 (April 17, 2008).

19   Jenia Iontcheva Turner, "Legal Ethics in International Criminal Defense," *Chicago Journal of International Law* vol. 10, no. 2 (2010), p. 2, 7–13, 30; Chandra Lekha Sriram, *Confronting Past Human Rights Violations: Justice vs Peace in Times of Transition*

Building upon such a normative foundation, we might ask, how can such institutions not be subject to ethical regulations? Are they not meant to promote norms of the greatest importance in international law? Their legitimacy might be expected to be secure precisely because of the norms and goals they purport to promote.[20] There has been what some analysts consider a "euphoria" surrounding institutions such as the International Criminal Tribunals for the former Yugoslavia and Rwanda, as well as the International Criminal Court, as it has been almost an article of faith for liberal international lawyers that such bodies could do good, rectifying past evils such as genocide, war crimes, and crimes against humanity.[21] However, if we examine the institutions more closely, we find that the guiding norms of their operation are procedural rather than substantive, and that they were created in general some time after the institutions themselves. While today, staff may be removed for reasons of professional misconduct, the emphasis upon such formal professional norms only followed serious breaches such as corruption scandals at both ad hoc tribunals, rather than being put in place at the inception of the tribunals. Further, such rules and penalties imposed on violators have not prevented serious acts and allegations of misconduct, particularly at the ICTR. Before turning to scandals at each tribunal that should give us cause for concern, it is worth first examining the formal codes of professional conduct in place at the ICTY, the ICTR, and the ICC.

International Criminal Tribunals: The Formal Protections

Professional regulations for judges
International criminal tribunals have more fully developed ethical regulations than the other, non-criminal, international courts noted briefly above. The International Criminal Court's regulations in particular represent an advance upon those of the ad hoc tribunals: the ICC has a code of judicial ethics governing acceptable behavior by judges regarding duties of confidentiality, impartiality, independence, public expression, and extra-judicial activities. They also note the need to avoid not only impropriety, but the appearance of impropriety.[22]

(London: Frank Cass, 2004), pp. 1–14; Sriram, *Globalizing Justice for Mass Atrocities: A Revolution in Accountability* (London: Routledge 2005), pp. 53–8.

20   Wayne Sandholtz, "International Criminal Tribunals: Authority and Legitimacy" draft manuscript at www.cgpacs.uci.edu/files/ /sandholtz_criminal_tribunals.doc (no date); see generally Bruce Cronin, *Institutions for the Common Good: International Protection Regimes in International Society* (Cambridge: Cambridge University Press, 2003).

21   Payam Akhavan, "The International Criminal Court in Context: Mediating the Global and the Local in the Age of Accountability," *American Journal of International Law* vol. 97 (2003), p. 712. Akhavan, formerly a legal adviser in the Office of the Prosecutor of the ICTY, is well placed to note the euphoria and its limitations.

22   *Code of Judicial Ethics* ICC-BD-02–01–05 http://www.icc-cpi.int/library/about/officialjournal/ICC-BD02–01–05_En.pdf. The presence of such ethical guidelines, however,

Extra-judicial activities, or activities prior to the initiation of judicial service, are less clearly regulated and can raise significant concerns, particularly with regard to the appearance of bias and impropriety whether or not either actually exist. Thus a serious challenge was mounted at the Special Court for Sierra Leone to remove Lord Robertson as a justice because of comments he had made with a book *Crimes against Humanity* about the nature of the Revolutionary United Front.[23] The ad hoc tribunal for Yugoslavia, too, had to grapple with assessing the fact or appearance of judicial bias.[24]

Professional regulations for staff
Staff regulations similarly place a number of ethical obligations upon employees of the court, and also require them to act in accordance with the "core values" of the court: fundamental human rights and dignity and respect for all cultures.[25] There exists a code of ethics for interpreters and translators as well, which also require them to behave in a "courteous, polite, and dignified manner at all times" in addition to specific professional ethics, such as confidentiality and refraining from exercising power or influence over their listeners.[26]

Professional regulations for counsel
International criminal tribunals clearly need strict guidelines for the practice of counsel, both prosecutorial and defense. There is no reason to presume that all those engaged in the lofty practice of international justice will necessarily behave morally, ethically, or even legally. However, both the ICTY and the ICTR experienced long delays in the creation of the formal rules that they do now have, in respect of both prosecution and defense counsel, and neither has a formal set of rules regulating judges. While counsel before the ICTY and ICTR were already

---

is no guarantee of consistency of rules of consensus on substance. See "Toward the Development of Ethics Guidelines for International Courts," (July 24, 2003). http://www. brandeis.edu/ethics/resources/publications/EthicsGuidelines.doc. On judicial independence, see Theodor Meron, "Judicial Independence and Impartiality in International Criminal Tribunals," *American Journal of International Law* vol. 99 (April 2005), pp. 359–69; see also William A. Schabas, "Judicial Ethics and the International Criminal Judiciary" in this volume.

23   Robertson refused to recuse himself despite defense claim of the appearance of bias, but he was removed pursuant to rule 15 of the Court. Melissa Pack, "Developments at the Special Court for Sierra Leone," *The Law and Practice of International Courts and Tribunals* vol. 4, no. 1 (2005) pp. 184–6. On the circumstances in which judges should recuse themselves, see Meron, "Judicial Independence and Impartiality." See also Mégret, "The judge who talked too much," in this volume.

24   Human Rights Watch, "Ethics" at http://hrw.org/reports/2004/ij/icty/10.htm.

25   *Staff Regulations* ICC-ASP/2/10 (8–September 12, 2003) http://www.icc-cpi.int/ library/about/officialjournal/Staff_Regulations_120704-EN.pdf.

26   *The Code of Ethics for Interpreters and Translators Employed by the International Criminal Tribunal for the Former Yugoslavia* IT/144 at http://eee.un.org/icty/basic/ codeinter/IT144.htm.

required to be licensed in their home jurisdictions, most of which would have ethical codes of conduct, these vary widely across legal systems. Further, counsel who are sanctioned by the tribunals can be removed from service, but further sanction such as disbarment is at the discretion of the home jurisdiction. Thus the importance of uniform rules for counsel at each institution.

Nonetheless, each institution did not impose such professional regulations until well after its creation. The ICTY did not have an enforceable code of conduct for counsel until a decade after it came into existence. An initial code of conduct for counsel appearing before the tribunal was created in 1997, some four years after the establishment of the tribunal, but without significant enforcement. An association for defense counsel practicing at the ICTY was created only in 2002.[27] A set of standards of professional conduct were only set forth for the office of the prosecution at the ICTY in 1999 and comprised three pages.[28] There are no specific codes of professional conduct in place for judges at the ICTY.[29] The ICTR similarly put in place a code of conduct for defense counsel in 1998 and one for prosecutors in 1999, but no specific code of judicial ethics has been promulgated.[30]

By comparison, in addition to the code of judicial ethics, the ICC has a code of professional conduct for counsel operating before it, each adopted about three years after the statute of the court entered into force.[31] The code of conduct for counsel, while quite detailed, and providing that counsel are "personally responsible for the conduct and presentation of the client's case and shall exercise personal judgment on the substance and purpose of statements made and questions asked,"[32] does not indicate what counsel should do should a client decide to lie. There is no guidance as to whether counsel should prevent such testimony, a genuine challenge given that defense counsel also have a clear duty to their clients.[33] However, while a draft code of professional conduct was prepared in 2003 for the Office of the Prosecutor

---

27 Judith McMorrow, "Creating Norms of Attorney Conduct in International Tribunals: A Case Study of the ICTY," *Boston College International and Comparative Law Review* vol. 30 (2007), p. 158. See also *Code of Professional Conduct for Counsel Appearing before the International Tribunal* (As Amended July 12, 2002 and June 29, 2006), IT/125 Rev. 2.

28 McMorrow, "Creating Norms of Attorney Conduct in International Tribunals," pp. 162–3.

29 Ibid., p. 165.

30 International Criminal Tribunal for Rwanda, *Code of Professional Conduct for Defence Counsel* (June 8, 1998); International Criminal Tribunal for Rwanda, *Prosecutor's Regulation No. 1 of 1999; Prosecutor's Regulation No. 2 of 1999; Prosecutor's Regulation No. 1 of 2005.*

31 *Code of Professional Conduct for Counsel* ICC-ASP/4/Res.1 (December 2, 2005); *Code of Judicial Ethics* ICC-BD/02–01–05 (2005).

32 ICC Code of Conduct, Article 24(2).

33 Turner, "Legal Ethics in International Criminal Defense," pp. 38–44.

(OtP), it was never adopted.[34] While in 2009 the OtP developed its own internal regulations, they include limited reference to professional ethical standards, referring to wider staff regulations requiring efficiency, competence and integrity.[35]

Protection of victims, witnesses, and the rights of the accused
Procedural regulations requiring the professional behavior of staff are not the only ways in which ethical concerns and the rule of law might be safeguarded before international criminal tribunals. Given that these institutions are relatively unique in prosecuting some of the most serious crimes in international law, particular concern for the needs and safety of victims and witnesses is merited. The ad hoc courts, the ICC, and hybrid courts such as the Special Court for Sierra Leone, have victims and witnesses sections to protect and in some cases to offer counseling to individuals who come before the courts in one or both of these capacities.[36] These are all formal regulations without any evident wider ethical aspirations, save for the regulations pointing to core values, or those seeking to offer special protections to victims and witnesses.

The rights of the accused should be protected in domestic or international criminal proceedings, regardless of the nature or seriousness of the charges leveled against her. This is both a matter of preserving the principle of due process, but also, according to some, an essential criterion for the legitimacy of international courts.[37] However, despite commitment to due process in international courts, the rules for protection of the accused have been relaxed in some cases. While in most instances the accused would have a right to know the source of accusations against them (although witness identities can be shielded in many instances for their own protection), the ICTY has recognized confidentiality privileges for both journalists and members of the International Committee for the Red Cross.[38]

---

34   Theresa Roosevelt, "Ethics for the Ethical: A Code of Conduct for the International Criminal Court Office of the Prosecutor," *Georgetown Journal of Legal Ethics* vol. 24 (2011), pp. 835–51.

35   Roosevelt, "Ethics for the Ethical," p. 847.

36   See, for example, "Tenth Annual Report of the International Criminal Tribunal for the Prosecution of Persons Responsible for Serious Violations of International Humanitarian Law Committed in the Territory of the Former Yugoslavia Since 1991," Report of the Secretary General (2003) at http://www.un.org/icty/rappannu-e/2003/AR03e.htm, paras 288–91; the Office of Victim and Witness Support is in the Registry of the Special Court for Sierra Leone: http://www.sc-sl.org/registry.html.

37   Aaron Fichtelberg, "Democratic Legitimacy and the International Criminal Court: A Liberal Defence," *Journal of International Criminal Justice* vol. 4, issue 4 (2006), pp. 765–85.

38   This was done to recognize the professional ethical requirements of the journalistic profession and, more unusually, of the ICRC. Emily Ann Berman, "In Pursuit of Accountability: The Red Cross, War Correspondents, and Evidentiary Privileges in International Criminal Tribunals," *New York University Law Review* vol. 80 (April 2005), pp. 241–77; Kelly Buchanan, "Freedom of Expression and International Criminal Law:

Despite expanding regulatory structures for the professional conduct of judges, counsel, and staff at international criminal tribunals, serious violations have occurred, which might give rise to concerns that formal rules are not enough. The scandals at both the ICTY and ICTR as well as controversies which emerged at the ICC during the trial of Thomas Lubanga illustrate this risk.

Scandals at the ICTY and ICTR

A brief discussion of the corruption scandals that have occurred at the ICTR and the ICTY makes clear that, at a bare minimum, professional regulations are necessary.[39] Following a report by the UN Office of Internal Oversight Services detailing the extent of corruption in each tribunal, the registrars of both tribunals issued a joint statement in March 2002 declaring their intent to eradicate corruption.[40] Many of these violations occurred after codes of conduct were put in place. In addition, as I discuss briefly later, even with formal protections in place, as we shall see, distinct concerns have arisen about the potential sacrifice of justice to efficiency, with the projected closing of the two ad hoc tribunals. I turn first to the scandals before each tribunal.

The ICTR experienced a range of corruption scandals, involving staff, defendants, and lawyers.[41] In March 2001, the ICTR fired 21 members of defense teams for violations of regulations, including defense counsel, co-counsel, legal assistants, and investigators. Among the allegations were claims that detainees and attorneys engaged in "fee-splitting", and that some defense attorneys offered their clients expensive gifts or employed relatives of the accused to act as official defense team investigators. The scandal increased when it was revealed that three people who were on the Rwandan government's list of genocide suspects were among those employed as investigators for defense teams.[42] In several instances, defense attorneys at the ICTR were sanctioned for delaying proceedings unduly, and in at least one instance the sanctioning chamber explicitly accused the counsel

---

An Analysis of the Decision to Create a Testimonial Privilege for Journalists," *Victoria University of Wellington Law Review* vol. 35 (October 2004), pp. 609–55.

39   While there have been a number of controversies over the handling and provision of evidence by the Office of the Prosecutor of the ICC in the case against Thomas Lubanga Dyilo, in Februt

40   United Nations Office for the Coordination of Humanitarian Affairs," "Measures to Curb Corruption at ICTR," (March 2002), at http://www.irinnews.org/report. asp?ReportID=24683.

41   Thalif Deen, "UN War Crimes Courts Embroiled in Corruption Charges," Inter Press Service (March 11, 2002), at http://www.globalpolicy.org/nations/ corrupt/2002/0311courts.htm.

42   Sukhdev Chhhatbar, "ICTR Fires 21 Defense Team Members,"; Sukhdev Chhhatbar, "Top Genocide Suspects on ICTR's Payroll," Sukhdev Chhhatbar "UN Finds Defense Corruption at War Crimes Tribunals," *Internews* (March 2001), at http://www. internews.org/activities/ICTR_reports/ICTRnewsMar01.html.

of doing so to earn more money through delay.[43] The ongoing imposition of penalties has not, however, ended the troubles with corruption: in September 2005 the ICTR's chief of external relations was fired for allegedly leaking confidential information, including the identities of prosecution witnesses, and sanctions for delay have been imposed as recently as 2009.[44]

The ICTY has not experienced the large-scale corruption scandals that the ICTR has, but several smaller scandals emerged, including one in which a detainee who claimed to be indigent and therefore received tribunal-sponsored counsel was found to have purchased real estate while in detention.[45] Several contempt proceedings have been brought against counsel before the ICTY. In one instance, in a case involving Dusko Tadic, an attorney accused of manipulating witnesses, putting forth false evidence, and bribing witnesses was found to have engaged in sufficiently serious breaches that he was removed from the list of assigned counsel before the court.[46]

The International Criminal Court and the Lubanga Case

Criticism regarding professional ethics at the International Criminal Court has focused on a different subject: the Office of the Prosecutor. In the first case before the court to reach a judgment, that against Thomas Lubanga Dyilo of the Democratic Republic of Congo, the defendant was convicted despite serious concerns regarding the treatment of evidence by the prosecutor's office as well as the use of intermediaries to identify and obtain witnesses. In 2008, the Trial Chamber of the court stayed proceedings against the accused based on evidence that the OtP had failed to disclose significant potentially exculpatory evidence. The Chamber imposed yet another stay in relation to non-disclosure of the name of an intermediary. The concerns raised by what the Chamber viewed as prosecutorial intransigence, if not formal professional misconduct, were discussed at length in the judgment against Lubanga, which did not rely upon evidence viewed as

---

43   International Criminal Tribunal for Rwanda, *The Prosecutor v. Leonidas Nshogoza* Case No. ICTR-07-91-T, Further decision to sanction defence counsel for misconduct *(March 17, 2009); International Criminal Tribunal for Rwanda, "Alfred Musema Case", ICTR Update* ICTR/UPD/004 (November 19, 1997); "ICTR/Nzirorera—Chamber censures accused's lead counsel for professional misconduct," *Hirondelle News Agency* (December 4, 2008), at www.hirondellenews.com.

44   James Munyaneza and Eleneus Akanga, "Tribunal Spokesman Sacked over Corruption," *The New Times* (Kigali) (September 18, 2005), at http://allafrica.com/stories/200509180005.html.

45   Deen, "UN War Crimes Courts Embroiled in Corruption Charges."

46   *The Prosecutor v. Dusko Tadic* Case No. IT-94-1-A-R77, Judgment on allegations of contempt against prior counsel, Milan Vujin (January 31, 2000); McMorrow, "Creating norms of attorney conduct in international tribunals," p. 168.

affected by questionable intermediaries.[47] The controversies surrounding the Lubanga case have drawn attention to the absence of a formal code of conduct for the OtP, in contrast to the presence of codes of conduct for other counsel before the ICC outlined above.[48] As one analyst has observed, the absence of a strong code of conduct for the prosecutor is particularly troublesome given his/her symbolic normative importance and power within the system.[49] The absence of such formal regulations, and controversies over specific cases, have the potential to affect the legitimacy of the court in ways I have outlined above.

In Contrast: Ethics Regulations in Common Law Jurisdictions

In notable contrast to many international courts and tribunals, domestic courts, at least in functional democratic states adhering to principles of due process and rule of law, have far more detailed professional ethics rules for legal professionals, whether lawyers, barristers, or solicitors. And unlike many of the international tribunals examined above, they do have rules of professional conduct for judges. I examine rules from just two countries here—the United States and the United Kingdom—both notably common law countries with adversarial systems. The selection is made not to suggest that civil law countries do not have similar rules; for example Peru's code of judicial ethics prioritizes judicial independence, impartiality, and integrity and outlines criteria for behavior to preserve these principles.[50] However, here I focus on these two countries by way of illustration, to demonstrate that such regulations are not only aspirational principles but codified in national jurisdictions in ways which international courts might seek to replicate.

The United Kingdom has an extensive set of rules in the Guide to Judicial Conduct. This extensive set of rules, first published in 2004 in light of the UK's passage of the Human Rights Act, as well as the promulgation of principles on judicial conduct by the UN Human Rights Commission in 2003, also creates an oversight committee on judicial conduct.[51] The introduction to the guide notes a trend towards regulating judicial conduct, citing sets of principles in Canada, Australia, and Nigeria, the existence of the *Bangalore Principles of Judicial*

---

47   International Criminal Court, *Situation in the Democratic Republic of the Congo in the Case of the Prosecutor v Thomas Lubanga Dyilo. Judgment pursuant to Article 74 of the Statute* ICC-01/04-01/06-2492 14-03-2012 1/624 SL T (March 14, 2012), para 10 and generally; Roosevelt, "Ethics for the Ethical."

48   Roosevelt, "Ethics for the Ethical," p. 839.

49   Ibid., p. 843.

50   Código ética del poder judicial de Perú (October 14, 2003); similar legislation can be found elsewhere in Latin American civil law countries such as Venezuela and Mexico, and Puerto Rico, which is a civil law system with common law influence.

51   United Kingdom, Guide to Judicial Conduct (First Supplement published June 2006; Second supplement published March 2008).

Conduct which was developed with the support of the UN Special Rapporteur on the Independence of Judges and Lawyers. The principles emphasize that judicial independence is not merely a privilege which attaches to judges, but rather is essential to the rule of law and protection of citizens' rights. Critically, they also emphasize the importance of not only the reality but the appearance of impartiality and fairness, to ensure citizen confidence in the judiciary. Solicitors and barristers are also closely regulated by detailed codes of conduct.[52]

Its federal structure means that the United States has a complex legal system, in which federal courts are distinct from state courts, with, consequently, different sets of regulations for each. Further, each state's legal professionals are regulated by the state bar, further complicating matters. Nonetheless, there is a Code of Conduct for United States Judges, which covers Federal Court judges and a range of judges in specialized courts, first adopted in 1973. The rules emphasize the importance of propriety, fairness and impartiality in judicial behavior and the importance of public confidence in the integrity and independence of judges. It even suggests that judges should disqualify themselves where questions might be raised about partiality, apparently even where no impropriety arises.[53] The conservative approach to even the appearance of bias in both US Federal and UK judicial regulations might be placed in contrast to the controversy which arose before the Special Court for Sierra Leone with respect to Judge Robertson, noted above. Lawyers are regulated by the rules of individual bar associations, which vary but are extensive and include similar rules regarding ethical behavior towards clients.[54]

Both of the national legal systems discussed above are common law systems, with adversarial processes. It is worth noting that international criminal tribunals, in particular, increasingly combine elements of civil and common law systems, and therefore of adversarial and inquisitorial approaches to courtroom proceedings. This means, in practice, different obligations for counsel and for judges which may be reflected in professional ethics regulations. According to one analyst, it means that there are wider obligations on the prosecution to disclose exculpatory evidence than in purely adversarial systems, and a wider role for judges in managing the court proceedings. Further, practices such as witness proofing, or witness preparation, are therefore not permissible at the ICC, although common in adversarial systems.[55]

---

52   Code of Conduct of the Bar of England and Wales, at http://www.barstandardsboard. org.uk/standardsandguidance/codeofconduct/; Solicitors' Code of Conduct 2007, at http:// www.sra.org.uk/solicitors/code-of-conduct.page.

53   Code of Conduct for United States Judges (as amended July 1, 2009).

54   Codes of conduct for US federal courts can be found at: http://www.uscourts. gov/library/codeOfConduct/Code_Effective_July 01–09.pdf; UK judges at: http://www. judiciary.gov.uk/docs/judges_council/judicialconduct_update0408.pdf; for UK solicitors at http://www.sra.org.uk/solicitors/code-of-conduct.page, and UK bar standards at: http:// www.barstandardsboard.org.uk/standardsandguidance/codeofconduct/.

55   Turner, "Legal Ethics in International Criminal Defense," pp 22–3.

What Can International Tribunals Learn from Domestic Courts?

Clearly, international tribunals face a range of challenges which domestic courts seldom do. They involve lawyers and judges from a rage of legal traditions, whether the more inquisitorial, civil law countries, or adversarial, common law traditions.[56] Judges in international courts may have been appointed because of their professorial expertise, and in some instances may have a diplomatic background, without having operated previously as a judge. The levels of training and expertise in all legal staff may vary significantly, as may the legal cultures from which they come.[57] In particular, views about corruption, in extreme circumstances, and about consultation with colleagues, in more justifiable ways, may vary. However, this may be all the more reason to ensure that there are baseline consistent rules, of the sort in the proposed model rules noted above. Further, the US's plural legal system, with both federal and state courts and rules may suggest to us that the same basic rules can be enshrined despite the diversity of actors and regulations. The judicial ethics code for the ICC may offer a good starting point for elaboration of judicial rules in international courts. It does recognize that judges face particular challenges because they operate in a court of international character, and could be used as a foundation for more detailed regulations incorporating the principles and concerns that are more clearly articulated in domestic judicial codes.

In particular, the absence of judicial regulations before many international courts should be of concern, particularly given that many do face precisely the type of legitimacy and public confidence concerns that are of concern in domestic systems, which can be alleviated by clear rules insisting upon standards of judicial integrity. Given that international tribunals, and perhaps particularly international criminal tribunals, operate in highly charged political situations and are frequently accused of bias and political manipulation, such rules might be particularly important for promoting confidence in international rule of law.

The Need for More Coherent Regulations

International courts and tribunals, whether criminal or otherwise, would enhance their own legitimacy with coherent codes of professional conduct. These would help to signal, per Franck's legitimacy criteria, coherence in process and adherence to a normative hierarchy, and help to counter claims about selectivity in proceedings and externally imposed norms. This is not to say that international courts and tribunals should necessarily have codes modeled on those present in common law countries such as the UK and the US outlined above; these are rather presented to draw a contrast with the relative dearth of rules at international

---

56   Brandeis Institute for International Judges, "Towards the Development of Ethics Guidelines," p. 5.

57   McMorrow, "Creating Norms of Attorney Conduct in International Tribunals."

courts. Existing model codes developed by international actors might equally be used to guide the drafting of codes for judges, staff, and counsel at the many international courts and tribunals where there are none. These include principles developed to inform domestic jurisdictions, such as the *Bangalore Principles of Judicial Conduct* and principles espoused by the UN Special Rapporteur on the Independence of Judges and Lawyers, as well as principles developed by the United Nations for prosecutors and model standards of professional responsibility created by the International Prosecutors' Association.[58] Similarly, projects such as those undertaken by the Brandeis Institute for International Judges, and the Project on International Courts and Tribunals, have advocated for, and sought to develop the content of, ethics regulations which might be applied in the numerous international courts and tribunals that currently do not have them.[59]

A Distinct Challenge for the ad hoc Tribunals: Completion Strategies

Formal rules notwithstanding, at least two international courts now face a different challenge: completing their work efficiently without sacrificing "justice." Both the ICTY and ICTR are under pressure to complete their work, although the deadline for completion has been extended several times for each.[60] For the ICTY, this has meant changes in the statutes and rules of procedures and evidence, resulting in the transfer of cases to domestic courts, and changes in procedures for issuing new indictments, permitting judges, through the bureau, to participate in the process. Concerns have been raised with respect to the appropriateness of the domestic venues to which some cases will be transferred, as well as the infringement upon

---

58   *Bangalore Principles of Judicial Conduct*; webpage of the Special Rapporteur on the Independence of Judges and Lawyers at http://www2.ohchr.org/english/issues/judiciary/index.htm; United Nations Guidelines on the Role of Prosecutors, at http://www.unhchr.ch/html/menu3/b/h_comp45.htm; International Prosecutors' Association, Standards of Professional Responsibility and Statement of the Essential Duties and Rights of Prosecutors at http://www.iap.nl.com/ressources/Standards_English.pdf.

59   Brandeis Institute for International Judges, "Professional conduct in the International Justice System," (2009), at http://www.brandeis.edu/ethics/pdfs/internationaljustice/ethics/Topics_in_Ethical_Practice_2009.pdf; Project on International Courts and Tribunals, "The Hague Principles on Ethical Standards for Counsel Appearing before International Courts and Tribunals," (September 2010) at http://www.ucl.ac.uk/laws/cict/docs/Hague_Sept2010.pdf.

60   Daryl A. Mundis, "Note and Comment: The Judicial Effects of the 'Completion Strategies' on the Ad Hoc Criminal Tribunals," *American Journal of International Law* vol. 99 (January 2005), pp. 142–58. However, these are target dates rather than fixed deadlines. Compare Larry D. Johnson, "Closing an International Criminal Tribunal While Maintaining International Human Rights Standards and Excluding Impunity," *American Journal of International Law* vol. 99 (January 2005) pp. 158–74.

prosecutorial discretion to issue indictments.[61] Concerns have also been raised with reference to the possible effects upon the rights of the accused and the potential for serious perpetrators to escape with impunity.[62]

Conclusions

International courts and tribunals, including international and internationalized criminal courts, are important components of international rule of law. However, their legitimacy may be compromised by the relative dearth of professional and ethical rules for counsel, staff, and judges, as they will potentially be seen not to be rule-bound even as they purport to apply primary rules in a coherent and consistent fashion. As we have seen with political challenges to the ICC, states which wish to challenge the jurisdiction of an institution often choose to challenge its legitimacy, accusing it of bias and selectivity.[63] Conversely, such institutions' efficacy might be improved with greater legitimacy. While the creation of professional codes of conduct is but one element of legitimacy, it is an important one, and relatively easy to achieve. Such codes might be modeled on existing domestic codes, or international model codes, or the more elaborate codes which the ICC has.

Of course, codes alone are clearly insufficient, as the scandals at the ICTY and ICTR demonstrate; further there are ethical concerns that are not fully covered by professional codes. For example, protection of victims and witnesses, and specific standards of due process for defendants, are also responsibilities of the courts themselves which may be separately codified and provided for institutionally, as they have been at international criminal tribunals.

Further, many international courts and tribunals have been and may continue to be criticized as political, and therefore biased and illegitimate, regardless of

---

61   Mundis, "Note and Comment," pp. 146–54. On the justification and legitimacy of prosecutorial discretion, see Allison Marston Danner, "Enhancing the Legitimacy and Accountability of Prosecutorial Discretion at the International Criminal Court," *American Journal of International Law* vol. 97 (July 2003), pp. 510–52.

62   For example, it was implied by a dissenting judge in an interlocutory appeal in the Milosevic case that the completion strategy had taken priority over the rights of the accused. Johnson, "Closing an International Criminal Tribunal," p. 161. Obviously it is impossible to guarantee that all indictees will be arrested prior to the target ending dates.

63   This commonly takes the form of assertions that the ICC's caseload, involving situations only in Africa at the time of this writing, is a type of neo-colonialism or at a minimum demonstrates a problematic emphasis on the continent. For a discussion of and response to this critique, see Chandra Lekha Sriram, "The International Criminal Court Africa Experiment: The Central African Republic, Darfur, Northern Uganda, and the Democratic Republic of the Congo," in Chandra Lekha Sriram and Suren Pillay (eds), *Peace versus Justice? The Dilemma of Transitional Justice in Africa* (Durban: University of KwaZulu Natal Press, 2009, and Oxford: James Currey, 2010), pp. 317–30. See also Popovski, "Legality and Legitimacy of the International Criminal Tribunals."

procedural ethical protections, given that decisions are rendered by judges from specific nation states, who some will assume to be biased. Finally, institutions such as the ICC, which may receive referrals from the UNSC, an eminently political body, and whose proceedings may also be suspended by the UNSC, will continue to be subject to the criticism that they are susceptible to political manipulation. The controversy over the role of the UNSC, already significant with its referral of the situation in Darfur, was exacerbated with its referral of the situation in Libya to the ICC.[64] Improved ethics and professional regulations for counsel, judges, and staff will not eradicate the host of legitimacy challenges faced by these courts, but may yet have the potential to address significant concerns and enhance their legitimacy.

64　Lawrence Moss, "The UN Security Council and the International Criminal Court: Towards a More Principled Relationship," (Berlin: Friedrich Ebert Stiftung, March 2012) at http://library.fes.de/pdf-files/iez/08948.pdf.

Chapter 9

Judicial Ethics at the International Criminal Tribunals

William A. Schabas

The International Military Tribunal ('Nuremberg Tribunal') and the International Military Tribunal for the Far East ('Tokyo Tribunal') were the first genuinely international criminal courts, established to deal with the previously unimaginable atrocities perpetrated in the course of the Second World War. The institutions were a new phenomenon, premised on the prosecution of certain international crimes that hitherto had only been vaguely defined, if at all: crimes against peace, war crimes and crimes against humanity. These offences were addressed to the protection of fundamental values of humanity rather than collective or bilateral issues involved in suppression of what were in substance relatively ordinary crimes like piracy.

Each of the four powers that established the International Military Tribunal – France, the Soviet Union, the United Kingdom and the United States – appointed one judge and one alternate in a process that can best be described as opaque. But they were all jurists of considerable renown in their own countries, and there is little to suggest that their selection was inappropriate. They came close to unanimity in their judgment, with the Soviet judge dissenting on the acquittal of three offenders and the non-imposition of the death penalty with respect to some of the convictions. Eleven judges were appointed to the Tokyo Tribunal, each from a different country. The relationship was sometimes difficult, and there are reports of feuding. Moreover, some were absent for protracted periods during the proceedings. But critics of the two trials generally focus on the selection of the accused and the evident fact that no equivalent proceedings were held for crimes committed by the victors rather than aspersions about this first experiment with an international criminal judiciary.

In his memoir of the trial, the American prosecutor writes of his dissatisfaction with the Soviet judge, Nikitchenko, who had participated in the London Conference that had established the Tribunal and established its primary legal instrument. Taylor felt Nikitchenko's involvement in preparing the legal framework of the trial made him unsuitable to sit as a judge.[1] One of the issues that is often invoked by critics of Nuremberg is the handling of the Katyń forest massacre perpetrated by the Soviets against Poland's elite in the first part of 1940. There is the charge that

---

1   Telford Taylor, *The Anatomy of the Nuremberg Trials*, New York: Alfred A. Knopf, 1992.

political considerations triumphed in the Tribunal's handling of the episode, and that the judges were in some way complicit in the scheme. Close scrutiny suggests such criticism is not well-founded.

The Germans discovered the mass grave at Katyń in 1943 and promptly attributed the killing to the Soviets. But when the Red Army recovered the territory, the Soviets held their own commission of inquiry which blamed the Germans. At Nuremberg, the Soviet prosecutor insisted upon including Katyń in the indictment over the objections of Robert Jackson and the other prosecutors. It is not clear whether this was because Jackson or the others suspected the Soviets were themselves responsible. Jackson did not make such a claim when he testified before a congressional committee in the 1950s. The American, British and French prosecutors may simply have considered that responsibility for the massacre would be difficult to prove without lengthy testimony, given the conflicting versions. There were many other much clearer examples of Nazi barbarism, on a more awesome scale than Katyń, upon which to base their case. The Soviet prosecutors, who probably accepted in good faith their regime's official, albeit dishonest, explanation of the crime, did not themselves seem particularly enthusiastic about proving the crime. They confined their evidence to the perfunctory submission of the report of the Soviet commission of inquiry.

The judges allowed the accused Germans to call three witnesses in defence; the Soviet prosecutor was allowed three witnesses in rebuttal.[2] The result, on any fair reading of the transcript, was inconclusive. If anything, contemporary observers felt that the Soviets had made a strong showing and that the Germans had not had much success with their witnesses in making the case for Soviet responsibility. The judges were without any jurisdiction to blame the Soviets for the crime, although that would have been self-evident had they explicitly concluded that the Germans were not responsible. Instead, Katyń was not mentioned at all in the final judgment. Even the Soviet judge, Nikitchenko, avoided speaking of the matter in his dissenting opinion. This silence is often dismissed as evidence of cynicism and manipulation, something that is said to have tarnished the reputation of the judges for independence and impartiality. That is a harsh reading of the record. It seems most likely that the judges were simply perplexed by the evidence. Although Nikitchenko is usually dismissed as the least impartial of the judges, on Katyń he glistens with rectitude. His failure to mention Katyń indicates a man prepared to depart from the official narrative of his government, even if he only did so implicitly, by refusing to acknowledge the massacre at all.

The revival of international criminal justice in the 1990s brought with it more explicit attention to judicial ethics. This was probably a reflection of enhanced interest in such matters generally, driven by developments in international human rights law and the work of bodies like the quinquennial United Nations Congress on the Prevention of Crime and the Treatment of Offenders. In this respect, the

---

2   (1949) 17 IMT 274-383.

Basic Principles on the Independence of the Judiciary, adopted in 1985, is a document of great significance.[3]

In identical provisions, the statutes of the International Criminal Tribunals established by the Security Council in 1993 and 1994, and the United Nations courts that were established subsequently for Sierra Leone and Lebanon, contain the following: 'The judges shall be persons of high moral character, impartiality and integrity who possess the qualifications required in their respective countries for appointment to the highest judicial offices.'[4] This is really little more than international law boilerplate. The text is modelled on something very similar in the Statute of the International Court of Justice.[5] The judges of these international courts were left largely on their own in terms of the perception and enforcement ethical behaviour.

Appointed to relatively short terms of three or four years, it was probably felt that any lapses in judicial conduct could be dealt with by non-renewal of their terms. Indeed, there is some evidence of judges felt to be weak or inadequate failing to have their terms renewed. However, the voting for judges at the General Assembly is so fraught with imponderables that it is difficult to conclude this has been a factor, let alone a decisive one, in the electoral process.

Defence lawyers occasionally raised issues about a lack of impartiality, although this was generally a question of appearance rather than complaints based upon actual evidence of inappropriate behaviour or relationships. In any event, defence lawyers are notoriously reticent about challenging judges on such issues, lest their applications fail and they find themselves forced to continue before someone who is angry or unhappy about being attacked. In an early case before the International Criminal Tribunal for the former Yugoslavia, a judge frequently seemed to fall asleep during the proceedings. The problem was never raised directly before the trial court, probably out of fears that the judge in question would become embittered.[6] The matter became an issue before the Appeals Chamber. It agreed that there was evidence the judge had been asleep for short periods, and on one occasion for as much as 30 minutes, and said this could not 'be accepted as appropriate conduct for a judge … If a judge suffers from some condition which prevents him or her from giving full attention during the trial, then it is the duty of that judge to seek medical assistance and, if that does not help, to withdraw from the case.'[7] Although the Chamber did not grant the appeal, these words amounted to a form of sanction for unethical conduct. By then, there was nothing more to do, because the judge had retired from the international judiciary.

---

3   GA Res. 40/32, 40/146.

4   UN Doc. S/RES/827 (1993), annex, art. 13(1); UN Doc. S/RES/955 (1994), annex, art. 12(1).

5   Statute of the International Court of Justice, art. 2.

6   *Delalić* et al. (IT-96-21-A), Judgment, 20 February 2001, para. 644.

7   Ibid., para. 629.

The International Criminal Court Code of Judicial Ethics

Many perceived shortcomings in international justice were addressed when the International Criminal Court was created. One of them was the issue of judicial ethics. The Rome Statute of the International Criminal Court itself is silent on the subject of judicial ethics, except for the standard formulation in article 36(3) that judges be of 'high moral character, impartiality and integrity'. Adoption of a Code of Judicial Ethics is required by the Regulations of the Court, a subordinate instrument whose drafting and adoption is require by article 52 of the Rome Statute. The Regulations are to provide for the 'routine functioning' of the Court. They are adopted by the judges and remain in force in the absence of prompt objection from any of the States Parties.

Thus, it is the judges themselves, by means of Regulation 126, who have imposed the requirement of a Code of Judicial Ethics:

> Regulation 126, Adoption of the Code of Judicial Ethics
>
> 1. The Presidency shall draw up a Code of Judicial Ethics, after having consulted the judges.
>
> 2. The draft Code shall then be transmitted to the judges meeting in plenary session for the purpose of adoption by the majority of the judges.[8]

Unlike the Regulations of the Court, the Code of Judicial Ethics does not require any particular approval for entry into force once it has been adopted by a majority of the judges. The Code of Judicial Ethics was drafted by a working group established by the Presidency of the Court following consultation with the judges.[9] The Code was adopted on 9 March 2005 by the Plenary of the judges.[10]

The Code of Judicial Ethics has been described as 'an innovation for international criminal tribunals'.[11] Most of the legislative instruments of the International Criminal Court can be interpreted with regard to the *travaux préparatoires*, which generally consist of a collection of drafts, proposals and in some cases records of meetings that can assist in divining the intent of the drafters. However, the Code of Judicial Ethics is without any such background or explanatory materials.

The document is framed as an agreement of the judges of the Court ('The judges of the International Criminal Court ... Have agreed as follows ...'). The operative paragraphs are preceded by a five-paragraph preamble. The first preambular paragraph cites article 45 of the Rome Statute, which requires that upon taking office all judges are to make 'a solemn undertaking in open court to exercise his or her respective functions impartially and conscientiously'. The text of the undertaking is set out in the Rules of Procedure and Evidence, which are also

---

8   Regulations of the Court, Regulation 126.
9   Code of Judicial Ethics, ICC-BD/02-01-05.
10   'Report on the Activities of the Court', ICC-ASP/4/16, para. 40.
11   'Report of the International Criminal Court for 2004', UN Doc. A/60/177, para. 22.

referenced in the first preambular paragraph of the Code: 'I solemnly undertake that I will perform my duties and exercise my powers as a judge of the International Criminal Court honourably, faithfully, impartially and conscientiously, and that I will respect the confidentiality of investigations and prosecutions and the secrecy of deliberations.'[12]

The second paragraph of the preamble 'recall[s] the principles concerning judicial independence, impartiality and proper conduct specified in the Statute and the Rules'. Of particular importance in this respect is article 41 of the Rome Statute:

> Article 40. Independence of the judges
>
> 1. The judges shall be independent in the performance of their functions.
>
> 2. Judges shall not engage in any activity which is likely to interfere with their judicial functions or to affect confidence in their independence.
>
> 3. Judges required to serve on a full-time basis at the seat of the Court shall not engage in any other occupation of a professional nature.
>
> 4. Any question regarding the application of paragraphs 2 and 3 shall be decided by an absolute majority of the judges. Where any such question concerns an individual judge, that judge shall not take part in the decision.

During the trial, the presiding judge (three judges make up a Trial Chamber) has a special responsibility to ensure that proceedings are conducting 'in a fair and impartial manner'.[13]

International human rights law distinguishes between 'independence' and 'impartiality'. While independence is desirable in and of itself, its importance really lies in the fact that it creates the conditions for impartiality.[14] This leads to a further distinction, between the objective and the subjective dimensions of the norm. An individual judge or prosecutor may be above reproach from the standpoint of impartiality, yet the conditions of appointment, remuneration and tenure may lead a 'reasonable person' to suspect that justice cannot be done.[15]

Preambular paragraph 3 explains that the Code was adopted in recognition of 'the need for guidelines of general application to contribute to judicial independence and impartiality and with a view to ensuring the legitimacy and effectiveness of the international judicial process'. Paragraph 4 of the preamble

---

12   Rules of Procedure and Evidence, Rule 5(1)(a).

13   Rome Statute, art. 64(8)(b).

14   The distinction between independence and impartiality is discussed at some length in *Norman* (SCSL-2004-14-AR72(E)), Separate Opinion of Justice Geoffrey Robertson, 13 March 2004, para. 2.

15   Rules of Procedure and Evidence of the International Criminal Tribunal for the former Yugoslavia, Rule 15(A); Rules of Procedure and Evidence of the International Criminal Tribunal for Rwanda, Rule 15(A); Rules of Procedure and Evidence of the Special Court for Sierra Leone, Rule 15(A).

refers to the United Nations Basic Principles on the Independence of the Judiciary, adopted in 1985 by the General Assembly, 'and other international and national rules and standards relating to judicial conduct'. The preamble concludes with a reference to 'the international character of the Court and the special challenges facing the judges of the Court in the performance of their responsibilities'. This phrase suggests that there exist unique features of relevance to judicial ethics that are peculiar to courts of an 'international character'.

The Code of Judicial Ethics contains nine operative provisions. Article 1 notes that the Code was adopted by the judges pursuant to Regulation 126. It confirms that the Code is to 'be read subject to the Statute, the Rules and the Regulations of the Court'. In a sense, the idea of a normative hierarchy makes sense, in that the adoption of the Code is required by the Regulations, the adoption of the Regulations is to be in accordance with the 'Statute and the Rules of Procedure and Evidence',[16] and if there is a conflict, the Statute is to prevail over the Rules of Procedure and Evidence.[17] Nevertheless, it seems odd to suggest that judicial ethics could be subordinate to anything. Surely judges cannot behave unethically because of a perceived conflict with 'superior' legislation. Article 1 also seems to indicate that the obligation to behave ethically flows from the other normative instruments in the Rome Statute system, whereas it might well be argued that this is actually an autonomous duty whose source is not found in the Statute, the Rules and the Regulations.

Article 2 is a technical provision that specifies that the terms 'Court', 'Statute', 'Rules' and 'Regulations' are to have the meaning attached to them in the Regulations of the Court, where they are defined in Regulation 2(1).

Article 3 is entitled 'judicial independence', a matter already considered in article 40 of the Statute itself, as discussed above. Indeed, article 3(2) of the Code merely repeats the text of article 40(2) of the Rome Statute. Article 3(1) of the Code adds to the provisions in the Rome Statute: 'Judges shall uphold the independence of their office and the authority of the Court and shall conduct themselves accordingly in carrying out their judicial functions.'

Article 4 is labeled 'impartiality'. It reads as follows:

> 1. Judges shall be impartial and ensure the appearance of impartiality in the discharge of their judicial functions.
> 2. Judges shall avoid any conflict of interest, or being placed in a situation which might reasonably be perceived as giving rise to a conflict of interest.

The difficulty with impartiality, as article 4(2) of the Code implies, is that there are both objective and subjective dimensions. Article 36(3)(a) of the Rome Statute, which requires that candidates for the judiciary be impartial, points to an objective appreciate of the matter. But article 4(2) of the Code indicates this is also about

---

16   Rome Statute of the International Criminal Court, art. 52(1).
17   Ibid., art. 51(1).

'a situation which might reasonably be perceived as giving rise to a conflict of interest'. Indeed, this might be taken a step further: the fact that there actually is a conflict of interest does not mean the judge is lacking in impartiality, but it certainly makes a judge appear impartial. These issues are also addressed in the Statute itself. Article 41(2)(a) of the Statute dictates that a judge is not to participate in a case 'in which his or her impartiality might reasonably be doubted on any ground. A judge shall be disqualified from a case in accordance with this paragraph if, *inter alia*, that judge has previously been involved in any capacity in that case before the Court or in a related criminal case at the national level involving the person being investigated or prosecuted.' Rule 34(1) of the Rules of Procedure and Evidence provides greater clarification, by enumerating certain grounds where an appearance of a lack of impartiality is deemed:

> (a) Personal interest in the case, including a spousal, parental or other close family, personal or professional relationship, or a subordinate relationship, with any of the parties;
>
> (b) Involvement, in his or her private capacity, in any legal proceedings initiated prior to his or her involvement in the case, or initiated by him or her subsequently, in which the person being investigated or prosecuted was or is an opposing party;
>
> (c) Performance of functions, prior to taking office, during which he or she could be expected to have formed an opinion on the case in question, on the parties or on their legal representatives that, objectively, could adversely affect the required impartiality of the person concerned;
>
> (d) Expression of opinions, through the communications media, in writing or in public actions, that, objectively, could adversely affect the required impartiality of the person concerned.

Challenges based upon the alleged lack of impartiality of judges are discussed later in this chapter.

'Integrity' is the subject of article 5 of the Code of Judicial Ethics. It reads as follows:

> 1. Judges shall conduct themselves with probity and integrity in accordance with their office, thereby enhancing public confidence in the judiciary.
>
> 2. Judges shall not directly or indirectly accept any gift, advantage, privilege or reward that can reasonably be perceived as being intended to influence the performance of their judicial functions.

Again, as with impartiality the assessment of these factors is a combination of the objective and the subjective.

Article 6 of the Code of Judicial Ethics requires judges to 'respect the confidentiality of consultations which relate to their judicial functions and the secrecy of deliberations'.

Article 7 requires judges to 'act diligently'.

1. Judges shall act diligently in the exercise of their duties and shall devote their professional activities to those duties.

2. Judges shall take reasonable steps to maintain and enhance the knowledge, skills and personal qualities necessary for judicial office.

3. Judges shall perform all judicial duties properly and expeditiously.

4. Judges shall deliver their decisions and any other rulings without undue delay.

Article 8 governs the conduct of proceedings. Much of the provision actually concerns the behaviour of participants in the judicial debate, such as counsel, witnesses and members of the public who attend proceedings. According to article 8:

1. In conducting judicial proceedings, judges shall maintain order, act in accordance with commonly accepted decorum, remain patient and courteous towards all participants and members of the public present and require them to act likewise.

2. Judges shall exercise vigilance in controlling the manner of questioning of witnesses or victims in accordance with the Rules and give special attention to the right of participants to the proceedings to equal protection and benefit of the law.

3. Judges shall avoid conduct or comments which are racist, sexist or otherwise degrading and, to the extent possible, ensure that any person participating in the proceedings refrains from such comments or conduct.

Many national judges, even those with highly visible profiles as academics or politicians prior to their appointment, exercise great restraint in making any public statements or pronouncements. Upon appointment to the bench they withdraw into anonymity, speaking only through their judgments in judicial proceedings. When they occasionally speak out, about matters of concern such as sentencing norms or financing of the justice system, there will frequently be rebukes and charges that such conduct is incompatible with the required impartiality of the judiciary. But at the International Criminal Court, and other international criminal justice institutions, judges are frequent keynote speakers, lecturers and panellists at academic conferences and similar events. Their speeches are often published. They do not comment on pending cases, but it is not at all unknown for them to assess judgments that have already been delivered. Upon retirement, they may publish accounts that further explain their dissenting judgments[18] or recount their frustrations with the operation of the institution.[19] Indeed, there is probably a significantly greater tolerance for public pronouncements of judges

---

18   Georghios M. Pikis, *The Rome Statute for the International Criminal Court, Analysis of the Statute, the Rules of Procedure and Evidence, the Regulations of the Court and Supplementary Instruments*, Leiden: Martinus Nijhoff Publishers, 2010.

19   Patricia M. Wald, 'The International Criminal Tribunal for the Former Yugoslavia Comes of Age: Some Observations on Day-to-Day Dilemmas of an International Court', (2001) 5 *Washington University Journal of Law & Policy* 87.

at the international level than there is in the case of national justice institutions. According to article 9 of the Code of Judicial Ethics, which is entitled 'Public expression and association':

> 1. Judges shall exercise their freedom of expression and association in a manner that is compatible with their office and that does not affect or appear to affect judicial independence or impartiality.
> 2. While judges are free to participate in public debate on matters pertaining to legal subjects, the judiciary or the administration of justice, they shall not comment on pending cases and shall avoid expressing views which may undermine the standing and integrity of the Court.

Again, there is an acknowledgment of the subjective and objective assessment of such matters. The United Nations Basic Principles on the Independence of the Judiciary address the same issue, but somewhat differently. The relevant section is entitled 'Freedom of expression and association', and reads as follows:

> 8. In accordance with the Universal Declaration of Human Rights, members of the judiciary are like other citizens entitled to freedom of expression, belief, association and assembly; provided, however, that in exercising such rights, judges shall always conduct themselves in such a manner as to preserve the dignity of their office and the impartiality and independence of the judiciary.
> 9. Judges shall be free to form and join associations of judges or other organizations to represent their interests, to promote their professional training and to protect their judicial independence.

The United Nations text explicitly contemplates the freedom of association issues related to organizations of judges. Despite the reference to 'association' in article 9 of the Code of Judicial Ethics of the International Criminal Court, this matter is not serious considered. There is no professional organization of international judges that is mandated to 'represent their interests' analogous to what exists at the national level. Many judges of the Court would be members of professional bodies that promote professional training and judicial independence, such as the International Society for the Reform of Criminal Law and the International Law Association.

Article 10 of the Code concerns 'extra-judicial activity'.

> 1. Judges shall not engage in any extra-judicial activity that is incompatible with their judicial function or the efficient and timely functioning of the Court, or that may affect or may reasonably appear to affect their independence or impartiality.
> 2. Judges shall not exercise any political function.

This develops the idea expressed in article 40(2) of the Rome Statute: 'Judges shall not engage in any activity which is likely to interfere with their judicial functions or to affect confidence in their independence.'

Article 11 is an overarching provision entitled 'Observance of the Code' that has the effect of qualifying or limiting the scope of the Code itself. Article 11 describes the 'principles embodies in this Code' as 'guidelines on the essential ethical standards required of judges in the performance of their duties'. It also specifies that they are 'advisory in nature and have the object of assisting judges with respect to ethical and professional issues with which they are confronted'. Despite their 'advisory' status, the provisions of the Code might well be invoked in disciplinary proceedings conducted pursuant to articles 46 and 47 of the Statute. Article 11 concludes with a limitation: 'Nothing in this Code is intended in any way to limit or restrict the judicial independence of the judges'.

Impartiality

The issue of impartiality probably lies at the heart of ethical concerns. It is the matter most likely to lead to challenges in judicial proceedings. Litigants may not be terribly concerned about moral lapses, substance abuse, narcolepsy and similar matters when judges are concerned, because these may not be perceived as having any impact upon their rights in the proceedings. In the famous case of the judge who fell asleep before the International Criminal Tribunal for the former Yugoslavia, the Appeals Chamber found that the defence challenge on this point was 'opportunistic'.[20] The defence had not pressed the point at trial, perhaps unsure whether it might even work to its advantage.

On the other hand, defence counsel will be very concerned if they suspect that a judge cannot be impartial. The Code of Judicial Ethics addresses this matter, in particular in article 4. To date, however, there do not appear to have been any significant debates before the International Criminal Court concerning such matters. There are rumours that defence counsel may have questioned the competence of the first Japanese judge elected to the Court, who did not have a law degree. That matter did not involve an issue of impartiality. However, the same cannot be said of the international criminal tribunals established by the United Nations on an ad hoc basis, where there are many examples.

According to a Trial Chamber of the International Criminal Tribunal for Rwanda, the test is one of a 'reasonable apprehension of bias'.[21] In *Furundžija*, the Appeals Chamber of the International Criminal Tribunal for the former Yugoslavia said 'there is a general rule that a Judge should not only be subjectively free from bias, but also that there should be nothing in the surrounding circumstances which

---

20   *Delalić* et al. (IT-96-21-A), Judgment, 20 February 2001, para. 650.

21   *Karemera* et al. (ICTR-98-44-T), Decision on Motion by Nzirorera for Disqualification of Trial Judges, 17 May 2004.

objectively gives rise to an appearance of bias'. The Appeals Chamber said that aside from the case where actual bias exists, there is an unacceptable appearance of bias if a Judge is a party to the case, or has a financial or proprietary interest in the outcome of a case, or if the Judge's decision will lead to the promotion of a cause in which he or she is involved, together with one of the parties. As for apprehended bias, the Appeals Chamber said that the 'reasonable person must be an informed person, with knowledge of all the relevant circumstances, including the traditions of integrity and impartiality that form a part of the background and apprised also of the fact that impartiality is one of the duties that Judges swear to uphold'.[22] Judges benefit from a presumption of impartiality, which can only be rebutted on the basis of adequate and reliable evidence.[23]

The only successful motion for disqualification before an international criminal tribunal concerned President Geoffrey Robertson, of the Special Court for Sierra Leone. His independence and impartiality was questioned because of comments he had made about crimes committed by certain combatants in the Sierra Leone civil war in his celebrated book, *Crimes against Humanity: The Struggle for Global Justice*, which had been published prior to his appointment to the international bench. Robertson had described one of the leaders of the combatant forces, Foday Sankoh, who was actually accused before the Court until his death in August 2003, as 'the nation's butcher'. More generally, he had made many pejorative observations about the Revolutionary United Front. Several of its members had pending cases before the Court. Robertson refused to withdraw, leaving the remaining four judges of the Appeals Chamber to rule that he should not sit in specific cases. The motion to disqualify submitted by the defence was actually supported by the Prosecutor.[24] According to Judge George King, who drafted the reasons, with which the other three members of the Appeals Chamber concurred:

> The learned justice is certainly entitled to his opinion. That is one of his fundamental human rights. The crucial and decisive question is whether an independent *bystander* so to speak, or the reasonable man, reading those passages will have a legitimate reason to fear that Justice Robertson lacks impartiality. In other words, whether one can apprehend bias. I have no doubt that a reasonable man will apprehend bias, let alone an accused person and I so hold.[25]

The Appeals Chamber concluded that Judge Robertson could continue to sit in the cases that did not involve accused members of the Revolutionary United Front.

The Appeals Chamber of the International Criminal Tribunal for the former Yugoslavia dismissed as 'frivolous' various challenges by accused Vojislav Šešelj

---

22 *Furundžija* (IT-95-17/1-A), Judgment, 21 July 2000, paras 189–90.

23 *Akayesu* (ICTR-96-4-A), Judgment, 1 June 2001, para. 91.

24 *Sesay* (SCSL-2004-15-AR15), Decision on Defence Motion Seeking the Disqualification of Justice Robertson from the Appeals Chamber, 13 March 2004, para. 7.

25 Ibid., para. 15.

directed at Judges Schomburg, Mumba and Agius, who were members of the Trial Chamber assigned to his case. Šešelj said that the judges possess 'certain personal characteristics which completely preclude them from being impartial'. He said that Germany, of which Judge Schomburg is a national, has 'traditionally been hostile towards Serbia and the Serbian people'. Moreover, he argued that because Germany is a member of the North Atlantic Treaty Alliance whose people 'committed aggression against Serbia', Judge Schomburg should be disqualified. Šešelj described Judges Mumba and Agius as 'ardent and zealous Catholics', adding that the Roman Catholic Church had 'contributed to the destruction of Yugoslavia'. The Bureau said 'the nationalities and religions of Judges are, and must be, irrelevant to their ability to hear the cases before them impartially'.[26]

In *Furundžija*, the accused challenged the impartiality of Judge Mumba because she had served as the Zambian delegate to the United Nations Commission on the Status of Women, and could be said to share its feminist legal and political agenda. He did not charge that she was actually biased, but noted that other participants in the proceedings, notably one of the prosecution lawyers and members of an *amicus curiae* team, had also been involved with the Commission. According to the Appeals Chamber of the International Criminal Tribunal for the former Yugoslavia, even if Judge Mumba shared the goals and objectives of the Commission, which were to promote and protect the human rights of women, 'she could still sit on a case and impartially decide upon issues affecting women'.[27] The Appeals Chamber noted that the Statute encouraged judges to be qualified in the area of international human rights, noting that a Judge should not be disqualified 'because of qualifications he or she possesses which, by their very nature, play an integral role in satisfying the eligibility requirements ... It would be an odd result if the operation of an eligibility requirement were to lead to an inference of bias.'[28]

A challenge to Judge Odio Benito based on her membership on the Board of Trustees of the United Nations Voluntary Fund for the Relief of Victims of Torture met a similar fate.[29] Similarly, the Appeals Chamber of the Special Court for Sierra Leone dismissed a challenge to Judge Winter, seeking her recusal from a motion on the legality of the crime of recruiting child soldiers. The defence argued that she had long been associated with a variety of children's rights organizations, and more specifically had participated in a UNICEF publication relevant to the work of the Special Court that supported prosecution of the offence of recruitment.[30]

---

26   *Šešelj* (IT-03-67-PT), Decision on Motion for Disqualification, 10 June 2003.

27   *Furundžija* (IT-95-17/1-A), Judgment, 21 July 2000, para. 200.

28   Ibid., para. 205.

29   *Delalić* et al. (IT-96-21-A), Judgment, 20 February 2001, paras 697–9, 707.

30   *Norman* (SCSL-2004-04-14-PT), Decision on the Motion to Recuse Judge Winter from the Deliberation in the Preliminary Motion on the Recruitment of Child Soldiers, 28 May 2004. Judge Winter reacted angrily, calling herself for the recusal of Judge Robertson from the hearing of the motion. She charged that there had been 'improper collaboration' between Judge Robertson and one of the defence counsel who happened to work in the

When her term came to an end, in 1997, and she was not re-elected, Judge Odio Benito was appointed Vice-President of Costa Rica. She took the oath of office for that position prior to completing an ongoing trial. The defence argued that having become a member of the executive branch of Costa Rica, she had ceased to possess the criteria required for an independent judge and had acquired an association which may affect her impartiality. The Bureau of the International Tribunal observed that her nomination as Vice-President of Costa Rica had been approved in advance by the Plenary of judges, based on her commitment not to assume any of the functions of that office until the completion of her duties as a member of the Trial Chamber. The Plenary also authorized her to take the oath of office. Citing authority from the European Court of Human Rights, the Bureau did not consider there to be grounds for disqualification: '[T]he mere fact that a person who exercises judicial functions is to some extent subject, in another capacity, to executive supervision, is not by itself enough to impair judicial independence.'[31] The Appeals Chamber upheld the findings.[32]

Diligence

Election or appointment as a judge at an international criminal tribunal constitutes a prestigious achievement. Often, senior members of national judiciaries step down from their positions to take up these international functions. They may work under difficult conditions, living far from home, in unfamiliar conditions and isolated from their families. On the other hand, the salaries and other benefits are often greatly superior to what they could earn at home. The lengths of the judicial terms vary from one tribunal to another. At the ad hoc tribunals, the general rule is that judges are elected every three or four years, although several of them have been on shorter one-trial contracts as *ad litem* judges. At the International Criminal Court, the basic term is nine years, subject to certain exceptions. Trials are lengthy, and it is not that uncommon for the term of a judge to come to an end before the conclusion of the proceedings in which he or she is sitting.

That there may be a connection between the length of some trials and the desire of judges to continue working beyond the expiration of their terms is a matter of serious concern because of its evident impact upon the right of the accused person to trial within a reasonable delay. In the practice of the ad hoc tribunals, there are examples of very prolonged proceedings where one consequence was the extension of the term of one or more of the judges involved. Drafting of judgments at both the

---

chambers of which Judge Robertson was head. See: *Norman* (SCSL-2004-04-14-PT), Justice Winter's Response to Motion to Recuse her from Deliberating on the Preliminary Motion on the Recruitment of Child Soldiers, para. 19.

31   *Delalić* et al. (IT-96-21-T), Decision of the Bureau on Motion on Judicial Independence, 4 September 1998.

32   *Delalić* et al. (IT-96-21-A), Judgment, 20 February 2001, paras 651–93.

International Criminal Tribunal for Rwanda and the Special Court for Sierra Leone has taken excessive time, leading to suspicion that this was being unnecessarily delayed because the judges (as well as the lawyers in their Chambers, whose employment was also at stake) were in no hurry to complete their terms.

The phenomenon exists more generally in the context of the 'completion strategies' of the ad hoc tribunals. They have been pressed to finish their work, but have not been very good at meeting the targets they have set themselves not to mention those established by the Security Council. At the International Criminal Tribunal for Rwanda there has been great reluctance to transfer cases of lesser importance to national jurisdictions. By denying transfer applications, the judges have ensured that they have additional cases and may remain in office for a few more years. Although this does not directly engage the rights of the accused, who must be tried in one forum or another, it certainly imposes huge additional costs on the United Nations system. Transfer to national jurisdictions is a cost-effective alternative.

At the International Criminal Court, the term of one of the three judges appointed to serve on the Trial Chamber in *Lubanga*, which was the first case at the Court to go to trial, was due to expire in March 2009. The trial itself had been scheduled to start in 2008, but in fact did not begin until January 2009. Consequently, the judge who was due to retire had his employment extended until the trial was completed. Hearings did not finish until 2011, and it seems likely that the judgment will not be released until late 2011 or early 2012. As a result, in practice three years were added to the term of the judge.

It is of course virtually impossible to prove in any of these cases that proceedings have been unnecessarily delayed. Nevertheless, as with other aspects of judicial ethics, there may be both a subjective and an objective aspect to the issue of diligence. Judges must not only act with diligence, they must appear to be diligent.

At the International Criminal Court, several new judges were elected in late 2008 to replace those whose terms had expired. This required a reorganization of the Chambers, a matter that the Rome Statute leaves to the Plenary meeting of judges. Inevitably, this is a source of tension amongst the judges themselves. Some prefer to work in the Appeals Chamber, which may be viewed as being more prestigious than the Pre-trial and Trial Chambers. It is also the Chamber with the lightest work load, a feature some judges may find attractive. The departure of members of the Appeals Chamber upon expiration of their terms in March 2009 resulted in agreement to replace them with Akua Kuenyehia and Anita Ušacka, both of whom had previously been members of Pre-trial Chamber I. This may have been inconsistent with the requirement in the Statute that judges of the Appeals Division serve their full term in that Division.[33] The Assembly of States Parties questioned the wisdom of designating two 'contaminated' judges to the Appeals Chamber, so-called because they are prohibited from sitting on the pending cases

---

33   *Rome Statute*, art. 39(3)(b).

and situations before the Court with which they already have been involved.[34] According to the report of the Assembly's Committee on Budget and Finance:

> 1. 'Contamination' of judges
> 107. The Committee received a copy of the letter of the President of the Assembly to the President of the Court, dated 9 April 2009, expressing the concerns of the Bureau at the manner in which the Appeals Division had been composed by the plenary of judges. The Committee also received an informal paper from the Presidency on the matter.
> 108. The Committee recalled that as of its eighth session, it had 'agreed that, before any further proposals were made to increase the provision of legal support in Chambers, the Court should provide a revised staffing structure.' The Committee expressed concern with the financial implications that the composition of the Appeals Division could have in terms of the amount of work the two 'contaminated' judges may be able to engage in over the next few years, as well as the impact on any legal officers working with these judges. The Committee requested that a detailed report outlining the scope of the issues, the potential costs for major programme I and the impact on the establishment of efficiency measures within the Court be provided along with a revised staffing structure prior to its next session.[35]

The Plenary of judges convened to reconsider the matter, but by a close vote the earlier controversial decision was upheld.

Thus, two of the five members of the Appeals Chamber were effectively barred from a large number of the proceedings likely to come before them over the next two or three years. It is impossible to say with accuracy why this situation was created. At the very least, it is plainly illogical, to the extent that the best interests of the Court are the guiding principle in determining the composition of the Chambers. The situation seems to be one that raises concerns as to whether the judges 'conduct themselves with probity and integrity in accordance with their office, thereby enhancing public confidence in the judiciary'. At a minimum, it shows a lack of judgment. Apparently, personal interests and preferences triumphed over the welfare of the institution.

Discipline and Removal

One of the serious shortcomings of the ad hoc tribunals, including the early examples at Nuremberg and Tokyo, is the absence of provisions governing discipline and

---

34   See, e.g., *Katanga* et al. (ICC-01/04-01/07), Decision replacing judges in the Appeals Chamber, 3 July 2009.

35   'Report of the Committee on Budget and Finance on the work of its Twelfth Session', ICC-ASP/8/5 (reference omitted, bold face in the original).

removal of judges. Lack of clarity about both the grounds and the procedure for discipline and removal leaves judges in an unacceptable state of uncertainty. It is not illegitimate for the public to be concerned about the impartiality of judges who may themselves be concerned about the security of their appointment. It is probably a general principle of law that where no provision is made for removal from a position, this is by implication within the power of the body or person who made the appointment.

The International Criminal Court is the first international criminal tribunal to have codified rules concerning discipline and removal of judges. In the case of disciplinary measures, for 'misconduct of a less serious nature', judges may be subject to a reprimand and loss of salary for a period of up to six months.[36] Removal may be ordered for 'serious misconduct', which is defined as follows:

> (a) If it occurs in the course of official duties, is incompatible with official functions, and causes or is likely to cause serious harm to the proper administration of justice before the Court or the proper internal functioning of the Court, such as:
> (i) Disclosing facts or information that he or she has acquired in the course of his or her duties or on a matter which is *sub judice*, where such disclosure is seriously prejudicial to the judicial proceedings or to any person;
> (ii) Concealing information or circumstances of a nature sufficiently serious to have precluded him or her from holding office;
> (iii) Abuse of judicial office in order to obtain unwarranted favourable treatment from any authorities, officials or professionals; or
> (b) If it occurs outside the course of official duties, is of a grave nature that causes or is likely to cause serious harm to the standing of the Court.
> 2. For the purposes of article 46, paragraph 1 (a), a "serious breach of duty" occurs where a person has been grossly negligent in the performance of his or her duties or has knowingly acted in contravention of those duties. This may include, *inter alia*, situations where the person:
> (a) Fails to comply with the duty to request to be excused, knowing that there are grounds for doing so;
> (b) Repeatedly causes unwarranted delay in the initiation, prosecution or trial of cases, or in the exercise of judicial powers.

As can be seen, many of the core issues of judicial ethics are addressed.

The judges themselves are left to govern the conduct of their colleagues. In terms of procedure, a charge of serious misconduct where dismissal is at issue is to be examined by the Presidency, which may in turn rely upon one or more judges who are designated to provide assistance.[37] The drafting history of the Rules suggests that the 'assisting judges' are meant to conduct the investigation, thereby insulating the other judges somewhat from the challenge of being both prosecutor

---

36   Rome Statute, art. 47; Rules of Procedure and Evidence, Rule 25.
37   Rules of Procedure and Evidence, Rule 26.

and adjudicator in the matter. If the Presidency decides that the complaint or charge is not manifestly unfounded, the matter is submitted to the Plenary of judges. A decision to recommend removal from office must be accepted by two-thirds of the judges. If this occurs, the case then proceeds to the Assembly of States Parties, where a vote of two-thirds is required to effect removal from office.[38] Thus, the judges act as a filter on such cases. Without the agreement of a special majority, the Assembly of States Parties is powerless to proceed on removal.

Although there are detailed provisions governing the procedure for discipline and removal of judges, many questions about their implementation persist. Nothing is known about the procedure in practice because such matters are to remain confidential. It may well be that the procedure has never been employed. But serious concerns about how this procedure for removal of judges operates remain, precisely because it is shrouded in secrecy. On the one hand, judges may be expected to close ranks so as to collectively resist any serious oversight by an external body. On the other, where collegiality is not particularly strong individual judges may find themselves exposed to campaigns led by rival colleagues that are driven by concerns that are somewhat remote from the issues central to the Code of Judicial Ethics.

In the best national systems, carefully balanced mechanisms exist so that concerns about judicial ethics can be assessed in a manner that will inspire public confidence. This is a particular challenge at the international level, because the courts themselves are not part of a complete and coherent justice system. Preferably there will be some form of control or oversight that is external to the judiciary itself. Leaving the adjudication of ethical issues to the judges themselves, as is the case at the International Criminal Court, ultimately seems to be an inadequate solution.

---

38   Rome Statute of the International Criminal Court, art. 46(2)(a).

Chapter 10

Conclusion

Vesselin Popovski

This book examines the evolution of international rule of law and the role of the web of professional ethics, codes and standards, creating a normative framework, by which the international rule of law is evaluated. It reveals how the ethical behaviour of professionals, working in international organizations and tribunals – professions 'beyond borders' – can contribute to the ascendancy of the rule of law from the domestic to the international domain.

The first chapter 'From Domestic to International Rule of Law: A Long and Unfinished Journey' introduces the origins of the idea of the rule of law and charts its historical evolution from ancient to modern times. The rule of law places the law above the executive and makes it as a supreme governor, independent of the wealthy and the powerful, unbiased and consistent, a guarantor of equality and liberty. People are free and equal, when they are governed by the law; people are not free or equal when subject to the rule of a monarch, who can be driven by momentous desires. The *Rex Lex* (the King is the Law) has become *Lex Rex* (the Law is the King). The chapter introduces a number of tests for the rule of law: for example, the test of rule of law applicability in extreme emergencies and the legitimacy test, which examines the dialectical tension that exists between law and legitimacy. One extreme expression of the rule of law – *Fiat justitia et pereat mundus* (Make justice, even if the world disappears) – may invite a heavy moral dilemma and an argument, that even a supreme law can be subjected to ethical qualifications and re-interpretations. Shakespeare illustrates in his play the *Merchant of Venice* a dilemma and finds a solution in a legal reinterpretation, not in denial of the rule of law. In fact laws can be legitimate or illegitimate; oppressive regimes can introduce oppressive laws, and these laws can be challenged, amended or abolished.

The chapter records the progress of the concept of the rule of law from the domestic to the international sphere, raising definitional issues, one of them being that international rule of law can be confused with the supremacy of obligations from international law above those from domestic law, enshrined in modern constitutions. It argues that international rule of law is less statutory, rather a process of recognition of the ascendancy of law above power internationally, a result of gradual acceptance of the rule of law in more countries in the world, and application of the rule of law principles by international institutions, by international courts, etc. The international rule of law has a strong practical orientation and value – *what it delivers*, rather than *how we define it*, is more fundamental.

The chapter presents the development of international rule of law from a macro perspective, in the practice of the United Nations, and from a micro perspective, the ethical behaviour of individual professionals and how codes of conduct, standards, behavioural practices, impartiality and avoidance of bias of internationalized professions can contribute to the international rule of law. Though significant progress has been made, there is still a long way to go, because states may comply with the rule of law principles domestically, but could be less concerned with these in international affairs. They may declare acceptance and compliance with rulings of international tribunals or international ethical standards, but these should not remain rhetorical in statements and declarations, but rather be visible in actual compliance. The rule of law remains attractive and meaningful across continents and cultures, it can gain international support through ethical and institutional means and can serve as a fundamental governance value, supported on micro level with the ethics of international professions, and on macro level with the strengthening of international institutions.

A more in-depth review of international rule of law is undertaken in the second chapter, 'Unqualified Human Good' or a Bit of 'Ruling-Class Chatter?' This chapter engages in a long historical and geographical voyage – from the *Code of Hammurabi* (1760 BC Babylon) to the developments of Enlightenment, through to modern times. The journey also crosses many centuries, traverses many borders and engages with many cultural traditions – Anglo-Saxon, Continental Europe, Arabic, Chinese. The chapter provides a critical review of the formalistic ('thin') and the substantive ('thick') theories, and elaborates on the functionalist theories of rule of law. The 'thin' theories emphasize the formal instrumental limitations on the exercise of state power, whereas the 'thick' theories incorporate substantive notions of justice, fairness and human rights. The two approaches to the international rule of law are not necessarily detached from each other – the substantive approach can be built on the back of its more formalistic partner. The chapter presents three possible meanings of international rule of law: (1) application of rule of law principles to relations between states and other subjects of international law; (2) prevalence of international law over domestic law, establishing the primacy of human rights covenants over domestic legal arrangements; (3) 'global rule of law' or emergence of a normative regime that applies to individuals directly without formal mediation through existing national institutions.

The chapter further argues that the functionalist approach – what international rule of law does – is the essential one, as it requires assessing what needs to be undertaken, and how, for the rule of law to serve the society. It further discusses the rule of law from three definitional angles – first, the power of state cannot be exercised arbitrarily; second, the law must guide the sovereign state and the independent judiciary should apply the law to specific cases; and third, the rule of law should be applicable, consistent, and most importantly it must be implemented – it must result in action, rather than remaining an abstract notion ('on paper'). The chapter exemplifies how the rule of law has been promoted through international forums and organizations with a particular focus on its purposes, including the achievement of specific political ends on the core subjects of the modern international system, such as promotion of human rights, development, peace and security. It explores the extent to which international organizations, such as the United Nations, World Trade Organization, International Criminal Court, have adopted the rule of law in their procedures, and argues that they do not exist as autonomous jurisdictions comparable to national legal systems, which invites the larger question of whether the rule of law is a coherent concept at the international level. The chapter concludes that the manner in which the rule of law has been articulated at the international level – not so much as a political ideal, but rather as a tool with direct applicability to achieve peace, human rights and development – accurately reflects the development of the rule of law in national jurisdictions and appropriately highlights the political work that must be done, if power is to be channelled through the law.

The third chapter, '"Thin Theories" of the Domestic and International Rule of Law' by Charles Sampford, offers a critical perspective on the rule of law at the international level, delivered through the lens of the formalistic 'thin' theories of rule of law. The chapter reflects on the author's previous writings, prescribing that the international rule of law should adopt qualities from the 'thin' theory, such as clarity, predictability, consistency and stability. In the same way as no citizen should be above the law in domestic constitutions, in international affairs no state should be above the law and no state should seek to exercise powers other than those deemed acceptable under the law. Powerful states should recognize the international rule of law and demonstrate best examples of compliance, by subjecting their own behaviour to independent judicial institutions.

This, however, has not often been the case – powerful states have regularly denied or ignored international law. Regular examples of non-compliance certainly produce a deal of scepticism, which leads some to question the extension of the rule of law from the domestic to the international domain. The reservations harboured by sceptics can be placed in two categories: international reservations against the domestic rule of law, and arguments against the international rule of law *per se*. Sampford reminds us that from the times of Westphalia there has always been a clear division between national sovereignty and international affairs, with each having a distinct set of legal rules and institutions. Nation states exist as well-defined physical spaces, within which domestic political and legal structures arbiter legitimate behaviour, and taken together can form the cornerstone of an international legal system of states. However, globalization challenges the Westphalian system – some states may fail, other may abuse power – and one way to preserve the rule of law and to internationalize it is to re-conceive the liberal democratic principles and re-institutionalize them for a more globalized world.

Sampford further elaborates the fundamental value of the rule of law as a governance framework, noting that the 'thin' theory allows values, such as democracy, citizenship and human rights to be defined independently, enforced reliably and uniformly. He argues that the narrower discourse and the freedom from ideological manipulation in the 'thin' theory makes it a less controversial and preferable tool for internationalization of the rule of law, compared with the 'thick' theory, which includes legitimacy, justice, accountability and human rights. When the rule of law is 'thickened' with many other values, it becomes more difficult to develop a clear picture of interactions of these values and the roles of corresponding institutional mechanisms in supporting the rule of law. The 'thick' theory is more vulnerable, more exposed to misinterpretation, as a set 'imperialism of values'. Sampford concludes that the international rule of law might achieve the virtues of the 'thin' version – predictability, stability and effectiveness – if it is well-ordered and supported and if those who hold power are willing to accept the jurisdiction of independent international judiciaries.

The next chapter by John Barker, 'Reflections on the Rule of Law: Its Scope and Significance for Partners in Development', is based on lessons gleaned from field experience in the practical implementation of projects in support of the rule of law. The chapter adds the critically important views of a practitioner, which are used in this volume to supplement the academic perspective. Barker's chapter explores the relationship between the principle of the rule of law (and its various governance concepts) to its overall impact on the political and economic development of societies within the context of the North–South divide. The chapter begins by defining the core meaning of the rule of law and reveals the many layers of the concept. These layers include rules of law's relationship to law and order, justice and substantive rights, amongst others, to affirm its centrality in the firmament of the good governance concepts. To elaborate the link between politics, economics and the rule of law, Barker analyses the law comparatively in the context of both authoritarian systems and democratic settings, and argues that the origin of political and economic problems often lies within the weakness of the rule of law.

The author notes that increasing number of countries in both the North and South are confronted by widespread public dissatisfaction with perceived gaps in governance and objective global challenges; he questions whether greater attention to certain aspects of the rule of law provides a way forward in addressing seemingly intractable political and economic problems. The chapter further argues that a greater focus on democratic legitimization in law-making and the principles associated with structured, accountable decision-making, represent significant tools that, if promoted, could transform the political as well as the legal landscape, and also the economic prospects for many countries. The chapter then channels its attention to deficiencies in contemporary rule of law. It does this by highlighting the differences in the way governments and organizations – global, regional and bilateral – perceive the core meaning of the rule of law, with each trying to influence specific institutional mandates that define their orientation to the subject. An interesting observation is that the North, through the nature of its development relationship with the South, would discover how similar the challenges of the internationalization of the rule of law are, and such a realization of the similarities of the structural problems makes the North–South relationship more inter-independent – a two-way pursuit. The chapter concludes that the rule of law has a large impact on economic and political development, and leaves open the question of whether the rule of law can be, on the one hand, universal and recognized as such, and on the other, able to accommodate a wide range of informal legal and cultural traditions. With the prospect of assumed differences between North and South beginning to fade, states should realize the similarity of governance deficiencies mirrored on both sides of the North–South divide, and work together utilizing a common, international rule of law 'toolkit', towards good global governance.

Frédéric Mégret in his chapter, 'What is "International Impartiality"?' analyses the centrality and integral role of the concept of impartiality for the development of international rule of law. He traces the origins of the concept from the first cases of international and third-party arbitration and dispute settlement (late nineteenth century), when certain individuals, by vocation or necessity, rose above their national moorings to function in a truly international manner, leading to a remarkable new phenomenon – the international civil service. The de-nationalization of judges and technocrats and emergence of international independent experts resulted from the adoption of international impartiality, which implies that there are universal guiding threads beyond particular national interests, a commonality of criteria and principles, about which one can reasonably expect to be impartial.

These threads could either be linked with international law (international judges), international public interest (international civil servants) or a generic value, such as peace (international peacekeepers), and accordingly one can witness the ascendancy of these three global professions. International impartiality confronts and avoids biases – ethnic, cultural, religious, gender and age biases – all of which may have a negative impact on international decision-making. The chapter further asserts that much of the confusion that surrounds impartiality is linked to a certain tendency to portray it as a negative attitude of distance from, or absence of, prior commitments, prior ideas, prior opinions on a given case. Mégret proposes that to analyse international impartiality one must view the concept as less as a blank slate and more as a critical way of engaging one's own situation.

Mégret concludes that impartiality would have less of a quality, if existing in splendid isolation, and advocates that impartiality can benefit from collegiality and transparency. A contemporary take on impartiality would emphasize the degree to which it is a process rather than a status, something that must be reached, rather than assumed. The evolution of international institutions – legal, political, military – has generated a significant need for even-handedness, transparency and objectivity, and in many ways the legitimacy of these institutions was derived from the degree of de-nationalization afforded them by their membership. Mégret points out that international impartiality is still insufficient and limited by the inability of some to completely break free of their respective national identities and ideological biases, leading to a triple crisis – of plausibility, desirability and morality. The changing political circumstances of the post-Cold War world have re-framed some of the central dilemmas of impartiality and made epistemological shifts in the understanding of its cognitive texture. Mégret also problematizes impartiality, in fact arguing that, if impartiality is to be saved, it needs to be better problematized. While in ordinary circumstances the concept is defensible as a moral category, a form of blind impartiality may stand in tension with certain enlightened moral judgment. For example, to persist in the ways of impartiality, when faced with one party in an armed conflict committing crimes against humanity, creates a fundamental problem of favouring criminals. Impartiality has also, at times, become a code name for states to protect their sovereignty and oppose any form of international moral judgment, particularly in regards to human rights performance. Mégret stresses that the reproach against impartiality when faced with crimes or gross human rights violations is essentially that it abides by an ethics appropriate for a world of states in which international organization can only survive if seen to be above the fray. Instead, what is necessary is the development of an ethics for an integrated world, one in which the ethics of impartiality are tempered on occasion by the need to stand up against evil.

The chapter concludes that impartiality is a quality of governance that must emerge from fundamentally representative institutions, which avoid being an excuse for neutrality, and draw their strength, not on the denial of bias, but from their critical deconstruction. Impartiality is increasingly seen as secondary, when representation becomes a goal in itself and not merely a means to impartiality, reflecting politically realistic views of the nature of international governance and law-making, in which nothing is served by idealizing impartiality, even when something is lost by abandoning it.

The next chapter, 'Professions without Borders: Global Ethics and the International Rule of Law,' follows the line of the preceding chapter in analysing further the role of internationalized professions and the ethics of international professionals – lawyers and soldiers in particular – in supporting the international rule of law. It starts with the premise that the emergence of strong sovereign states with the Treaty of Westphalia turned the legal and the military professions – two of the most cosmopolitan ones before – into the least cosmopolitan, because sovereign nation states were able to determine the content of the law within their borders, which in turn allowed them to create purely nation-based armies. After the Treaty of Westphalia, states could determine which laws were to be applied, what form of economic regulation was to be adopted, and how to recruit and discipline soldiers through mandatory conscription.

The two professions – lawyers and soldiers – played a major role in strengthening the sovereignty of states through the articulation and institutionalization of key governance values. With the Enlightenment, the concept of sovereignty experienced a 'Feuerbachian' reversal in the relationship between the rulers and the ruled – if before it was the citizens who had to demonstrate allegiance and loyalty to the sovereign government, with the new social contract it was governments who had to justify their sovereign status, which could be proven by allegiance to the rule of law and the principles of good governance. The chapter then moves to our current time and argues that in the post-Westphalian world the two professions – lawyers and soldiers – spread 'beyond borders' and have become cosmopolitan once again. It is argued that the erosion of sovereignty has had profound impact for the legal profession and the ethics of how, and for what ends, it is practised, and the same can be said of the military. State sovereignty has been challenged by multiple developments: the rise of transnational law, free-trade treaties, and the development of universal jurisdiction. Furthermore, the rise of international and transnational organizations in the public, corporate and voluntary sectors has contributed to increasing pluralism and, given the absence of any equivalent to national governments within the international order – professions 'beyond borders', such as lawyers, civil servants and soldiers – may need to play an additional and disproportionate role in building and sustaining that international order.

The chapter recommends that the legal profession should take the lead and ally with the military, to break free from its Westphalia shackles, 'globalize' itself and become independent from any allegiance towards employers or states. Such independence would strengthen international rule of law and make it a fundamental component of a more effective global order. If the rule of law becomes a fundamental value of the profession and a value that it uses to justify the profession, lawyers need to reflect carefully and debate publicly its meaning and relationship to the nature of the profession and its work to a global community. In this respect the creation of codes of ethics is a top priority: lawyers can contribute to the articulation of such specific codes and high international standards for them and for others – not least the military, who are potential allies in building the international rule of law. Similarly, soldiers can give examples of high ethical standards, especially when acting as peacekeepers under UN mandates. In conclusion, the chapter re-asserts the notion that the legal and military professions should join forces, to become more actively involved in ethical support for the international rule of law and also through strengthening institutions that will support the rule of law as fundamental governance value. The international rule of law may be articulated, advocated and institutionalized to become the key goal of the newly cosmopolitan and globalizing professions 'beyond borders'.

The next chapter by Lorne Sossin and Vasuda Sinha, 'International Civil Service Ethics, Professionalism and the Rule of Law', follows the work of the previous chapter by critically examining the ethics and professionalism of another internationally employed group – the international civil service: those being the individuals who collectively comprise the staff of the international organizations and exercise authority through the auspices of entities recognized under international law. The two authors reflect on the potential of the operation of such ethics and professionalism to define and enhance the concept of the international rule of law. Sossin and Sinha start by hypothesizing whether an independent, global multilateral public service can serve as a necessary precondition for international rule of law. They answer in the affirmative, and continue their research and writing by looking at what mechanisms in the operation of bureaucracy in multilateral governance may strengthen (or erode) the international rule of law.

The first part of their analysis attempts to situate the international rule of law within the foundation principles of the UN and to ascribe tangible features that impose obligations on those engaged in decision-making at the UN level. Within this framework the authors point out that the principles of the rule of law are embedded in the UN Charter, which encompasses elements relating to state-to-state relations. Though, the authors argue, this gives the main UN organs, such as the General Assembly and the Security Council, the essential responsibility and mandate to carry on this action; they argue that it falls onto the international civil service and international judicial bodies to transform the commitment to the rule of law into tangible action.

Sossin and Sinha also discuss the implications of the independence of the international civil service and what mechanisms exist to resolve disputes which might arise around their potentially competing duties. They list various provisions within the UN Staff Rules and Regulations, the primary source to guide the ethical code for civil servants working for the UN. The UN Staff Rules stress the importance of the twin ethical pillars of 'internationalism' and 'independence' and require that international civil servants and institutions conduct themselves independently of the national interests, but in accordance with the multilateral interests of the UN. The authors argue that the independence of international civil servants is integral to their institutions' effective functioning, and this can only be sustained if all participants and stakeholders within the UN allow the international institutions and civil service to conduct their work and take decisions free from any external political pressure.

Sossin and Sinha also look at the case law of the ILO Administrative Tribunal and the UN Office of Administration of Justice as other exemplars of the evolution of the concept of independence, the improved infrastructure of the international civil service and the accountability of the oversight services of the UN. The authors diagnose some uncertainty that will need to be resolved if the international civil service is to effectively function as a primary guardian of the international rule of law; these raise questions and uncertainty about the nature and scope of the rule of law inexorably leading to the problem of whose definition of the concept should guide the international civil service. Do the international civil servants duly follow every directive from the General Assembly? Or can they question and even refuse to implement a directive that can contradict rule of law values? Must international civil servants be guided by how their supervisors approach the rule of law? Or is it up to international tribunals to delineate the scope of the rule of law? The chapter concludes by stating that these questions remain at the core of the definition of the independence of the international civil service and its functioning, and without answering them the international rule of law remains a hollow slogan rather than a concrete reality.

The last two chapters discuss the issues of impartiality and ethical behaviour of judges, prosecutors and counsel serving in international tribunals. Chandra Sriram, in the chapter entitled 'International Rule of Law? Ethics and Impartiality of Legal Professionals in International Criminal Tribunals', examines and offers a vigorous critique that international courts and tribunals have generally not been subject to the degree of professional ethical regulations that domestic courts have been, arguing that this might affect the consistency of their operation with basic principles of the rule of law.

Sriram refers to the work of Thomas Frank to support her opinion that this is indeed the category of legitimacy that pulls and encourages the greater compliance of nation states with the international legal regimes, as they are perceived as credible by the public. And here comes the challenge with relatively cleaner institutions, such as the two ad hoc tribunals – for former Yugoslavia and Rwanda (ICTY and ICTR) that faced corruption and impropriety charges, exposing weak professionalism and uncertain ethical regulations, characteristic of the gaps in the current system. The ad hoc tribunals developed ethical standards only for counsel, and the International Criminal Court (ICC) has also developed such standards for judges, though these are still very minimal when compared to domestic courts.

Sriram focuses on international and internationalized criminal tribunals, but it does observe that other international courts have relatively limited ethical regulations as well. The insufficient ethical codes should be of particular concern for criminal courts, because defendants lie at risk of losing their liberty and because these judicial institutions themselves purport to uphold human rights norms. International criminal trials are often expected not merely to prosecute crimes but to contribute to a range of other good social aims, such as reconciliation, establishment of historical record, protection and compensation of the victims, promotion of democratization and the rule of law in the affected societies. International tribunals, including international and internationalized criminal courts, are important components of the international rule of law and their legitimacy may be compromised by the relative dearth of professional and ethical rules. A loss of legitimacy is directly linked to the perception that the courts themselves are not bound by a set of rules, even as they purport to apply primary rules in a coherent and consistent fashion. The chapter lists examples of how the lack of ethical codes may lead to scandals of corruption.

Sriram then compares the lack of codes of conduct in international criminal tribunals with the well-developed rules for judicial conduct in common law jurisdictions, and also with the emergence of international standards – the *Bangalore Principles of Judicial Conduct*. She suggests that the international criminal tribunals can incorporate a lot from existing principles and codes and with the support of the UN Special Rapporteur on the Independence of Judges to elaborate and develop professional rules of conduct for all their employees – judges, prosecutors, counsel, registry and other staff. Codes alone are not sufficient, Sriram further argues; there are ethical concerns not covered by professional codes, such as protection of victims and witnesses, specific standards for defendants, etc. Such a comprehensive approach would positively affect the legitimacy of the whole international criminal justice system, otherwise it will continue to be seen as politicized, moreover, when the Security Council, an eminently political body, refer cases. International criminal tribunals have been and may continue to be criticized as biased and illegitimate, regardless of procedural ethical protections, given that decisions are rendered by judges from specific nation states, whom some will assume to be biased. Improved ethics and professional regulations for counsel, judges and staff will not eradicate the host of legitimacy challenges faced by these courts, but may yet have the potential to address significant concerns and enhance their legitimacy.

William Schabas in the last chapter of this volume, 'Judicial Ethics at the International Criminal Tribunals', begins by examining the International Military Tribunals in Nuremburg and Tokyo and the serious lack of impartiality and ethics which characterized these trials. The example of the Soviet Union's assertion that the mass killing of Polish prisoners of war in Katyń Forest was carried out by the Nazis is used as support for this argument (in fact the crimes were actually committed by the Soviet army itself). Schabas then moves to analysing the two ad hoc tribunals – ICTY and ICTR – noting the large discretion afforded to their judges. The revival of international criminal justice in the 1990s, partly driven by developments in international human rights law, brought with it a more explicit attention to judicial ethics, culminating in the attempt of the Rome Statute for the ICC to limit judicial discretion to a large degree.

Schabas then investigates the growth of the international judiciary and highlights questions relating to international judges' appearance of bias within the international criminal tribunals and within the overall theme of independence and impartiality of the judiciary. He – similarly to Mégret, Sossin and Sinha earlier in the book – distinguishes between the concepts of 'independence' and 'impartiality' by stating that while independence is desirable in itself, its importance lies in the fact that it creates the conditions for impartiality. Schabas considers the issues of impartiality to be at the heart of the ethical concerns that play an integral part in maintaining the credibility and legitimacy of the international criminal tribunals. The challenge is that impartiality is a blend of objective and subjective dimensions, which is encompassed within the tribunals' codes of ethics.

Schabas then explores various regulations concerning discipline and procedures governing the removal of judges, found in breach of impartiality. However, he does point out the dichotomy of enabling an oversight body to judge their actions versus the issue of judicial independence, which is critical to inspiring public positive perception and confidence. The only successful motion for disqualification before an international criminal tribunal happened when the independence and impartiality of Geoffrey Robertson, President of the Special Court for Sierra Leone (SCSL), was questioned, because he had already described as criminal some activities by the members of the Revolutionary United Forces in his book *Crimes against Humanity*, published before his appointment as a President of the SCSL.

Schabas also expresses disappointment with the length of some trials and the desire of judges to continue working beyond the expiration of their terms, suspecting deliberate delays by judges. This is a matter of serious concern, because of its evident impact on the right of the accused person to trial within a reasonable delay. The International Criminal Court is the first international criminal tribunal to have codified rules concerning discipline and removal of judges; however, the judges are left themselves to govern the conduct of their colleagues and there are confidentiality barriers in the procedures that create an element of non-transparency and secrecy. Schabas warns that the judges may collectively resist a serious oversight by an external body, or in case collegiality is not strong, judges may be exposed to campaigns by rival colleagues. He concludes that leaving the adjudication of ethics to the judges themselves in the ICC is an inadequate solution and there should preferably be some form of external control.

In conclusion, the chapters in this book problematize the international rule of law, both in theory and in practice, finding insufficient progress in the process of internationalization of the rule of law, but also opportunities in the way how the ethical behaviour of international professions, and the development of codes and standards of conduct can support international rule of law. The book explores the tension between the promotion of the rule of law internationally as a 'thin' concept, with no ethics and other values attached, as extrapolation around the world of the principle of supremacy of law, and the more ambitious goal of establishing international rule of law as a 'thick' concept in interaction with other values, such as ethics, human rights and freedoms. The first approach, argued by Sampford, would be that, given the slow evolution, it would be easier to develop the international rule of law – in definitional terms – having the 'thin', and even 'anorexic' version without complicating it in a holistic framework of many values. This is a good first step of focusing on necessity and feasibility. However, a more challenging question would then be whether the 'thin' version of the international rule of law would be a sufficient development, in particular in terms of serving as a guidance for international civil servants and employees of international tribunals. Certainly Mégret's emphasis on impartiality, as a value that is enhanced in international contexts critically engaging professionals with their own individual situation, is a valid argument that signals that an ethical grounding can be found for even a 'thin'-based internationalization of the rule of law. It also offers a balance of learning between best practices of ethical professionalism in the core of the international system – the United Nations, and the ethics of different regional and local institution, and of individuals.

The final judgment is still to come, but looking at both the critiques and the best practices that this book reveals, there are expectations that the international rule of law will advance in an enhanced international culture of professionals in international organizations and tribunals, acting with independence and impartiality, where principles of international professional ethics are understood and promoted. The ethical rules, codes and their implementation – either integral or imposed – can offer the necessary supports to strengthen the international rule of law. The impartiality and independence of the employees in international tribunals and other international institutions represent a solid platform for international rule of law to flourish; and on the opposite, corruption, bias, lack of transparency and lack of accountability jeopardize the advancement of international rule of law, as also illustrated in this book.

The advance of the international rule of law through learning from the best practices in domestic systems, and from the development of ethical standards and professional ethics in international organizations, is expected to inform the activities of professionals and solidify international rule of law, as a universal good, setting the basis of more stable global governance.

Index

www.ingramcontent.com/pod-product-compliance
Ingram Content Group UK Ltd.
Pitfield, Milton Keynes, MK11 3LW, UK
UKHW020354010325
455677UK00021B/447